To Robert Silans -

With very

best wishes

Howard R Penniman

# ELECTIONS IN SOUTH VIETNAM

# AEI-Hoover policy studies

The studies in this series are issued jointly
by the American Enterprise Institute
for Public Policy Research and the Hoover
Institution on War, Revolution and Peace.
They are designed to focus on
policy problems of current and future interest,
to set forth the factors underlying
these problems and to evaluate
courses of action available to policymakers.
The views expressed in these studies
are those of the authors and do not necessarily
reflect the views of the staff, officers
or members of the governing boards of
AEI or the Hoover Institution.

# ELECTIONS IN SOUTH VIETNAM

Howard R. Penniman

American Enterprise Institute for Public Policy Research
Washington, D. C.

Hoover Institution on War, Revolution and Peace
Stanford University, Stanford, California

AEI-Hoover Policy Study 4, December 1972
(Hoover Institution Studies 38)

Library of Congress Catalog Card No. L.C. 72-95776



*Printed in United States of America*

# Acknowledgments

The Republic of Vietnam is remarkably open in spite of invasion and civil war. Thousands of American and other foreign newsmen have filed literally hundreds of thousands of stories from Saigon since 1966 and their stories and films have not been blocked, delayed or censored. Inevitably, however, news coverage of campaigns and elections—some of it excellent—is often fragmentary, disjointed, and incomplete. The news audience is too general to justify the presentation of technical details of such events. Each election passes into history in a few days and reporters move on to the next events that have become the "news."

Anyone studying the politics and elections of South Vietnam can learn much from the press, but he must look elsewhere for details of election laws, ministerial decrees, court decisions, administrative practices, and even election results. Moreover, no single government agency or library, here or in South Vietnam, files all needed documents and analyses. The researcher, then, must seek help from many sources. And, because he has received help from so many, it becomes impossible to credit each with a full statement of his contribution. I have, therefore, been forced to that blunt instrument—the acknowledgment list.

American, British and South Vietnamese scholars, U.S. and South Vietnamese officials here and in the Republic of Vietnam, newsmen and political activists in Vietnam have provided unclassified information, read drafts of the manuscript, argued interpretations of events, and suggested further sources of help in developing this book. Among those to whom I owe thanks for one or more of such contributions are: Seymour R. Bolten, George A. Carver, Jr., Karl Cerny, Dennis J. Duncanson, Valerie Earle, Thomas Eliot, Edwin D. Goldfield, Allan E. Goodman, Jeane J. Kirkpatrick, Sven F. Kraemer, James McCusker,

Harold Meinheit, James P. Nach, Nguyen Ngoc Bich, Pham Huy Bach, Richard M. Scammon, Harry Sizer, Daniel Southerland, Gerald L. Steibel, John Sylvester, Richard S. Thompson, Richard Thornton, Tran Minh Tiet, Tran Quoc Buu, and Theresa A. Tull.

For the typing of revision after revision I owe thanks to Barbara Cayelli and Catherine Penniman.

No book is possible without the time and opportunity to prepare it. I am thankful to Georgetown University for a sabbatical leave during the academic year 1971-1972 when most of this manuscript was prepared; to the Earhart Foundation for allowing me to postpone the writing of another book in order to complete this one; to Frank N. Trager and the American-Asian Educational Exchange for a travel grant to the Republic of Vietnam to observe the 1971 presidential election (in 1967 I was fortunate to travel as an election specialist with the team appointed by President Lyndon B. Johnson to observe the presidential election of that year); and to the American Enterprise Institute for Public Policy Research for office space, the use of its excellent bibliographic facilities, and the expert assistance of its editorial and secretarial staffs.

My debt to Charles M. Lichenstein is great. He was responsible for encouraging, editing and publishing an earlier work on South Vietnam's 1967 election, and he has made major contributions to both the substance and readability of this book. For all his help I am very grateful.

Finally I wish to thank my wife who helped with the research, read drafts, and maintained her patience throughout the long months that this book was in preparation.

All errors of fact and interpretation are, of course, my responsibility.

Howard R. Penniman

# Contents

# 1
# Introduction

South Vietnam has regularly conducted national elections since 1966 in spite of civil war and invasions from the North. This book will examine seven national elections, beginning with the September 1966 election of a Constituent Assembly to write a new constitution that, on its face at least, measures up to the accepted norms of a democratic system. Since then, voters have twice elected members of the lower house and Senate and twice a president.

Almost everyone has an opinion about the electoral institutions of South Vietnam—and almost no one has bothered to study them. Evaluations often appear to be more a function of the observer's "hawkishness" or "dovishness" than of their own inherent quality. The efficacy of these institutions, and their future prospects, depend mostly on the political will of that country's leaders and people of course. But they also depend on eventualities inside and outside South Vietnam that are themselves largely unpredictable—for example, developments in the war or at the peace table in Paris, the magnitude of U.S. military and economic aid (in turn dependent on U.S. politics and elections), possible changes in strategy on the part of North Vietnam and the National Liberation Front (NLF), Russian and Chinese attitudes toward both the United States and North Vietnam, and the like. In the face of so many imponderables, about all one can do is describe the operation of the electoral system and point out certain factors that augur well or ill for its success as a system.

The difficulty of creating and maintaining a system of popular elections in a developing country is generally acknowledged in the literature of the social sciences. The standard list of pitfalls confronting a traditional society on the way to modernization includes the shift from rural to urban dominance, the need for unavailable expertise, and the evolution of a new secularism—a matter both of attitude and of institutional development. The additional difficulty of establishing not only a modern society but a viable *democratic* system in such circumstances is almost universally recognized.

By any such standard, South Vietnam was a most unlikely candidate for instant modernization *or* democratization with the onset of independence in 1954. The whole of Vietnam—the three regions of Tonkin, Annam, and Cochinchina—had been controlled for roughly 80 years by a colonial power whose policies could most generously be termed unenlightened. Virtually every effort by the Vietnamese to develop indigenous political institutions was stifled by the French. In 1954, more than 80 percent of the people of South Vietnam lived on the land—much of which was controlled by absentee landlords. There were a half-dozen or more religious, ethnic, and linguistic groups in a land area smaller than the state of Missouri. Warring sects and organized armies of criminals fought to prevent any effective government from developing in Saigon. Then add to all this a continuing state of civil war, supported (some would say organized) by North Vietnam. By 1972, when the Viet Cong (VC)—the NLF's military arm—was sharply reduced in numbers and effectiveness, the North Vietnamese launched a full-scale invasion of the South.

These military realities multiplied and magnified the political/electoral problems that face any developing country. Just to hold elective office at the village or hamlet level greatly decreased life expectancy in areas where the Viet Cong was powerful.[1] During the Tet offensive of 1968, retreating enemy soldiers and guerrillas murdered at least three thousand persons who had been identified with the government of Vietnam. In 1972, the invading North Vietnamese armies and the local VC, according to intelligence sources quoted in the *New York Times,* executed not only hamlet and village officials but hundreds of other

---

[1] See U.S. Department of Defense, *United States-Vietnam Relations, 1945–1967* (Pentagon Papers), 12 vols. (Washington, D. C.: Government Printing Office, 1971), vol. 2, pp. 58–59: "*The New York Times* estimated that 3,000 local government officials were killed or captured during 1960." Throughout this book, the Government Printing Office 12-volume edition of the Pentagon Papers has been used. There appear to be no major differences between it and other editions except that in some respects the GPO edition is more inclusive.

citizens in Binh Dinh province.[2] Some of the latter were, at most, marginally political.

The complications do not end with the influence of the war on the evolution of South Vietnamese political institutions. The American presence has also had a profound impact. The very fact that there have been competitive elections from the local to the national level has been partially the result of the encouragement of U.S. officials. Tacit U.S. support of the coup d'etat in 1963 was widely believed to have provided the necessary "clearance" for those in the military who wanted to get rid of President Ngo Dinh Diem. And this, in turn, has apparently created a presumption among Vietnamese politicians that U.S. intervention in local affairs is more likely than not in any future crisis.

Actually, since 1963, the United States has generally kept hands off internal Vietnamese politics. The U.S. government has supported every South Vietnamese government that has been in power. While doubtless pleased with the relative stability of the post-'67 period, it has not intervened in behalf of President Nguyen Van Thieu. On the contrary, most of the evidence suggests that Ambassador Ellsworth Bunker, to the extent that he played any role at all, sought to make the 1971 presidential election something other than the one-man race it eventually turned out to be.

It has evidently been difficult for many Americans and South Vietnamese to credit this appearance of neutrality as real. Some of Thieu's opponents, possibly thinking back to the overthrow of Diem, have operated as if their political futures depend more on editorial and political support in the United States than on the decisions of the voters in South Vietnam. Duong Van ("Big") Minh, for example, seemed to be relying on a U.S. constituency when he held more than a dozen press conferences with American reporters between the time he announced his presidential candidacy in late November 1970 and the time he withdrew from the race in August 1971. By contrast, for at least the first eight months, *he did not hold a single conference with members of the South Vietnamese press corps.*[3] They were forced to write their stories, if any, by recourse to American wire services or newspapers.

The confusions of war and the peculiarities of the U.S.-Vietnam relationship should not obscure the possible relevance of a position first

[2] *New York Times,* August 4, and August 10, 1972.

[3] See Chapter 7 for an extended discussion of the phenomenon of the dependence of South Vietnamese opposition politicians on American support.

argued by Professor I. Milton Sacks some years ago. He suggested that the "continuation of the . . . effort to create an elected government in South Vietnam and to 'make the constitution work' might create the conditions of stability."[4] Unlike those who worry about the difficulties of holding elections in wartime, Professor Sacks submits that the very fact of elections in the crisis periods of a transitional society might have a stabilizing influence on that society. In December 1971, he said: "The efficiency of electoral administration [in South Vietnam] is an established fact. Perhaps more significantly, electoral experiences have had a socialization effect. They have had, that is, enough meaning so that all Vietnamese political leaders must now recognize electoral processes as established institutional facts."[5] These are hypotheses only, but they are put forward by a distinguished scholar on South Vietnam and should be given some weight.

**The Problem of Elections under Stress.** Elections in periods of stress, even in a mature democracy, often deviate from the norms of the going electoral model. During periods of war or civil war when the very life of a country may be at stake, elections are least likely to measure up to the model—if they are held at all.

The United Kingdom, for example, is generally regarded as an exemplar of mature democracy. Yet the British postponed elections during World War II, prevented some parties from operating, jailed a member of Parliament who was thought to be sympathetic to the enemy, and reduced the access of the press to governmental and war news. Most people in Britain and elsewhere accepted these wartime restrictions as necessary, even desirable, or at the very least as understandable.

During the American Civil War, martial law was declared in border regions of the North deemed to be militarily sensitive by President Lincoln. Civilians there who sympathized with the South and called for immediate negotiations were sometimes jailed, and the writ of habeas

[4] I. Milton Sacks, "Restructuring Government in South Vietnam," *Asian Survey,* August 1967, p. 520.

[5] "Report of the Meeting: Vietnam, Laos, and Cambodia Panel Seminar of the Southeast Asia Development Advisory Group" (SEADAG), December 10–11, 1971, p. 3. The quotation is from the minutes and may not be Professor Sacks' precise words. SEADAG, an organization with government and foundation support, was created in 1965 to further research by university and government scholars to help fill wide gaps in U.S. knowledge about the area. See Samuel P. Huntington, "Introduction: Social Science and Vietnam," *Asian Survey,* August 1967, pp. 503–506.

corpus was suspended, thus effectively denying critics access to relief through the courts.

The national election in 1864 created special difficulties for the Lincoln administration. As late as October of that year, the President is said to have predicted his defeat by General George McClellan who advocated a negotiated settlement based on acceptance of Southern secession. With presidential approval, Lincoln's subordinates took vigorous action to maximize his reelection prospects. Troops were furloughed home to vote, especially in states where the election was expected to be close. When Governor Horatio Seymour (D., N.Y.) sought to counter by sending a commission to the field to persuade New York troops to vote Democratic, Secretary of War Edwin Stanton intercepted the commissioners and put the three Democratic members in jail until after the election.[6]

In less mature democracies, the threat to electoral institutions may be more immediate and their successful defense more difficult. In Italy, for example, democratic institutions, electoral and otherwise, were destroyed by the rise of fascism during the economic and political crises of the 1920s. And as Professor Robert A. Dahl has pointed out, some Italian intellectuals who were deeply committed to democracy and freedom in the abstract almost certainly contributed to their demise in fact. He cites three leading intellectuals of the period—Gaetano Mosca, Benedetto Croce, and Gaetano Salvemini—who scoffed at the inept, immature, and sometimes corrupt democratic institutions of Italy as unworthy of their allegiance. Perfection was the price they demanded; and what they got, of course, was the "perfection" of fascism under Mussolini. The real world only rarely offers a choice among the full gamut of conceivable options, a fact the Italian intellectuals discovered too late. In 1945 Salvemini said, "As for the results of the Fascist dictatorship in contrast with those of Italian democracy in the making,

---

[6] Benjamin P. Thomas and Harold M. Hyman, *Stanton: The Life and Times of Lincoln's Secretary of War* (New York: Alfred A. Knopf, 1962), pp. 325–335, provides a detailed account of the machinations of the secretary and the Union Army in assuring that the soldiers vote in the first place, that the vote be counted by sympathetic counters, that New York elections be honestly conducted by sending Union troops to New York City to oversee the voting and counting, etc. Generals were dispatched to speak at rallies both for civilians and for soldiers. Where it was possible to segregate the soldier vote, it ran 119,754 for Lincoln to 34,291 for McClellan. The authors estimate that the soldier vote was worth 101 electoral votes or enough to elect Lincoln to a second term.

they are here before our very eyes. Let us hope that the Italians will not be the only ones to learn from that frightful experience." [7]

**Questions about the Electoral Process in General.** After describing each of the elections held under the current Vietnamese constitution, I will attempt to make some sense of them by answering a number of questions, broken into three categories, that might well be posed about any electoral system, anywhere, anytime.[8] The first category of questions involves the electorate, its composition, and its freedom of action:

1. Is the electorate constitutionally and legally defined in a manner that is generally inclusive of adults and therefore of potential voters, or are large numbers of them arbitrarily excluded from casting ballots for national and local candidates?
2. Is the registration of voters conducted in a manner that assures the maximum listing of legally qualified voters, thus making heavy participation at the polls possible?
3. Is secrecy of the vote protected for the citizen casting his ballot?
4. Is there adequate protection against multiple voting and other forms of voting fraud?
5. Is the system for counting ballots open and public so that an honest count is probable?

The second category involves the levels of candidate competition as allowed by the constitution and the laws and as actually practiced:

6. Do constitutional and legal rules make it possible for a reasonable number of candidates to compete for voter support?
7. Does the system provide for roughly equal opportunity for candidates who have been nominated to compete for support?

---

[7] Quoted from an essay by Salvemini in Robert A. Dahl, *Polyarchy: Participation and Opposition* (New Haven: Yale University Press, 1971), pp. 18–19. The entire second chapter, "Does Polyarchy Matter?", makes very rewarding reading.

[8] This list of questions is similar to an earlier list drawn up in the spring of 1971 in response to a request from Eugene Patterson for suggestions about advice to give readers of the *Washington Post* on how to follow that year's lower house and presidential elections in South Vietnam.

Although these questions were developed earlier, the reader will notice that they parallel the two major concerns of Robert A. Dahl (ibid., pp. 5–7) in his discussion of "polyarchy." Professor Dahl stresses the importance of an "inclusive" electorate and of "public contestation." He reserves the use of the word "democracy" for a society in which subnational and even some organizations traditionally considered private are controlled by the people who belong to or work for them.

8. In the case of the legislature, where there are many positions to be filled, does the system encourage the selection of candidates representing the various religious, ethnic, and other minority groups in the society?

The third category of questions involves institutions closely related to the electoral process:

9. Is the press free to criticize the government and its policies and to offer alternatives to the personnel and programs of the incumbent regime?

10. To what extent does the political party system provide the organization and perform the functions generally thought to be required of parties in a democratic system?

From time to time—to bring the analysis into sharper perspective—comparisons will be drawn to the most obvious alternative to the electoral system now existing in South Vietnam, namely that of North Vietnam.

**U.S. Involvement in Vietnam.** This book is about Vietnamese elections and not about U.S. foreign policy. Nevertheless, it is pertinent to note that the presence or absence of a system of free elections was no part of the reason for U.S. intervention in Vietnam in the first instance; nor has it been cited by any President since 1954 as a principal reason for continued military and economic aid to the South.

The Pentagon Papers provide a compilation of public pronouncements by the highest U.S. government officials concerning the reasons for this country's involvement in the Vietnamese war. They devote 239 pages to a section titled "Justifications of the War—Public Statements." [9] The general theme of the "justifications" has remained the same under four administrations over 20 years. Assuming that these arguments represent a valid cross-section of official views, the presence of democracy was never a *condition* for support of South Vietnam's independence: it was and is a "bonus."

President Dwight D. Eisenhower, at a Gettysburg College convocation, April 4, 1959, spoke directly to the problems of South Vietnam:

> Strategically, South Viet-Nam's capture by the Communists would bring their power several hundred miles into a hitherto

[9] Department of Defense, *United States-Vietnam Relations, 1945–1967.* Statements on U.S. policy concerning Vietnam are scattered through the 12 volumes in this edition. None of the statements in other editions, so far as I could discover, contradict those which appear in vol. 7, pp. A1–A6, B1–B53, C1–C46, and D1–D134. Section A includes the statements of the Truman administration, B those of the Eisenhower administration, C those of the Kennedy administration, and D those of the Johnson administration.

free region. The remaining countries in Southeast Asia would be menaced by a great flanking movement. . . . The loss of South Viet-Nam would set in motion a crumbling process that could, as it progressed, have grave consequences for us and for freedom. . . .

We reach the inescapable conclusion that our own national interests demand some help from us in sustaining in Viet-Nam the morale, the economic progress, and the military strength necessary to its continued existence in freedom.[10]

President John F. Kennedy, who as senator had long been an advocate of the defense of South Vietnam, addressed a Democratic party dinner in Chicago, April 28, 1961:

In Viet-Nam . . . a small army of guerrillas, organized and sustained by the Communist Viet Minh in the north, have assassinated over four thousand civil officers, two thousand state employees and two thousand police, believing that if they can "spill the wine," they can win control of the population. And when they have won, they do not intend to give way.

Now our great responsibility is to be the chief defender of freedom, in this time of maximum danger. Only the United States has the power and resources and the determination. We have committed ourselves to the defense of dozens of countries stretched around the globe who look to us for independence, who look to us for the defense of their freedom.[11]

In January 1962, President Kennedy asserted: "The systematic aggression now bleeding that country [South Vietnam] is not a 'war of liberation'—for Vietnam is already free. It is a war of attempted subjugation—and it will be resisted." [12]

Speaking at the Economic Club of New York, April 22, 1963, Secretary of State Dean Rusk replied to the argument that South Vietnam must be a democracy to justify American support:

Critics have complained that South Viet-Nam is not a full constitutional democracy and that our aid has been subject

---

[10] Ibid., p. B49. Note that, without explicitly using the phrase, the President stated the "domino" theory in the first paragraph of the quotation. Note also that use of the word "freedom" does not speak to the nature of the internal organization of the country. During the Eisenhower administration, government spokesmen cited in the Pentagon Papers sometimes spoke of "Free Viet-Nam" when referring to South Vietnam, and "free" meant free from control by North Vietnam.

[11] Ibid., p. C10.

[12] Ibid., p. C15.

to waste and mismanagement. Let us be clear that these criticisms are not merely alibis for inaction. For in passing judgment, let us recall that we are talking about a nation which has been responsible for its own affairs for less than a decade, about a people who have had no peace since 1941 and little experience in direct participation in political affairs. . . .[13]

President Lyndon B. Johnson, in his message to Congress, August 5, 1964, summarized American policy "in four simple propositions":

> 1. *America keeps her word.* Here as elsewhere, we must and shall honor our commitments.
>
> 2. *The issue is the future of Southeast Asia as a whole.* A threat to any nation in that region is a threat to all, and a threat to us.
>
> 3. *Our purpose is peace.* We have no military, political, or territorial ambitions in the area.
>
> 4. *This is not just a jungle war,* but a struggle for freedom on every front of human activity. Our military and economic assistance to South Vietnam and Laos in particular has the purpose of helping these countries to repel aggression and strengthen their independence.[14]

"Our own security," said President Johnson in his 1965 State of the Union message, "is tied to the peace of Asia. Twice in one generation we have had to fight against aggression in the Far East. To ignore aggression now would only increase the danger of a much larger war." [15]

President Richard M. Nixon, when asked whether assistance to South Vietnam should be continued in view of the one-man race for South Vietnam's presidency in 1971, told newsmen that

> in only 30 of those [91] countries [receiving military aid] do they have leaders who are there as a result of a contested election by any standard that we would consider fair. In fact, we would have to cut off aid to two-thirds of the nations of the world to whom we are presently giving aid, if we apply the standards some suggest we apply to South Vietnam.[16]

---

[13] Ibid., p. C33.

[14] Ibid., pp. D14–D15. (Italics in original.)

[15] Ibid., p. D25.

[16] *Weekly Compilation of Presidential Documents,* vol. 7, no. 38 (September 16, 1971), pp. 1282–1283.

In response to another question, President Nixon commented on "how difficult the process of democracy is. It took the British 500 years to get to the place where they had what we could really describe as a democratic system under the parliamentary setup and it didn't spring up full-grown in the United States." [17]

Subsequently, after the invasion by the armies of North Vietnam in the spring of 1972, President Nixon on April 26, 1972, again explained why the United States supports South Vietnam; his reasons included no mention of democracy:

> If one country can invade another nation and succeed in conquering it, other countries will be encouraged to do exactly the same thing—in the Mideast, in Europe, and in other international danger spots. If the Communists win militarily in Vietnam, the risk of war in other parts of the world would be enormously increased. If the Communist aggression fails, it will discourage others [from doing] the same thing. . . .
>
> We will not be defeated; and we shall never surrender our friends to Communist aggression.[18]

This is not to exclude the possibility that the evolution of a democratic system in South Vietnam *might* have been used to rationalize U.S. support, or even that it *should* have been. The blunt fact remains: it was not so used, although a lack of democracy has often been cited by critics as an argument for a change in U.S. policy.[19]

To sum up: reasons other than the character of the political system in South Vietnam engaged the U.S., and have kept it engaged, in the war. On the other hand, Presidents Johnson and Nixon in particular have

---

[17] Ibid., p. 1283.

[18] Ibid., vol. 8, no. 18, p. 793.

[19] The situation during these past 20 years is not unlike that of the late 1930s when the issue of U.S. intervention in World War II was being debated. President Franklin D. Roosevelt justified aid to the allies in terms of the danger of continuing Nazi conquests, the need to protect our allies from defeat, and our own stake in preventing the success of aggression. Opponents of aid to the anti-Nazi countries, aside from pacifists, criticized assistance to the anti-democratic "Cliveden set" in England and the "reactionary" government of France. The support of neither country, they said, was worth the risk of U.S. involvement. When the Nazis invaded the Soviet Union in June 1941, there was a rush by some of these same critics to support the President, but then the "isolationists" found in Stalin's totalitarianism still another reason for not offering U.S. aid. The President continued to send aid to the anti-Nazi forces and let his justifications for that policy stand.

encouraged the development of democratic institutions there. This study may help to measure progress toward that goal.

**The Organization of the Study.** Chapter 2 provides a brief history of Vietnam, and of elections and other key developments prior to the drafting of the current constitution. Chapter 3 examines the election for the 1966 Constituent Assembly. Chapters 4 through 7 describe the national elections held thereafter. Chapters 8 and 9 examine press freedom and political parties, respectively. A concluding chapter draws together the materials in the descriptive chapters and seeks to answer the questions raised in this introduction. Some attention is also given, in two brief interludes, to subnational elections and other institutional developments in South Vietnam—to the "historical setting." These interludes follow chapters 3 and 5, fill gaps in both time and circumstance, and add material that is literally extrinsic to the national electoral process but highly relevant nonetheless.

# 2

# Vietnam Before 1966: A Short Course

Elections are not the usual means for selecting leaders in a traditional society. Culturally developed as it may have been, pre-1966 Vietnam was no exception to this political norm. Nearly a century of colonial status afforded the Vietnamese no serious electoral experience, nor did the nine-year regime of Ngo Dinh Diem immediately after independence or the four-year military interlude that followed Diem's overthrow. When a Constituent Assembly was elected in 1966, the Vietnamese people were getting their first real taste of national politics and elections.

## French Rule

The French gained full control of Vietnam in the 1880s. For the greater part of the three preceding centuries that country had gone through three distinct phases. First, it had been divided into two virtually independent nations separated at almost exactly the present demarcation line. Two centuries later, the whole country came under the control of the Tay-son brothers—three bandits turned military-politicians—and was split into northern, central, and southern regions, each ruled by one of the brothers. Then, at the beginning of the 19th century, Nguyen Phuoc Anh defeated the descendants of the Tay-son brothers and united Vietnam. After his victory, he assumed the title of Emperor Gia Long and again divided the country into three regions for administrative purposes —Tonkin, Annam, and Cochinchina.

Professor McAlister says of the Gia Long reign that "beneath the surface of apparent political unity the governors of the various regions held the real power while acknowledging the sovereignty of the emperor.

# INDOCHINA DURING FRENCH OCCUPATION

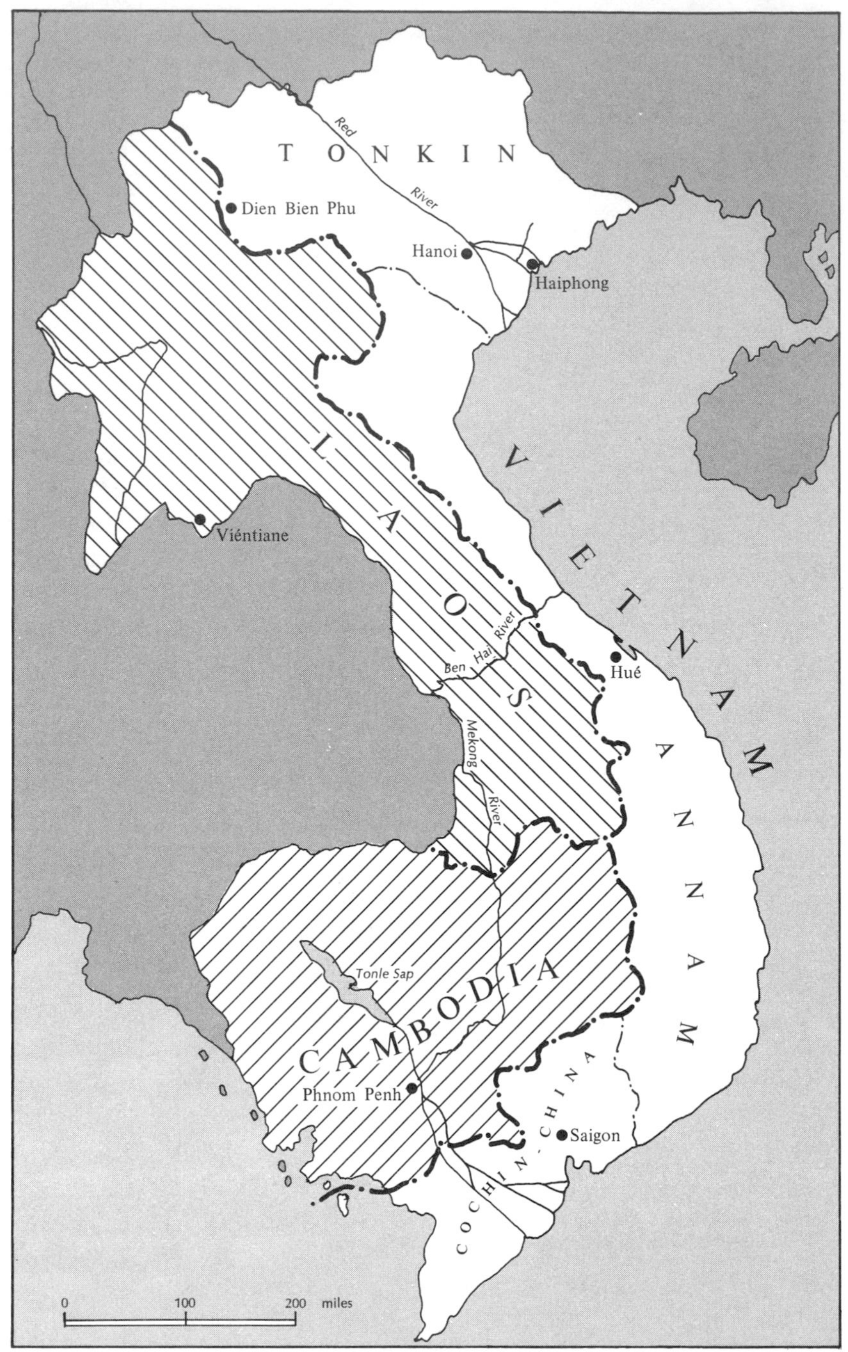

Unfortunately for the future of Vietnamese politics, even this promising trend toward unification was ended with Gia Long's death. . . ." [1]

Gia Long's successors were short-sighted and incompetent. They offended Westerners with massacres of thousands of Christians. They neglected the dikes (causing flooding in the north) and pursued disastrous economic policies that drove starving peasants into revolt. The country was ready for almost anything when French forces began their conquest in 1858.

After the French consolidated their hold, they followed the example of Gia Long and divided the country into three districts. Cochinchina in the south was a colony, while Annam in the center and Tonkin in the north were protectorates. All were thoroughly dominated by France.

A traditional society existed in Vietnam when the French reduced all of Indochina to colonial status. And so it remained—in spite of some changes in political and economic institutions forced on it by French colonialism—until after World War II. French rule was more efficient than that of the emperor, but life in the villages hardly changed. Taxes were higher and collected more efficiently. The French made heavier demands on the peasants for both work and taxes but offered the Vietnamese no tutelage in self-government in the process.

**Government and Politics in the Villages.** When the French took control, more than 90 percent of the Vietnamese were peasants who lived in the villages.[2] The villages were small, tightly knit units. The peasant had almost no contact with any level of government above the village Council of Notables or Council of Elders. If he were to have meaningful electoral experience, it had to be focused in the village.

Professor Scigliano quotes a Vietnamese historian to the effect that village chiefs were "elected by the adult male populations as early as 1461." [3] But other commentators make no mention of popular elections,

[1] John T. McAlister, Jr., *Vietnam: Origins of Revolution* (New York: Alfred A. Knopf, 1969), p. 37.

[2] Even today, it is probable that about 70 percent of the people live in rural areas. U.S. census experts suggest that figures of 40 percent urbanization, which are sometimes mentioned for South Vietnam, are based on a misunderstanding of the character of the villages. They are geographic areas like middlewestern townships so that even a population of 20,000 may not mean a high concentration in discrete areas.

[3] Robert Scigliano, "The Electoral Process in South Vietnam: Politics in an Underdeveloped State," *Mid-West Journal of Political Science,* vol. 4 (May 1960), p. 138.

either of the council or the village chief. Douglas Pike says that council members were selected by co-optation and served for life. The council was a self-perpetuating body that was not legally responsible to the village. Pike describes the process, however, as one in which the villagers were consulted and influenced the ultimate choice of each new councilman.[4]

Gerald Cannon Hickey asserts that, after 1904, the French colonial administration sought to integrate the villages into the larger society. To this end they gave greater power to higher levels of government and reduced the village councils' prerogatives.[5]

After World War I, the French for a time substituted election for co-optation, while increasing central government control of council acts.[6] By the time of the Japanese invasion in 1941, elections had been dropped and the council once more co-opted its replacements—now subject to approval by the provincial government.[7]

When the French returned to power after World War II, they resumed council selection by co-optation. Bao Dai, the hereditary head of state of Vietnam in 1945 and of the Associate State of Vietnam from 1949 to 1955, introduced universal suffrage and direct election of village councils in 1953 in the French-controlled areas. Shaplen says that in reality "the right to vote was restricted to about a million persons out of some thirteen million theoretically eligible: only those in villages regarded as relatively safe from Vietminh infiltration were permitted to cast ballots and they had to have been registered in a 1951 census con-

[4] Douglas Pike, in *War, Peace, and the Viet Cong* (Cambridge, Mass.: M.I.T. Press, 1969), pp. 68–71, provides a fascinating description of the selection of council members that involved consultation with the villagers but not formal control by them. Joseph Buttinger, in *The Smaller Dragon* (New York: Praeger Publishers, Inc., 1958), pp. 315–316, suggests that the council was chosen from among the rich landowners "to whom one or two poor old men of great respectability were frequently added." This arrangement, he quotes a former French administrator as saying, kept control of the villages in the hands of the wealthy. Jeffrey Race, *War Comes to Long An: Revolutionary Conflict in a Vietnamese Province* (Berkeley: University of California Press, 1972), pp. 6–12, argues the same point as Buttinger but stresses the period since 1938, during and after the French era.

[5] Gerald Cannon Hickey, *Village in Vietnam* (New Haven: Yale University Press, 1964).

[6] Robert Scigliano, *South Vietnam: Nation Under Stress* (Boston: Houghton Mifflin Co., 1963), p. 10.

[7] Ibid. Scigliano quotes Paul Mus as saying that the reason for dropping elections and returning to the system of co-optation was "the sullen opposition of the local rural leaders." Scigliano credits the Petain regime with the end of elections. Hickey, by contrast, speaks of council co-optation of replacements as early as the 1920s and 1930s.

ducted as a prelude to possible conscription." [8] The voters in these elections gave such strong support to the opponents of Bao Dai that promised provincial and national elections were promptly cancelled.

**Elections above the Village Level.** The French granted the Vietnamese limited elective representation on the councils of a few of the larger cities. Two-thirds of the seats on the Saigon council were held by Frenchmen representing the city's 5,000 French inhabitants. The remaining one-third were held by Vietnamese who represented 120,000 native inhabitants.[9]

Alexandre Varenne, governor-general of Indochina for two years in the mid-twenties, gave slightly increased opportunities for consultation to a limited Vietnamese electorate by creating regional assemblies with some consultative powers in Tonkin and Annam. In Tonkin most of the Vietnamese assembly members were appointed, while in Annam most were selected by an electorate of "high officials, district chiefs, and some other Vietnamese controlled by the administration." [10] These regional assemblies were roughly comparable to the Cochinchina colonial council in which the Vietnamese had 10 representatives and the French 14. The Vietnamese representatives were chosen by an electorate of 10,000 out of perhaps 2,000,000 persons in the region who were at least 18 years of age.[11]

---

[8] Robert Shaplen, *The Lost Revolution: The U.S. in Vietnam, 1946–1966* (New York: Harper and Row, 1966), p. 92. The Viet Minh, founded by the Indochina Communist party in 1941, was the party's most inclusive front organization. It was the mass organization through which the Communist party carried on the war against France from 1945 to 1954. After independence the Viet Minh in North Vietnam became the Fatherland Front. In South Vietnam it was replaced in 1960 by the National Liberation Front. The new organizations were also controlled by the Communists.

[9] Joseph Buttinger, *Vietnam: A Dragon Embattled,* 2 vols. (New York: Frederick A. Praeger, 1967), vol. 1, pp. 551–552, footnote 88. In part because of French suppression of a Vietnamese nationalist party, the VNQDD, these minor elections strengthened both the Communists and the Trotskyists. See I. Milton Sacks, "Marxism in Vietnam," in Frank N. Trager, ed., *Marxism in Southeast Asia: A Study of Four Countries* (Stanford: Stanford University Press, 1959), p. 114 ff., for a description of the activities of the Marxist parties in the Saigon elections of the 1930s.

[10] Buttinger, *Dragon Embattled,* vol. 1, pp. 551–552, footnote 88.

[11] Ibid. See also Scigliano, "The Electoral Process in South Vietnam," p. 139. The Council of Cochinchina, according to Professor Scigliano, was chosen by an electorate of 12,000; it had 16 members of whom six were Vietnamese. None of the councils at the regional level had much power and all were dominated by French civil servants and colonists.

Cochinchina, but neither Annam nor Tonkin, was allowed to name one deputy to the French Chamber of Deputies. He was elected by French citizens—that is, by the French men in southern Vietnam and the handful of Vietnamese who were naturalized citizens. A Frenchman always held the post and clearly thought of himself as the representative of the colons, not of the Vietnamese.[12]

**Last Days of French Rule.** French influence deteriorated rapidly following World War II, but French governments and the French in Vietnam were slow to recognize this fact.

At home, the French assembly generally divided along left-right lines in proposing solutions to the Vietnamese "problem," but the Communist party alone insisted that there should be no negotiation between Paris and Vietnam except through Ho Chi Minh. The democratic left called for "negotiations with nationalists rather than the Vietminh, and even were prepared to accept the necessity of promising independence to a non-Communist regime . . ." while the center and right still demanded a "military solution." [13]

Aside from the Communists, most articulate Frenchmen wanted to create a government that would compete for Vietnamese support with Ho Chi Minh and the Viet Minh and, at the same time, would demand something less than full independence—a virtually impossible solution.

The French government and Bao Dai exchanged letters in 1949 establishing the State of Vietnam, independent but within the French Union. The French made concessions to Vietnamese aspirations for independence, but the concessions were hedged: control of defense and foreign affairs was retained by the French, and their control over the economy remained largely untouched.[14]

In 1954, the French recognized the need to reintegrate Cochinchina into Vietnam. To carry this off legally, it was necessary to select an assembly for the "Republic of Cochinchina" to approve the change of status. A mini-election was held in which, according to Bernard Fall, "abstentions in the district embracing Saigon and Cholon ran 90 percent,

---

[12] Buttinger, *Dragon Embattled,* vol. 1, pp. 552–553.

[13] Buttinger, *Dragon Embattled,* vol. 2, pp. 673–674. Buttinger provides a detailed story of the steps leading up to the "Bao-Dai solution" of 1949.

[14] Ibid., pp. 723–725.

and the total number who voted was 1,700 out of an adult population of 3 million." [15]

After several days of debate in May 1954, the newly elected assembly voted 55–6 with two abstentions to join Vietnam. A month later, after the French government ratified the action, Bao Dai returned to Saigon as the new head of the government of Vietnam. A handful of Vietnamese turned out to welcome him on his arrival in Saigon.[16] "Independence" for Vietnam, if indeed that is what it was, began inauspiciously at best.

## Ngo Dinh Diem Regime: 1954–1963

In 1946, Ngo Dinh Diem, who was to become first president of the Republic of Vietnam, rejected an offer to serve in the government of the Communist-dominated Viet Minh because he blamed its leader, Ho Chi Minh, for the murder of his brother. In 1949, he refused to be premier under Bao Dai because Vietnam was still a colony. Finally, in 1954, he accepted a new offer from Bao Dai after receiving the latter's promise of "full and complete civilian and military powers." [17]

During the first years of the Diem regime, South Vietnam was so badly divided that there were times when the government controlled little outside Saigon. But these were the years that Bernard Fall once called "Ngo Dinh Diem's finest hour." [18] Shaplen says of the early period of Diem's regime that "except for his family and a few Vietnamese friends and his American supporters, he literally stood alone." [19]

Premier Diem was generally opposed by the French who accepted him as the Vietnamese leader only after the United States made it clear that unless Diem were continued as premier, U.S. aid would be curtailed or stopped altogether. While it was U.S. policy to support Diem, some Americans in Saigon did so only reluctantly, either because they felt that the French alone could resist North Vietnamese attacks or because they were skeptical of Diem's ability to administer the country.

---

[15] Bernard Fall, *The Two Vietnams,* 2nd rev. ed. (New York: Praeger Publishers, Inc., 1967), p. 214.

[16] Ibid.

[17] Ibid., p. 244. Shaplen, *Lost Revolution* (1966 ed.), p. 114, says that Bao Dai retained some power of appointment under the new regime.

[18] Fall, *Two Vietnams,* p. 245.

[19] Shaplen, *Lost Revolution,* p. 115.

Diem's problems were legion. The commander of the South Vietnamese armed forces, a French citizen, refused to obey his orders. After the commander openly talked of a coup d'etat, Diem finally forced his withdrawal to France.

In the spring of 1955, Diem had to deal with the Binh Xuyen, a curious organization of 2,500 to 6,000 armed gangsters, river pirates, and gamblers, which controlled both the police and gambling and prostitution in the Saigon-Cholon area. Again in the face of French opposition, Diem ordered the army to attack; the Binh Xuyen was driven out of the city and its private army destroyed.[20]

By 1955, Diem had also broken the opposition of both the Hoa Hao and Cao Dai religious sects, which together could claim 2.5 million adherents. Some observers have argued that General Edward G. Lansdale, the U.S. advisor to Diem, bought off the Cao Dai and Hoa Hao leaders on behalf of Diem. General Lansdale flatly denies the story.[21]

Having defeated the major local opposition, Premier Diem convened a council in June 1955 to demand the abdication of Bao Dai and the transfer of all national political power to himself.[22] A national referendum was set for October to test public support for Diem and Bao Dai. Under any circumstances, Diem, who was perceived as both honest and successful in establishing a genuine national government free from French control, was assured a huge victory. The conduct of the campaign enhanced his chances. Campaign posters, political broadcasts, and

---

[20] In some respects the most useful description of the battle against the Binh Xuyen is to be found in Department of Defense, *U.S.-Vietnam Relations, 1945–1967* (Pentagon Papers), 12 vols. (Washington, D. C.: Government Printing Office, 1971), in the chapter "U.S. and France's Withdrawal from Vietnam, 1953–1956," vol. 1, pp. 27–32. The most detailed study in English is in Buttinger, *Dragon Embattled,* vol. 2, pp. 876–885.

[21] Shaplen, *Lost Revolution,* p. 117.

[22] Once again there are several versions of the repudiation of Bao Dai. Buttinger (*Dragon Embattled,* vol. 2, p. 890) states that the decision was made by "the archaic Council of the Royal Family at Hue." Fall, *Two Vietnams,* p. 27: "A gathering of the imperial clan was convened at Hue (under the protecting shadow of Ngo Dinh Can, Diem's brother); it obediently proclaimed Bao-Dai's dethronement on June 15, 1955." Department of Defense, *U.S.-Vietnam Relations, 1945–1967,* vol. 1, "The U.S. and France's Withdrawal from Vietnam, 1954–1956," p. 33: Ambassador Collins had recommended to Diem that he reconstitute the government. "Diem followed this advice. He invited some 700 elected counselors from 39 provinces to consider Bao Dai's legality. An Estates General composed of 50 counselors drew up a program demanding Bao Dai transfer all civilian and military powers to Diem who would exercise them until the assembly met—within six months—to draw up a constitution."

news stories all stressed Bao Dai the "pleasure-seeker," while portraying Diem as "miracle worker for the nation." The ballot itself showed pictures of Diem as the handsome young Vietnamese and of Bao Dai as an older man in traditional court clothes. Voters were to deposit in the ballot box the half of the ballot with the picture of the preferred candidate and throw away the other half.[23]

The announced vote was 98.2 percent for Diem and 1.1 percent for Bao Dai, with the remaining ballots spoiled. Denis Warner observed that "the 'referendum was not, and was not intended to be, an exercise in democratic procedures'; it was intended to be 'a collective demonstration of loyalty to the ruling authority.' "[24] In October 1955, the new Republic of Vietnam was proclaimed and Diem assumed the title of president.

**The Constitutional Assembly of 1956.** Late in January 1956, President Diem issued decrees calling for the election of 123 delegates to a National Constitutional Assembly charged with writing a constitution for the new republic.

Descriptions of the election vary greatly.[25] Professor Robert Scigliano says that 85 percent of the eligible voters turned out. There were 431 candidates, or an average for all districts of about 3.5 candidates per seat. The greatest competition was in the Saigon area. The fewest candidates per district were in the area which includes the mountains and some lowlands between Saigon and the region south of Danang

---

[23] J. A. C. Grant, "The Viet Nam Constitution of 1956," *American Political Science Review,* vol. 52 (June 1958), pp. 439–440. See also Buttinger, *Dragon Embattled,* vol. 2, pp. 890–891.

[24] Warner is quoted in Buttinger, *Dragon Embattled,* vol. 2, p. 891. George McTurnan Kahin and John W. Lewis, in *The United States in Vietnam,* rev. ed. (New York: Dial Press, 1969), pp. 71–72, limit themselves to giving the percentages for the two candidates and stating that Diem "conducted a grossly unfair election."

[25] Fall (*Two Vietnams,* pp. 258-259) and Buttinger (*Dragon Embattled,* vol. 2, pp. 942–943) suggest that the elections to the Constituent Assembly were controlled by the government. Scigliano in his article, "The Electoral Process in South Vietnam," p. 152, states: "The actual voting, however, was secret . . . in Saigon." And his article does not suggest the absence of secrecy elsewhere, although it does not exclude other pressures on the voter.

Professor Grant notes that in many of the single-member districts there were seven or eight persons contesting the seat so that frequently delegates were elected with less than half the votes of the district. His description does not preclude control of the elections but raises doubts that it occurred. See Grant, "Viet Nam Constitution of 1956," pp. 440–441.

(II Corps area). The three major parties in the campaign all supported President Diem and won 83 of the 123 seats. Among those elected were Madame Ngo Dinh Nhu, President Diem's sister-in-law, and four members of the Diem cabinet.[26] Scigliano concludes that

> the Government's tactics in the two campaigns [1956 for the convention and 1959 for the assembly] ranged from scrupulous fairness in observing the letter of elections laws to behind-the-scenes manipulations to violate their spirit. In general, it appears that the voting was carried on in fairness and secrecy and that the ballots were honestly counted, although improprieties could have been carried out in the provinces.[27]

Professor Scigliano also argues that the real issue in both elections was not the government's victory or defeat, "but how many people could be led to the polls and how big a victory the government could extract from them in the face of communist and other opposition. In other words, the elections were more a test of the government's strength than of its popularity." [28]

The heaviest turnout in 1956 and the heaviest vote for government candidates were in the rural areas. The strongest opposition took the form of a smaller turnout and a larger vote for anti-Diem candidates in the metropolitan Saigon area. This pattern is worth noting: it recurs again and again, through all subsequent Vietnamese elections.

**Provisions for Elections under the 1956 Constitution.** The new constitution provided for an elected president and National Assembly.[29] The latter was to consist of a single house whose members "shall be elected by universal and direct suffrage with secret ballot, according to procedures and conditions fixed by electoral law." There was to be one representative for every 50,000 eligible voters, with a minimum membership of 100. With minor exceptions, all persons age 18 and older could participate in the election of both the president and the assembly. The

---

[26] There are, in fact, two Scigliano accounts of the elections. The first, already cited, appeared in 1960. The second is in his excellent book, *South Vietnam: Nation Under Stress* (Boston: Houghton Mifflin Co., 1963), pp. 85–100. The accounts are similar except that the 1963 version suggests more government control over voting than the earlier essay.

[27] Scigliano, "The Electoral Process in South Vietnam," p. 150.

[28] Scigliano, *Vietnam: Nation Under Stress,* p. 95.

[29] Grant ("Viet Nam Constitution of 1956," pp. 444–457) provides the most complete description and discussion of the details of the constitution. The materials that follow are drawn from his article unless otherwise indicated.

term of assembly members was three years, but it could be extended "in case of war or internal disturbances," and the president could extend the term of particular representatives whose district had been "placed in a state of emergency, of alert or of siege."

The assembly was scheduled to meet twice a year for sessions not to exceed three months each. Special sessions could be called by the president or by a majority of the assembly. Meetings were to be public. When the assembly set its own rules of procedure, it urged the establishment of a "bloc" system with the goal of developing a two-party system.[30]

The president was to be elected to a five-year term and limited to three terms in all. President Diem's then current term was extended to April 30, 1961. All native-born citizens of 40 and over were eligible for the presidency. President Diem had asked the Constitutional Assembly to lower the age to 35, but his request was blocked by a coalition headed by Madame Nhu.[31]

The Constitutional Assembly turned down a committee proposal to give the president power to dissolve the National Assembly in case of an executive-legislative dispute "which may harm the interests of the nation." Instead, the assembly substituted a provision for a national referendum dealing with the matter in dispute. The results of the referendum would be binding on all parties.

A bill of rights guaranteed freedom of speech and press, with some limitations. At the same time, the constitution provided that anyone who might jeopardize "the republican form of government, the democratic regime, national freedom, independence, and unity shall be deprived of his rights." Other powers were granted to the president to suspend or restrict the liberties of individuals and organizations.[32]

The Constitutional Assembly then declared itself to be the first National Assembly, with its term to expire in 1959 when an election for a new assembly was scheduled.

---

[30] The bloc system never worked. Some 98 of the 123 members joined the majority bloc.

[31] Diem had favored the lower age because he wanted Nguyen Huu Chau to be eligible, but Madame Nhu opposed this friend and supporter of Diem and defeated the move.

[32] Grant, "Viet Nam Constitution of 1956," p. 462. While deploring some aspects of the constitution and of the Diem regime, Grant reminded his American audience that "our own First Amendment, it will be recalled, was followed by the Alien and Sedition Acts under conditions certainly far less explosive than those facing Vietnam. In fact, many of our present-day conceptions of justice that we like to attribute to the Constitution were actually post-18th century developments."

**Election of 1959.** Three elections were held under the 1956 constitution. Legislative elections were held in 1959 and again in 1963—a year behind schedule. A presidential election was held in 1961.

In general, the 1959 election followed the pattern of 1956. There were fewer parties in 1959—one large party and three small ones. The Can Lao party, which was controlled by Diem's brother Ngo Dinh Nhu, ran no candidates of its own but influenced the selection of candidates of the National Revolutionary Movement, the official government party.

There were 441 candidates seeking 123 seats, or an average of 3.6 candidates per seat.[33] The government won 89 seats (it had backed 94 party candidates). Professor Scigliano estimates that parties associated with the government received 79 percent of the total vote. Their strongest support came from the "communist-infested areas," while "the principal opposition to the government was in the secure—and freer—cities." (And by "freer," one might mean freer to indulge in the luxury of opposition and freer as well for more voters to go unhampered to the polls.) Winning legislative candidates in 1959 averaged 57 percent of the vote in the 22 urban districts of Vietnam, in contrast with an average of 84 percent in rural districts. In Saigon, the winning pro-government candidates averaged only 42 percent of the total vote.[34]

A coup d'etat was attempted on November 11, 1960, by paratroop and other military units. It failed for want of support among the bulk of the military leadership. Apparently many, perhaps a majority, of the civilians in Saigon supported the move, but the rest of the country was hardly aware of the attempt, much less involved in it.[35]

The attempted coup did suggest something of the increasing level of discontent in Saigon and elsewhere in the country. Reports to Washington spoke of "discontent with the Diem government [that] has been prevalent for some time among intellectuals and elite circles and . . . , to a lesser extent, in labor and urban business groups." The discontent focused on the Ngo family, the "pervasive influence of the Can Lao, the semi-clandestine apparatus of the regime; Diem's virtual one-man rule; and growing evidence of corruption in high places."[36] Discontent in

---

[33] Scigliano, "The Electoral Process in South Vietnam," p. 144.

[34] Scigliano, *Vietnam: Nation Under Stress,* p. 97.

[35] See Frank Trager, *Why Viet Nam?* (New York: Frederick A. Praeger, 1966), p. 158.

[36] Department of Defense, *U.S.-Vietnam Relations, 1945–1967,* vol. 10, pp. 1298–1299.

the cities was accompanied by reports of increasing rural unrest as well. A heralded land reform program had made little impact on peasant discontent. Attempts to protect villagers from the Viet Cong by transplanting them to strategic hamlets sometimes angered the peasants more than it protected them.

In 1958 and 1959 the Viet Cong had "fully resumed its campaign of terror in the countryside. . . ." [37] The rate of civilian assassinations and kidnappings rose rapidly over the next three years. Government figures showed the murders up from 193 in 1958 to 233 in 1959 to 780 in the first five months of 1960.[38] Bernard Fall asserts that the government

> lost almost 20 percent of its village chiefs in 1957 and 1958, and that by the end of 1959, they were becoming casualties at the rate of more than 2% per month. . . . The *New York Times* estimated that 3,000 local government officials were killed or captured during 1960. . . . The U.S. "White Paper" of 1961 cited losses of 1,400 local officials and civilians during 1960. . . . The violence was real, anti-government, rising in intensity, and increasingly organized.[39]

**The Elections of 1961 and 1963.** It was under this Communist pressure and the increasing opposition of intellectuals among others that President Diem faced the voters for the first time since the 1955 referendum against Bao Dai. In the April 1961 election Diem's opposition came from two virtual unknowns. The head of one ticket, Nguyen Dinh Quat, was a wealthy businessman who had formerly been a business associate of Diem's brother, Ngo Dinh Nhu. The other ticket was "headed by a 75-year-old practitioner of 'oriental medicine,' Ho Nhat Tan, who was too feeble even to read his speeches." [40]

Against this competition and with all the advantages of incumbency, Diem received 88 percent of the vote from a turnout of about 75 percent

---

[37] Ibid. (quoting Shaplen), vol. 2, pp. 56–57.

[38] Ibid., p. 58.

[39] Ibid. (quoting Bernard Fall and the *New York Times*), vol. 2, pp. 58–59. Race (*War Comes to Long An,* pp. 113–114) tells of the change in Long An province. "During the previous year (1959) . . . only three individuals had been assassinated in the whole province. Now in one week—the most solemn week of the year [Tet]—twenty-six people were killed: hamlet and village chiefs, youth leaders, Cong An, etc. Some were simply shot, while others died more agonizing deaths. Moreover, the Party [Communist] had planned a great many more than twenty-six executions . . ." but some of those marked for assassination escaped before the assassins arrived.

[40] Fall, *Two Vietnams,* p. 276.

of the eligible voters. Quat received 4 percent of the vote and Tan about double that amount. Diem ran least well in Saigon where he received only 64 percent of the vote. In the "Communist-infested" province of An Xuyen, he got 98 percent. In Kien Tuong, a "Communist-base area in the Plain of Reeds, and in the highland province of Pleiku, the opposition presidential candidates together got 7 votes to [Diem's] 102,031." [41]

The National Assembly elections were scheduled for the fall of 1962, but in July of that year the constitution was amended to extend assembly terms to four years. The elections were next scheduled for August 1963 but were again postponed until September 27 because of the violent conflict with the Buddhists.

The assembly election was finally held less than six weeks before the coup d'etat that toppled the Diem regime. The returns showed the number of invalid ballots to be 480,000 or 7.6 percent, a significant increase over earlier elections. As usual, the percentage of those voting in Saigon was lower than the national average; the number of invalid votes reached an amazing total of 25 percent.

As expected, Diem's National Revolutionary Movement won the largest number of seats of any party, 55. Independents, many of them committed to Diem, won 66 seats. Two socialists were elected. Some 60 deputies were reelected, 27 of whom had also served in the first National Assembly. Twenty-eight deputies who sought reelection were defeated. Another 35 did not seek reelection. More than one-third of all incumbents running (43) ran unopposed.

The new National Assembly met October 7 and had served three weeks when President Diem and his brother were overthrown and assassinated. The incoming military regime dissolved the National Assembly on November 2, 1963—and the disintegration of the Diem organization throughout the whole of South Vietnam rapidly ensued.

## Military Interregnum

The end of the Diem regime ushered in a period of heightened instability. For nearly four years the military dominated the government, while the country itself went largely ungoverned. Junta followed junta in a virtually continuous game of musical regimes. New constitutions or charters were quickly adopted with each change and as quickly discarded.

[41] Scigliano, *Vietnam: Nation Under Stress,* p. 97.

Government disarray was reflected in the collapse of its control over the countryside. The last years of the Diem regime had seen ever-increasing Viet Cong intimidation, murders, and abductions, and stepped up infiltration of northern soldiers into the South. Still, the Diem period was one of enemy harassment, not conquest. By contrast, during the early years of military government, the fortunes of Saigon declined sharply in the Mekong Delta as well as in the highlands and the provinces of the north. By April of 1966 the Reverend Hoang Quynh could assert that the "government controlled only 10 percent of the country's territory." [42] The priest may have exaggerated the situation, but not by much.

Buddhist dissent did not disappear with the death of Diem. The number of self-immolations was higher in 1966 than in 1963. The number of demonstrations increased during these same years. Thich Tri Quang and the An Quang Buddhists attempted to destroy governments and dictate national policy. Their continuing militancy invited charges of Communist control of the Buddhists or, at the least, of Buddhist politicization. This militant Buddhist effort was confined largely to the cities of the north and to a handful of activists in Saigon. It had little impact in the Delta. The leadership of the Buddhist church was itself divided between Thich Tri Quang and the more moderate Thich Tam Chau.

The military interregnum was least successful in its early days when it was led by older, French-trained generals. The government later was run more competently by younger officers who often had been trained in the United States. It was this latter group that eventually started the country back on the road to elective government.

**The Military Revolutionary Committee.** The Military Revolutionary Committee, chaired by Major General Duong Van ("Big") Minh, took control immediately after the coup of November 1, 1963. In a partial list of 22 members published four days later, the name of Lt. Col. Nguyen Van Thieu was number 18. Nguyen Cao Ky was not mentioned.

The committee suspended the 1956 constitution, dissolved the cabinet and the newly elected National Assembly, and adopted "a form of democracy consistent with the discipline required of a nation at war." All non-Communist parties were permitted "to operate within the limits

---

[42] L. A. Sobel, ed., *South Vietnam: U.S.-Communist Confrontation in Southeast Asia, 1966–67,* vol. 2 (New York: Facts on File, Inc., 1969), p. 224.

required by national defense security." [43] The committee promised to continue the struggle against the VC and North Vietnam.

The committee adopted a provisional constitution with the following principal features: (1) South Vietnam would remain a republic; (2) legislative and executive powers would reside in the Military Revolutionary Committee; (3) the chairman of the committee would exercise the powers of chief of state; (4) executive power was delegated by the committee to a provisional government with a committee-appointed prime minister, who would choose his cabinet subject to committee approval; (5) the legislative power was also delegated to the provisional government, with the exception of matters relating to the budget, fiscal legislation, defense, and security; and (6) existing laws and regulations would remain temporarily in force, with the exception of those "contrary to the spirit of the November 1 revolution." [44]

General Minh, whom Fall described as "friendly but inert," was chief of state, while the provisional government consisted of "faceless technicians led by Nguyen Ngoc Tho, an economist and Diem's former Vice President." [45]

A Central Executive Committee of 12 generals was to be responsible for "all major decisions until civilian rule was reestablished." General Minh chaired this committee too. A Council of Notables, consisting of 60 nongovernmental civilians appointed by Minh, was set up to advise on ways to "carry out the revolutionary policy in conformity with the people's aspirations." [46]

During the first weeks after the takeover, the new regime was recognized by most western European countries and the non-Communist countries in the Pacific—and by the U.S. France was slow in giving

---

[43] U.S. Agency for International Development (Saigon), *Public Administration Bulletin,* no. 9 (November 5, 1963), p. 1. This bulletin, which is issued periodically by the Public Administration Division of USAID (Saigon), includes compilations of English translations of major Vietnamese decrees, laws, national election returns, et cetera.

This publication is sometimes entitled *Public Administration Bulletin Vietnam* (or *Public Administration Bulletin USAID-Vietnam*), but is cited herein simply as *Public Administration Bulletin.*

[44] *Keesing's Contemporary Archives* (Bristol, England: Keesing's Publications Ltd.), April 18–25, 1964, p. 20016; hereinafter cited as *Keesing's.*

[45] Fall, *Two Vietnams,* pp. 285-286.

[46] *Keesing's,* April 18–25, 1964, p. 20017.

its recognition and made bad relations worse by supporting neutralization of all of Southeast Asia.[47]

The provisional government lasted only until January 30, 1964, when Generals Nguyen Khanh and Tran Thien Khiem overthrew it in a bloodless coup. The new government, with the approval of the Council of Notables, broke diplomatic relations with France. General Minh continued as chief of state while General Khanh took over as prime minister.

In March, General Khanh called on the Council of Notables to dissolve itself. The council refused, so the government dissolved it anyway a week later and announced that general elections would be held in the next four to six months "depending upon the degree of security in the country." [48]

For more than a year "governments" followed one another at a bewildering pace. Elections were promised but not held. Civilian leaders were brought in to "cosmeticize" the military government, but they were incessantly dropped, or reappointed, or replaced by other civilians.

General Khanh survived all efforts to oust him throughout 1964. As premier or president or chairman of something called the High National Council he remained the most powerful person in Saigon. The council even drafted a constitution that provided for an elected government. No elections were held. In late October 1964, civilian Phan Khac Suu was named chairman of the council and Tran Van Huong premier. But Buddhist opposition continued and even increased. So violent and unyielding were the Buddhists in their demands for the overthrow of the cabinet that Huong publicly linked them with the Viet Cong.[49] A bloodless December coup by the Armed Forces Council—a group of younger army officers—abolished the High National Council and ousted Huong and Suu. Characteristically, General Khanh landed on his feet: he became chairman of the new group.

In late 1964, General Minh was sent on a goodwill tour of Europe and General Khiem was posted to the United States as ambassador. Khanh thus got rid of the two men who had shared power and public attention with him. General Minh, in Robert Shaplen's words, had been

---

[47] Ibid.

[48] Ibid., p. 20018.

[49] Shaplen, *Lost Revolution,* pp. 276–277. Writing of the Buddhist demonstrations in August of 1964, Shaplen said that the demonstrators were sometimes persons who had been armed with clubs, "whipped into a frenzy," and paid to go screaming through the streets of Saigon.

a "thorn in his [General Khanh's] side—one that many felt the Americans should have helped him remove sooner . . . [Minh was] the inactive and sulky Chief of State, whose post the new charter [of August 16] abolished." [50]

General Khanh, against whom the Buddhists had so frequently demonstrated, now made common cause with them to denounce the United States and to intervene in the dispute between Huong and Suu over the issue of Buddhist activities. Huong was fired as prime minister, a position he had reassumed earlier in the month, while Suu, who supported the Buddhists, was retained as chief of state.[51] In February 1965, another coup led by the Armed Forces Council finally ended General Khanh's political career. He was sent to New York as ambassador-at-large and served as Vietnam representative to the U.N.

**First Days of the Thieu-Ky Regime.** In June 1965, the generals set up a new National Leadership Committee under General Nguyen Van Thieu. Marshal Nguyen Cao Ky became premier. Typically, the new government adopted a new charter or "convention." Its final article helps to sum up the problems of the preceding months: "The present Convention will take effect from the day it is promulgated until a permanent constitution is issued. The Provisional Charter No. 1 of November 4, 1963; the Provisional Charter No. 2 of July 2, 1964; the Charter of August 16, 1964; and the Provisional Charter of October 20, 1964, and all documents and laws contrary to the present Convention are hereby abolished." [52]

Also typically, the "convention" promised a new constitution. Untypically, however, the new regime proved to be relatively stable; and, after a year's delay, it made good on its promise to call elections for a constituent assembly to write a new constitution.

---

[50] Ibid., p. 271. Shaplen's reporting on the intricacies of government and Buddhist politics from the fall of Diem to the rise of Thieu and Ky in June 1965 is most perceptive. So also is Charles A. Joiner, "South Vietnam's Buddhist Crisis: Organization for Charity, Dissidence, and Unity," *Asian Survey,* July 1964, pp. 915–928. For another very useful report from a somewhat different perspective see Adam Roberts, "Buddhism and Politics in South Vietnam," *The World Today,* June 1965, pp. 240–250.

[51] Shaplen, *Lost Revolution,* p. 301.

[52] Fall, *Two Vietnams,* Appendix VII, pp. 451–454, where the full text of the charter is printed. The National Leadership Committee first included 10 generals, but was later expanded to include 10 civilians as well. The Central Executive Committee, whose chairman was Prime Minister Nguyen Cao Ky, carried out the functions of a cabinet.

The Ky-Thieu regime did bring a measure of stability—but it did not pass miracles. Buddhist militancy and divisiveness of leadership in Saigon in 1964-65 made national survival itself problematic. Even in the zone of highest priority, the six provinces immediately surrounding Saigon, the Viet Cong held the upper hand in many, perhaps most, villages and hamlets. A highly publicized pacification program, *Hop Tac,* failed to achieve much in the way of pacification. In March 1966, Shaplen reported that "less than a third of the hamlets are now candidates for construction (i.e., pacification) programs," which was to say that two-thirds of the hamlets were not under government control within a radius of 40 miles from the center of Saigon. He quoted a former chief of Hau Nghia province (which touches directly on Saigon) as saying: "There are two hundred and twenty thousand people in Hau Nghia, and two hundred thousand of them are ruled by the Vietcong, which made me a hamlet chief, not a province chief." Of the 300 hamlets in Hau Nghia only 28 had chiefs in March 1966, and only half of those dared "to spend the night in their hamlets." [53] Nationally, of 16,000 hamlets, "some thirty-eight hundred are listed . . . as 'pacified,' but it has been estimated that as many as half of these are still under some degree of Vietcong penetration or influence." [54]

---

[53] Robert Shaplen, *The Road From War: Vietnam, 1965–1970* (New York: Harper and Row, 1970), p. 45. See also Race, *War Comes to Long An,* pp. 105–140, for a detailed description of VC control during that period; Long An once included Hau Nghia and so is treated as part of that province by Professor Race.

[54] Shaplen, *Road From War,* p. 47.

# 3

# The Constituent Assembly and the Constitution, 1966-1967

With government fortunes at their nadir since 1954 and Thich Tri Quang still presiding over Buddhist disorders, General Thieu issued a decree of April 14, 1966, authorizing an election commission to prepare the way for elections of a Constituent Assembly. Its job, in turn, was to write a constitution as the first step toward the creation of representative government. Thich Tri Quang then called a halt to the Buddhist demonstrations. But, when the National Leadership Committee announced in May 1966 that it would continue to hold power even after the Constituent Assembly elections, and presumably until the new constitution was in force, the Buddhists started up again. The government reestablished control over Danang by force, and after new fighting broke out in Hue, the government simply took over (again by force) in mid-June.[1]

Meantime, on May 5, 1966, the National Leadership Committee had appointed a representative 32-member commission to draft a law for the election of a Constituent Assembly. The commission recommended that this body double as a national legislature, but its recommendation was turned down by the committee.

The Constituent Assembly was directed to write a constitution within six months of its convening. Its draft would then go to the National Leadership Committee chairman (General Thieu) who could suggest changes. His proposed changes would take effect unless the

[1] For an excellent discussion of the Buddhist-Government of Vietnam problems and interrelations between the two in the winter and spring of 1966, see John C. Donnell and Charles A. Joiner, "South Vietnam: 'Struggle' Politics and the Bigger War," *Asian Survey*, January 1967, p. 53ff.

assembly disapproved them by a two-thirds vote, and he was to promulgate the new constitution within 30 days after first receiving the draft text. If he failed to meet this schedule the "constitution will be effective *de facto*." [2] The committee was then responsible for setting up the institutions called for in the constitution within three to six months after the date of promulgation.

**Election Rules.** The rules for the September 11, 1966, elections were extremely detailed but in essence provided the following:

1. All persons age 18 or older who met the voter requirements could participate, i.e., virtually everyone except felons, the insane, Communists, and "pro-Communist neutralists."
2. The assembly was to consist of 117 members, with 13 seats reserved for various minority ethnic groups.
3. Generally, there was to be one representative for every 50,000 registered voters but there had to be at least one for each independent city and province.
4. Each province or independent city was a single constituency except for Saigon and Gia Dinh which were subdivided into three and two smaller constituencies, respectively.
5. Constituencies entitled to more than one representative were to use the list system of proportional representation for making their choices. Each list was to include as many names as there were seats apportioned to the constituency. The number of persons elected from a list depended on the proportion of the total vote cast that was received by the list. For example, if there were four seats to be filled and a list received 50 percent of the votes cast, the two top names on the list were declared elected. No candidate on a list receiving less than 5 percent of the votes could be elected under the 1966 rules. One multi-member constituency in Saigon was assigned six seats; the other two Saigon constituencies and the two in Gia Dinh each were allotted five seats. No other constituency was large enough to have more than four seats.
6. Candidates had to be Vietnamese by birth or by naturalization, be at least 25 years old, enjoy the full rights of citizenship, and not be in violation of obligations of service in the armed forces.

[2] Article 20, Decree-Law No. 021/66, June 19, 1966, on the organization of the election for the national Constituent Assembly, in U.S. Agency for International Development (Saigon), *Public Administration Bulletin,* no. 29 (July 1, 1966), pp. 3–34.

7. Persons convicted of certain crimes, the insane, and "persons who work directly or indirectly for communism or neutralism" were excluded from candidacy.

8. Also excluded were officials in provinces or districts, magistrates, high police officials, and commissioned and noncommissioned officers who were "commanders or deputy commanders of an administrative or military area or in charge of any unit from company size upward."

9. Electoral campaign committees representing all candidates were to lay down rules for the campaign and assure equality of treatment for all candidates.

10. Electoral expenses within a stipulated amount were to be covered by the central government, but each candidate had to deposit enough to cover his expenses; this deposit would be returned to him if he received at least 5 percent of the votes cast in his district.

11. Except in multi-member districts, as noted above, there was to be a separate ballot for each candidate. In either case, a slogan and an identifying emblem were allowed to appear on the ballot; but the emblem "should not be ridiculous, nor similar to any international emblem, nor to any familiar religious emblem." [3]

12. To receive his ballots, the voter had to present both his voter card and identity card to be checked.[4]

13. To vote, he had to take all ballots and an envelope into a booth where he made his selection and placed it in the official envelope

---

[3] George McTurnan Kahin and John W. Lewis, *The United States in Vietnam,* rev. ed. (New York: Dial Press, 1969), pp. 258–259. The authors make much of the allegation that the rules discriminated against the Buddhists. They suggest that "many multimember constituencies were established in areas of greatest Buddhist strength, [thus] the number of candidates that the Buddhists could expect to elect was thereby reduced." No other commentator makes this point, perhaps because more multi-member districts electing more candidates were created in areas of *non-Buddhist* strength, e.g., Gia Dinh and Saigon. In any case it is not the fact of multi-member districts that is relevant. (The Buddhists won 22 of 24 seats in I Corps in 1971 mainly in multi-member districts.) The list system of proportional representation could have an impact but it could help any organized minority in a district—Buddhists, for example. Kahin and Lewis also stress the restriction on the use of religious symbols and the reduction in the assembly membership from the 171 originally proposed to 117. Both figures were based on the number of registered voters, so it is difficult to see how there would be any significant discrimination against a group as numerous as the Buddhists.

[4] The identity cards were the result of research sponsored by Michigan State University and were developed in order to provide maximum security for the cards and for use in citizen identification.

while destroying the remaining ballots. He then dropped the envelope into the voting box.

14. Four copies were made of the election results. One was posted locally, one kept for the files, and the other two sent forward to the central voting station for each constituency.

15. The right to file complaints was recognized and the courts had 10 days within which to hand down a decision.

The rules have been given in some detail because, except for the proportional representation system, essentially the same rules have applied to all later elections. As is so often the case with South Vietnamese political processes, the rules closely follow French precedents.[5]

**The Election.** Nguyen Duy Lien, the South Vietnamese observer at the United Nations, requested the U.N. to send a team to "supervise the elections." Arthur Goldberg, the U.S. delegate, supported the request—an earnest that the Vietnamese government was seeking to conduct "fair, honest, and representative elections." The U.N. Security Council never met on the subject, and no observers were sent.[6] Invitations for foreign neutral observers have been issued for each subsequent national election in South Vietnam.

Professors Donnell and Joiner, viewing it against the backdrop of civil war and government instability, conclude that "the election of September 11 for members of the Constitutional Assembly was unquestionably the most significant symbolic and perhaps actual political event of the year" in Vietnam. They further stress the relatively large turnout in all regions in spite of opposition from Buddhist Thich Tri Quang and Catholic Reverend Hoang Quynh. "The opportunity to participate in a referendum proved a potent incentive to all regions." [7]

There were 532 candidates for the 117 seats, or roughly 4.5 candidates per seat. The registration lists included 5,288,572 voters from an estimated total population of 16,400,000. The turnout amounted to 4,274,872, or about 80.8 percent of eligible voters. The figure for registered voters was considerably below those for the 1963 and 1961

---

[5] The full statement of the rules is to be found in *Public Administration Bulletin,* no. 29, pp. 3–34.

[6] *Keesing's,* August 13–20, 1966, p. 21564.

[7] Donnell and Joiner, " 'Struggle' Politics and the Bigger War," pp. 58–59. For a very different description of the turnout and election, see Kahin and Lewis, *United States in Vietnam,* p. 258 ff.

elections for the National Assembly and president, respectively. The lower figure may simply be more accurate than the earlier ones. But also it doubtless reflects loss of territory and population under the control of the South Vietnamese government.

In addition to the highlanders and the ethnic Cambodians who had been assured of election in advance, 30 persons of northern Vietnamese origin were elected, 28 central Vietnamese, and 43 southern Vietnamese. Three Chinese were elected from the Cholon area.

The religious breakdown showed 35 Catholics, 34 Buddhists, 10 Hoa Hao, 5 Cao Dai, 4 Therevada, 1 Protestant, and 20 unspecified. The better organization or greater cohesion of the Catholics was clearly reflected in the results: of the total population, only about 10 percent was Catholic. At the same time, as Professor Sacks has noted, fewer than half the Catholics elected were displaced northerners, suggesting that the day of refugee dominance was passing.[8]

In occupational terms, heaviest representation went to four groups: civil servants 21; military 20; teachers 20; and merchants 16. After them came lawyers with 9, farmers 8, doctors 5, journalists 3, while 13 were not identified.[9]

Twenty-one of the delegates, or 15 percent, were associated with two of the traditional Vietnamese parties. Twelve were members of the Vietnam Democratic Nationalist party (VNQDD) and nine were from "various factions of the Dai Viet (Great Vietnam National party)." [10]

Robert Shaplen, commenting on the outcome, said it was "without doubt the fairest election ever held in South Vietnam" up to that time.[11] Earlier he had questioned the willingness of the military to keep hands off and thus allow a substantial civilian majority. In fact only 20 of 58 military candidates won. Shaplen seemed to agree with Sacks that the winners represented a fair cross section of the population of South Vietnam under government jurisdiction. They both saw some hope for a reduction in the bitterness of religious division.[12]

---

[8] I. Milton Sacks, "Restructuring Government in South Vietnam," *Asian Survey,* August 1967, p. 522; he gives the number of Catholic winners as 32.

[9] These figures and those on religious affiliation come from the U.S. Department of State *Fact Sheet* for October 1967.

[10] Sacks, "Restructuring Government," p. 522.

[11] Shaplen, *The Road From War: Vietnam, 1965–1970* (New York: Harper and Row, 1970), p. 83.

[12] Ibid., p. 85, and Sacks, "Restructuring Government," p. 522.

**Principal Constitutional Provisions.** The Constituent Assembly convened in November and submitted its final draft of the constitution on March 18, 1967, well within the fixed timetable. The assembly elected Phan Khac Suu, onetime chief of state, as its president. Suu was an active politician, clearly identified with civilian government. A member of the Cao Dai sect, he was also acceptable to the northern Buddhists.

The civilian leanings of the assembly were evident early when it adopted, by a vote of 75-8, an article that prohibits "soldiers on active duty from holding office or belonging to political parties." [13]

The constitution "advocates" equality of all citizens "without discrimination as to sex, religion, race or political party" (Article 2); opposes communism in any form and prohibits any activity "designed to publicize or carry out communism" (Article 4); and includes a Bill of Rights (Articles 6–22) that provides the usual guarantees but limits speech, press, and publishing by excluding the freedom to say those things that "harm personal honor, national security and good morals." Censorship is permitted in motion pictures and the theater, and the constitution provides that "press regulations shall be prescribed by law." The statement of rights is followed by a statement of duties, i.e., to defend the country, the constitution, and the law, to fulfill military duty, and to pay taxes (Articles 25–29).

The constitution provides for a two-house legislature or National Assembly. Members of the House of Representatives or lower house are elected from provincial or autonomous city districts by secret ballot. Terms are four years. To be eligible, a candidate has to be of Vietnamese birth or be naturalized for at least seven years, be at least 25 years of age, enjoy full citizenship, and "have draft status in order" (Articles 30–32). The size of the House may range from 100 to 200 members and is based on the number of registered voters in the country.

The Senate has 60 members [14] elected at-large on lists that include candidates for one-sixth of the total seats, i.e., lists of 10. Terms are six years with half the membership elected every three years. Candidates have to be at least 30 years of age and meet the other requirements for members of the House of Representatives (Article 33).

---

[13] Lester A. Sobel, ed., *South Vietnam: U.S. Communist Confrontation in Southeast Asia, 1966–67,* vol. 2 (New York: Facts on File, Inc., 1969), p. 242.

[14] The constitution actually provides for either 30 or 60 Senate members, but there have always been 60.

Members of both houses are protected in their freedom of speech and vote on the floor and are free from arrest and prosecution except with the concurrence of three-fourths of the members of both houses or in cases of *flagrante delicto*. Even in the latter cases, prosecution must stop if "the house concerned so requests." Members are prohibited from holding other offices except that they may teach in universities and advanced technical schools (Article 37).

Sessions of both houses are open unless voted to the contrary by 50 percent of the members of either. Two sessions are required each year. The right to call special sessions is given to the president and to one-third of the members of both houses (Articles 47–49).

The House of Representatives is the more powerful of the two bodies. If the Senate fails to agree with the House version of a bill, it still becomes law if repassed by a two-thirds vote of the House. In the event the House cannot muster the necessary vote, the Senate version is enacted (Article 43). (In 1971, the House overrode objections of the Senate by the required two-thirds majority and thus enacted the government-proposed presidential voting act. In 1972, the House failed on one occasion to override a Senate refusal to grant the president emergency powers after the North Vietnamese invasion.)

The president, in whom executive authority is vested, is elected along with a vice presidential running mate by universal suffrage for a term of four years. The president and vice president can be reelected only once. To be eligible, a candidate has to be Vietnamese from birth and have continuously resided in the country for at least 10 years before election. (Time spent abroad on official assignment or in political exile is excepted.) He has to be at least 35 years old and meet the legal draft requirements (Articles 51–53).

The Supreme Court, to be established after the new National Assembly meets, is authorized to "establish a list of candidates [for president and vice president], . . . control the fairness of the election, and . . . announce the result." Candidates are to receive equal government financing in the election campaign. "Procedures and conditions governing candidacies and elections of the President and Vice President are to be prescribed by law" (Article 54).

As under the French system, the president appoints the prime minister and cabinet. In other areas he is given appointive powers subject to approval by the Senate. "In special situations, the President [is given authority to] sign decree-laws declaring a state of alert, curfew or emergency over part or all of the national territory," which the legislature can "ratify, amend or reject." In periods of war and when elections cannot be held, the president with approval of two-thirds of both houses can "extend the terms of office of certain elected bodies and appoint some province chiefs" (Articles 56–65).

Villages and municipalities are guaranteed elective governments, but even elective legislative and executive officials can be "dismissed by the President if they [have] violated the Constitution, laws of the nation, or national policy" (Articles 71–75).

The members of the Supreme Court are chosen by the National Assembly from a list of eligible lawyers who have been nominated by organizations of judges, prosecutors, and lawyers. The Supreme Court is granted not only electoral functions but is authorized to "decide on the dissolution of a political party whose policy and activities oppose the republican form of government" (Articles 80–84).

An ethnic council is authorized to represent the various ethnic minorities on salient matters of public policy and law enforcement (Articles 97–98).

Articles 99–102 are concerned exclusively with political parties:

> Article 99 (1) The Nation recognizes that political parties have an essential role in a democratic society. (2) Political parties may be organized and may operate freely, according to the procedures and conditions prescribed by law.
>
> Article 100. The Nation encourages progress toward a two-party system.
>
> Article 101. The Nation recognizes the formalization of political opposition.
>
> Article 102. Regulations governing political parties and political opposition shall be prescribed by law.

Finally, several articles prescribe the general rules for election of the legislature and president. The National Assembly is empowered to establish "a list of candidates and shall control the legality and shall announce the result of the election of the first President and Vice President." During his first term, the president is authorized to appoint province chiefs. Elections for president and vice president are to be scheduled within six months of the promulgation of the constitution, and the National Assembly and the Supreme Court must be set up and operating within 12 months (Articles 113–116).

In the interim, the National Constituent Assembly elected in September 1966 is to assume national legislative powers (Article 110). Robert Devereux has noted in his commentary on the new constitution that this provision threatened the adoption of the entire draft. The National Leadership Committee objected to the decision of the assembly ignoring provisions of the decree that established it and "extending [its] own mandate [which] was a brazen attempt at self-aggrandizement. The deputies refused to alter their position even at the risk of seeing their work rejected, and in the end the military leaders gave way." [15]

The assembly approved the draft on March 18, 1967. Nine days later the National Leadership Committee followed suit, and Chief of State Nguyen Van Thieu promulgated the new constitution of the Republic of Vietnam on April 1, 1967.

[15] Robert Devereux, "South Vietnam's New Constitutional Structure," *Asian Survey,* August 1968, pp. 644–645.

# Historical Setting: One

*(In which subnational institutions and electoral processes are described.)*

**Local Elections, 1966–1970.** In December 1966, prior to the writing of the constitution, new and uniform governmental structures for villages and hamlets were established by decree. Elections at both levels were scheduled for the spring of 1967.[1]

The villages were to be governed by people's councils elected by all persons age 18 and older. (Villages with populations of less than 2,000 were to have councils of six members while villages of more than 10,000 were to elect 12 members.) A smaller administrative committee was

[1] Subnational elections for province and autonomous city councils were held two years earlier. (John C. Donnell, in "Expanding Political Participation—The Long Haul from Villagism to Nationalism," *Asian Survey,* November 1970, refers to them as "province advisory councils.") The elections were in May 1965, shortly before Nguyen Van Thieu and Nguyen Cao Ky first came to power. Government and army officials were ineligible. Roughly 1,000 candidates sought 471 seats. Some 4.7 million voters were registered, and, of this number, 3.5 million or 74 percent cast ballots.

Professor Donnell states in the above article that the impact of these councils has been "minimal." Council members have frequently sought membership in the National Assembly—especially in the lower house—but they have not been particularly successful. Nine were elected in 1967 and 13 in 1971.

A second round of elections for province and city councils was held June 28, 1970. The elections attracted relatively little voter attention. Some 73 percent of the voters turned out. In the six autonomous cities (the number was increased to 11 in the fall of 1970), 323 candidates sought 76 positions. In the provinces, 1,627 candidates campaigned for 478 seats. For all provincial and city returns, see U.S. Agency for International Development, *Public Administration Bulletin,* no. 54 (September 1970), pp. 46–48.

Province chiefs, who dominate government and administration in the provinces, are not now elected. Until they are, interest in province elections is not likely to be great. Constitutionally, province chiefs could be appointed by the president during his first term of office. Presumably, therefore, elections are to be held sometime during the second presidential term.

created as the executive arm of the village. The council was authorized to choose one of its members as chairman of the administrative committee, and he in turn named the remaining members of the committee subject to approval by the council. Each member of the committee had administrative responsibility for one or more policy areas.[2]

The special commissioner for administration, a national official, was empowered to "dissolve the Village Council upon the recommendation of a committee" composed of the province chief or his representative, a local presiding judge of a court of first instance or a court with extended powers or a justice of the peace, and one member of the provincial council. Dissolution could be ordered if the council was "inoperative or there [was] evidence that activities of more than half of the Village Council members [were] pro-Communist or neutralist in favor of Communism." [3]

The hamlets were under the administrative control of a hamlet management committee composed of the hamlet chief, an assistant for security, and another for propaganda and civic action. In hamlets that exceeded 3,000 persons, a deputy hamlet chief assisted the hamlet chief. Hamlet chiefs and deputy chiefs were elected by universal suffrage. The two assistants were appointed by the village administrative committee on the recommendation of the hamlet chief and with the concurrence of the village council. In general, the hamlet chief's function was to represent the village government in the hamlet and to speak for the hamlet at the village level.

Elections for the village councils were scheduled for five successive Sundays from April 2 to April 30, 1967, while the hamlet elections were scheduled for another five successive Sundays from May 14 to June 11, 1967. The elections at the two levels were set at separate times to prevent administrative and voter confusion; late spring was chosen as a period of relative freedom from farming tasks for the peasants.

Candidates for the three-year terms for village council or for hamlet chief or deputy had to be citizens by birth or by naturalization (for five years in the latter instance), be residents of the village for one year,

---

[2] For a full description of the village and hamlet governments, see Decree No. 198-SL/DUHC of 24 December 1966, reprinted in *Public Administration Bulletin,* no. 35 (February 1, 1967), pp. 36–72. This description is supplemented by a long memorandum from the special commissioner for administration to the province chiefs of January 9, 1967. See *Public Administration Bulletin,* no. 36 (April 1, 1967), pp. 5–37.

[3] See Article 7, Decree No. 198-SL/DUHC of 24 December 1966, reprinted in *Public Administration Bulletin,* no. 35 (February 1, 1967), p. 38.

must not have been deprived of civic rights or convicted of a felony, or be bankrupt or insane, and must have met military draft requirements. The age requirement was 25 for the village councils and 21 for hamlet chief or deputy.

A board at the province level was required to review the list of voters and to check the candidates and the election returns for each village. The province board included the province and district chiefs or their representatives, a senior judge in the province, and two provincial councillors (or two notables chosen by lot to represent the people). A comparable board at the district level was set up for hamlet elections.

Would-be candidates submitted applications to the boards along with birth certificates, up-to-date court record forms, and certificates of residence. The candidates were screened to see that they met the requirements listed and "to eliminate any Viet Cong agents, known criminals or others proscribed from running for office by the Constitution."[4] In 1967, some 286 possible candidates were rejected as "pro-Communist or neutralist in favor of Communism." Of these, 25 were former village and hamlet officials.[5]

In the village elections, the candidate receiving the largest number of votes was to be the council chairman (i.e., village chief) and the candidate receiving the second highest number, the vice chairman. Consistent with Vietnamese custom, in case of ties the older candidate wins.

Campaigns lasted no more than seven days. Campaign costs were defrayed by the candidates who made equal contributions to a central pot administered by representatives of all of them.

The village and hamlet elections were characterized by the government as "the first truly free elections at the local level in Vietnam's history." In the local elections of an earlier period of this century the "reins of power . . . usually were held by hereditary mandarins steeped in the Confucian tradition. These village chiefs and their councils derived their authority from an acquiescent people's ritual votes of confidence at the polls. . . . Their choices were limited because the candidates were self-recruited village gentry. . . ."[6]

Elections for 993 of the 2,552 villages (39.3 percent)—an indication of the level of pacification—were scheduled for early 1967. Another

---

[4] Ibid., pp. 59–60 (see Articles 3–7 of Decree No. 199-SL/DUHC).

[5] *Public Administration Bulletin,* no. 38 (June 1, 1967), p. 6.

[6] *Viet-Nam Bulletin* (Info series No. 2), distributed by the Embassy of the Republic of Vietnam, August 1969, p. 4.

275 (10.8 percent) were to be held later, contingent on the success of the pacification programs. Elections were postponed in six villages for security reasons and in three because there were not enough qualified candidates. The highest percentage of villages secure enough for elections were in III Corps (44.3 percent) and IV Corps (42 percent). Six candidates were killed, one wounded, and 18 turned up "missing" during the campaign and election. Another 22 were captured but had been released in time for the elections.[7]

Elections were next held in 4,608 hamlets, or 33.3 percent of the 13,005 hamlets in the country. Still another 972 hamlets (7 percent) were scheduled for later in the year, subject to further pacification. The highest percentage of eligible hamlets were found (again) in III Corps (37.1 percent) and IV Corps (35.8 percent). At least seven candidates were murdered by the Viet Cong during the campaign, but elections were postponed in only one instance.[8]

Turnout in the villages was 77 percent of the registered voters and in the hamlets, 78.7 percent. The heaviest turnout was in the Mekong Delta and the lightest in the area just outside Saigon, in the strip of provinces from the Cambodian border to the South China Sea.

At the hamlet level, 45.4 percent of those elected were farmers and 33.3 percent were either village or hamlet officeholders. No other category won as many as 5 percent of the positions. Farmers also dominated the village elections, winning 57 percent of the council seats. Next in line came the incumbent village and hamlet officials with 13.1 percent of the seats, merchants with 11 percent, and the "liberal professions" with 4.7 percent. None of the other "occupational" categories elected as many as 4 percent of the 8,964 new council members.

Hamlets and villages in recently pacified areas held their first local elections in the spring of 1969. By the end of June 1969, there were fully elected councils in more than 88 percent of South Vietnam's villages and elected hamlet chiefs in over 81 percent of the hamlets.

In 1970, the three-year terms of the first councillors had expired and new elections were held. The turnout of registered voters reached

---

[7] All figures on the village elections for the spring of 1967 are found in *Public Administration Bulletin,* no. 38 (June 1, 1967), which was a special issue devoted exclusively to village elections.

[8] All figures on the hamlet elections of May and June of 1967 are in *Public Administration Bulletin,* no. 40 (August 15, 1967), which was a special issue on hamlet elections.

nearly 85 percent. Roughly half the council members elected in 1970 were persons who had not previously held that office.

**Reorganization, 1972 Decree.** In late August 1972, President Thieu issued a decree reorganizing village and hamlet governments.[9] The decree abolished the election of hamlet chiefs, and gave the province chiefs power to appoint members of the village administrative committees (except for the village chief who has to be a member and, indeed, chairman of the committee) and the hamlet management boards. At the same time these administrative bodies were sharply reduced in size.

The timing of the move, according to some U.S. officials, may have been prompted in part by the invasion from the North [10] and was also intended to tighten provincial control of local administration. Cutting the size of the village administrative councils from 14 to eight and the hamlet management boards (in the larger hamlets) from 11 to six might also result in substantial financial savings.

As a result of the decree, the village council lost the power to approve appointments to the village administrative committee. The village chief, on the other hand, who is the one elective member of the committee and its chairman, emerged with increased power. His office has also been given back some functions that have been exercised in recent years by an appointed member of the village administrative committee whose position was abolished by the decree. Some U.S. officials believe that the village chief's nomination of members of the village administrative committee will generally be accepted by the province chief.

Village elections were unaffected by the decree. And, all across the board, it is not yet possible to say what practical effect the decree will have: as of publication date, authoritative evidence is simply lacking.

[9] Decree No. 120 SL/VN, 22 August 1972.

[10] President Thieu had proposed a somewhat similar action to the National Assembly in August 1971 but had failed to win support for it.

# 4
# The Presidential Election of 1967

## Rules, Processes, and Candidates

Following the new constitution's promulgation on April 1, 1967, the National Assembly began at once devising laws to govern the next round of presidential and legislative elections. The National Leadership Committee was sometimes at odds with the assembly concerning the specific provisions. The committee could recommend changes in the assembly's proposed rules and could overrule those that had been adopted by less than an absolute majority. The committee was itself often divided—divisions that generally reflected the political struggle between Marshal Ky and General Thieu.

On one issue there was no apparent disagreement. After first proposing a two-tier presidential election, Thieu backed off. All other officials consistently opposed the idea of a runoff between the top two candidates in the event that no one received an absolute majority on the first ballot. U.S. embassy personnel, who feared that without such a second election the winner might receive only a relatively small percentage of the total vote, tried hard to persuade the Vietnamese of the merits of such a system. But the National Assembly rejected the runoff by a wide margin. The Vietnamese, according to embassy officials, opposed the idea on the ground that the leading candidate in the first round might well lose in the second. They were quite right: such a possibility is, of course, the principal justification for a second round of elections to begin with.

The question of candidate eligibility was one major area of conflict between the National Leadership Committee and the National Assembly. The assembly originally proposed the endorsement of presidential candidates by at least 30 "popularly elected officials"—that is, 30 signatures from among the 117 members of the National Assembly or the members of the provincial and municipal councils elected in 1965. This proposal was similar to the one that did become law in 1971.

In 1967, Premier Ky asserted that the requirement of 30 endorsements "doesn't bother anybody who has the ability to run." [1] General Thieu, by contrast, argued that such a requirement was unconstitutional. The National Assembly voted to retain the requirement of endorsements but by a vote of less than 50 percent of the full membership, which left the National Leadership Committee free to make its own decision. A majority of the committee joined Thieu in opposing the rule, and the finished product included no such requirement.[2]

A second area of disagreement between the National Assembly and the National Leadership Committee involved senatorial election rules. The committee wanted voters to select president and senators the same day, perhaps on the theory that the senatorial candidates favored by the winning presidential candidate would thus receive added strength.[3] The committee also wanted all voters to select six slates of 10 candidates each; the National Assembly initially favored limiting each voter to selecting only one slate. The committee's preference meant that the voters would be selecting the entire membership of the Senate at-large at one time. The assembly agreed to the simultaneous election of the Senate and president but then sought to limit each voter to the selection of two slates. The committee went back to six in the final version. The assembly could not muster enough votes to override and denounced this change as "flouting the will of the people." [4] The electoral laws were officially promulgated on June 15, 1967.

**Election Preliminaries.** In South Vietnam, the government takes the initiative in registering voters, as is the case in most countries except the United States. For voters in the military services, registration is the responsibility of each unit commander. In 1967, the tentative lists of

---

[1] *Chronology of Major Internal Political Developments in Viet-Nam Since Diem,* a chronology given to the Presidential Observer Team appointed by President Lyndon B. Johnson to observe the 1967 elections (mimeographed), p. 8 (hereinafter cited as *Chronology*).

[2] Ibid., pp. 8–9.

[3] If that was the theory, it was apparently incorrect. Later voting patterns would indicate no perceptible "coattail" effect.

[4] *Chronology,* p. 9.

voters were posted for the first time on July 10. Any citizen was allowed until July 25 to complain if his name had not been included on the list or if it had been incorrectly recorded (as to home district, for example). When the final list was posted on August 14, 390,000 names had been added.

Eligible voters were persons of Vietnamese nationality who, "irrespective of sex, [were] 18 years of age as of December 31, 1966, and who [were] inscribed on the electors' list and holders of regular electors' cards except those deprived of the rights of citizenship." The latter category included criminals, the insane, and Communists.

Each eligible voter was given a voter card (see page 53) which he showed along with his regular identification card to verify his right to vote. Voter cards were distributed at the time and in the manner prescribed by the election committee of each province to take into account differences in security in various sections of the country.[5] In some less secure areas, for example, they were not distributed until a day or two before the elections. In Saigon, the cards were ready more than a week in advance but could be picked up as late as 3:00 p.m. election day.

Ballots for every slate were printed by the Special Commission for Administration (the central body in charge) and distributed to the autonomous municipalities and provinces. Each carried the full names of the presidential and vice-presidential candidates, their photographs, and the name and symbol of the slate. The ballots looked like the public posters for each slate, already recognizable to the voters, except that they were smaller (of course) and did not include the three- or four-line statement of principles. Envelopes for the ballots were also distributed by the commission.

The number of polling places in the country exceeded 8,800, considerably more than there had been for the 1966 election to the National Constituent Assembly: pacification programs had increased the number of hamlets and villages in which elections could be held, and the Special Commission for Administration had directed the provinces and autonomous municipalities to increase the number to avoid the overcrowding found at some voting places in the preceding election. When possible, a polling place was set up in every hamlet. Special voting places were authorized for servicemen.

---

[5] Law No. 001/67, June 15, 1967, Articles 4 through 9. For the entire law, see U.S. Agency for International Development (Saigon), *Public Administration Bulletin*, no. 39 (August 1, 1967), pp. 1–19.

Each voting place was supervised by a commission which included a chairman and two deputy chairmen (one for the senatorial and one for the presidential election) plus an even number of committee members (at least two had to be named). Province chiefs and mayors selected the chairman and vice chairmen. On election morning, the chairman selected another seven workers from among the early voters.

Each slate of presidential and senatorial candidates was entitled to name poll watchers at all voting places. If every ticket had gone all out there would have been 59 watchers for each polling place, or a total in excess of half-a-million for the whole country. But, of course, some slates had no appreciable support in many areas and thus no watchers. One rough estimate suggests that there were about four or five lists represented at a typical polling place.[6]

**Election Procedures.** The polls opened at 7:00 a.m. on election day 1967. Voters presented their voting cards to be checked against the registration list and then they were given 11 presidential ballots and an envelope. In the voting booth they selected one ballot, which they placed in the envelope, and discarded the remaining 10. The voter emerged from the booth and dropped the envelope into a double-locked ballot box. If the envelope contained more than one ballot for president, the vote was invalid. If the voter wished to show his opposition to the whole process, he could drop an empty envelope into the box and no one was the wiser. After completing his vote for the presidency, the voter then repeated the process for the senatorial vote.

Once his ballots were cast, the voter presented his voter card to a worker who stamped it and clipped off the corner marked "A"—the corner designated for the September 3 election. Thus, the card could not be used again at any other polling place that day. The clipped corners were strung on a flexible wire, with a white marker after every 10. When a hundred corners were on the wire it was closed and a new one started. Anyone could estimate at a glance the number of persons

[6] The three political scientists who were consultants to President Johnson's 1967 observer team visited voting places in Saigon, Long Xuyen in An Giang province, and in Tay Ninh. In the several voting places visited, they saw from one to seven watchers. The consensus among all observers suggests that an average of four or five per polling place might have been about right, but it gives no assurance of coverage for all polling places.

who had voted at any given time. Officials reported the number of voters to the district polling office every two hours throughout the day.

As soon as the polls closed at 4:00 p.m., election workers collected the undistributed ballots to send back to district headquarters. The

**Figure 1**

VOTING CARD ISSUED IN 1967 AND ITS ENGLISH TRANSLATION

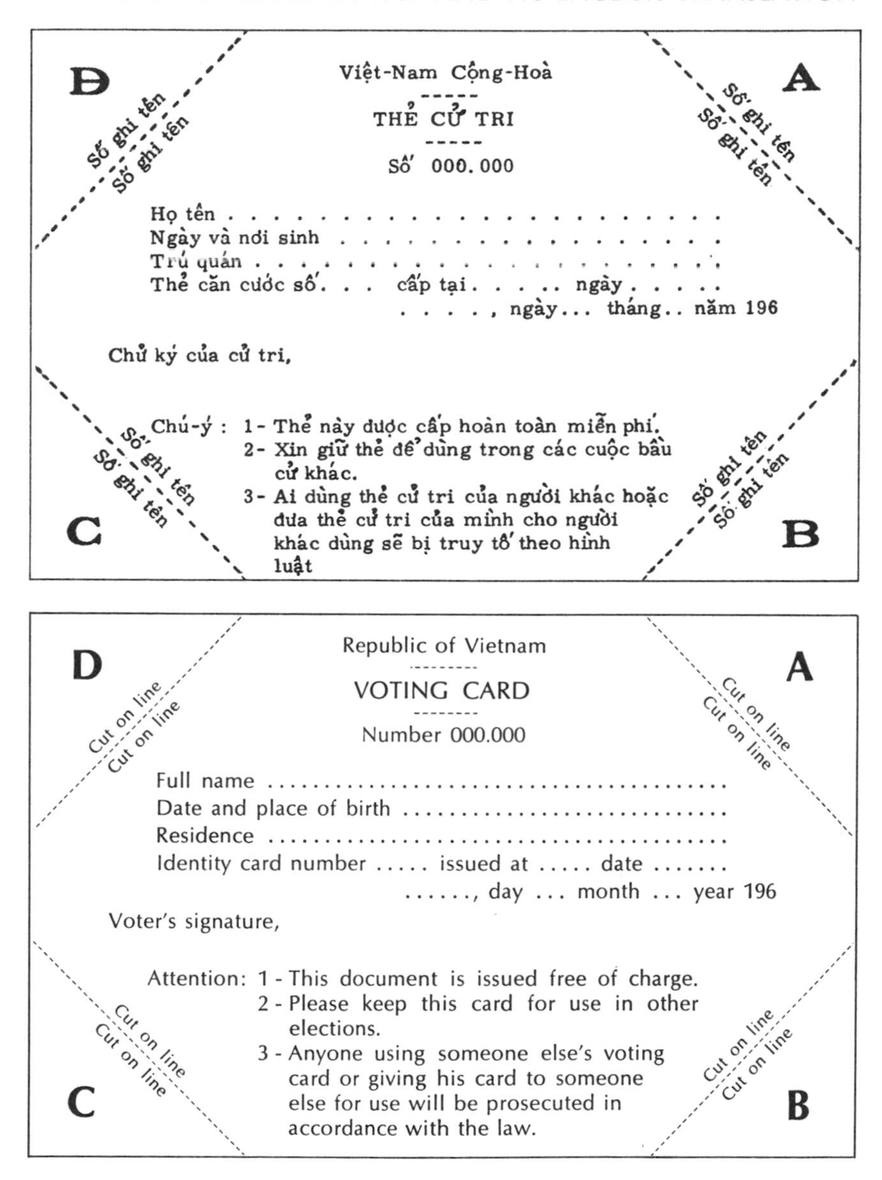

Đ | A | B | C

Số ghi tên

Việt-Nam Cộng-Hoà

THẺ CỬ TRI

Số 000.000

Họ tên . . . . . . . . . . . . . . . . . . . . . .
Ngày và nơi sinh . . . . . . . . . . . . . . . .
Trú quán . . . . . . . . . . . . . . . . . . . . .
Thẻ căn cước số . . . cấp tại . . . . . ngày . . . . .
. . . . . , ngày . . . tháng . . năm 196

Chữ ký của cử tri,

Chú-ý : 1- Thẻ này được cấp hoàn toàn miễn phí.
2- Xin giữ thẻ để dùng trong các cuộc bầu cử khác.
3- Ai dùng thẻ cử tri của người khác hoặc đưa thẻ cử tri của mình cho người khác dùng sẽ bị truy tố theo hình luật

D | A | B | C

Cut on line

Republic of Vietnam

VOTING CARD

Number 000.000

Full name . . . . . . . . . . . . . . . . . . . . . . . . . . . . . . . . . . . . . .
Date and place of birth . . . . . . . . . . . . . . . . . . . . . . . . . . .
Residence . . . . . . . . . . . . . . . . . . . . . . . . . . . . . . . . . . . . . .
Identity card number . . . . . issued at . . . . . date . . . . . . .
. . . . . . , day . . . month . . . year 196

Voter's signature,

Attention: 1 - This document is issued free of charge.
2 - Please keep this card for use in other elections.
3 - Anyone using someone else's voting card or giving his card to someone else for use will be prosecuted in accordance with the law.

chairman unlocked one of the locks on the presidential ballot box and the deputy chairman for the presidential election unlocked the other. The contents were then dumped on the table and the envelopes counted. The total was compared with the number of clipped corners. If there was a difference in the number, this fact had to be noted on the tally sheets kept by two of the election workers. (At the polling place where I watched the ballot-counting, there was one more voting card corner than there were envelopes.)

One worker opened each envelope, and handed the ballot to another worker who held it up and called the name on the ballot; the vote was then recorded by still other workers who kept the records. If there was no ballot inside or more than one, this fact was also noted and the content of the envelope declared illegal. The process continued until all ballots were counted and the totals announced. (Exactly the same process was carried on for the counting of senatorial votes except, of course, that each envelope could contain up to six ballots for as many different slates. If there were two for the same slate only one of these could be counted, along with the ballots for the remaining five slates.)

When the ballots for both the senatorial and the presidential races had been tabulated and all the necessary notations had been made about the empty envelopes, spoiled ballots, and so on, a report was prepared in quadruplicate. The chairman of the committee posted one copy at the polling place, filed one in his office for the record, and sent two on to district headquarters along with any irregular ballots that had been noted in the reports.

At district headquarters, all the reports were collated and a new report prepared, also in quadruplicate, for the province offices. Again one report was posted, one filed, and two sent on to the province. The provinces sent unofficial results on to the national office as soon as possible and then prepared the official tabulations. Spoiled ballots and other pieces of evidence concerning notations on the reports were forwarded to Saigon as well. At the national level, the unofficial results were posted as soon as received by the Office of the National Assembly. Copies of all reports were also sent to the Central Election Council, the Special Commission for Administration, and the directorate of the National Archives and Libraries.

Final decision on questions of legality of the presidential election rested in 1967 with the National Assembly; the deadline was October 3. The assembly's ultimate decision was contingent on the Central Election

Council's examination of all the documents, including complaints, and the council's recommendation.[7]

**Candidates.** Phan Khac Suu, president of the Constituent Assembly, announced his candidacy for the national presidency three days before the constitution was promulgated. His running mate was Dr. Phan Quang Dan. Suu had been head of state during the regime of General Nguyen Khanh. Dr. Dan was a long-time opponent of the Diem regime who had been jailed and exiled after being barred from a National Assembly seat that he had apparently won at the polls in 1959.

Tran Van Huong, former prime minister and former mayor of Saigon, provisionally declared himself a candidate shortly thereafter.[8] He did not officially confirm his candidacy until mid-June when he announced that his vice-presidential running mate would be Mai Tho Truyen, a retired civil servant.

By the time the law was promulgated on June 15, Premier Ky had already campaigned throughout the Delta in violation of the spirit, if not the letter, of the law and the rules of the National Leadership Committee. He had announced a "rice bonus" for civil servants, the military, and their families. He had signed a land distribution decree that abolished back rents for land that had been controlled by the Viet Cong, and he forbade the use of government troops as rent collectors. To top it off, "government officials posted signs reading 'The Nguyen Cao Ky government is the government of the poor.' "[9] Ky denied that he had ordered the signs prepared and put up, but his denial was not widely accepted.

---

[7] For the rules on counting and checking presidential returns at all levels, see Law No. 001/67, Articles 26–34 and 50–59, in the *Public Administration Bulletin,* no. 39, pp. 11–15 and 18–19.

[8] Frances FitzGerald, *Fire in the Lake: The Vietnamese and the Americans in Vietnam* (Boston: Atlantic Monthly Press Book, Little, Brown and Company, 1972), p. 335, speaking of the presidential election in 1967 says that "of the ten civilian candidates, only three had any political reputation—*the ancient* Dr. Phan Khac Suu, the former chief of state and president of the Constituent Assembly; Tran Van Huong, the former premier, who, reportedly, had strong support among province notables in certain parts of the Delta; and Dr. Phan Quang Dan, the renegade of the Diemist assembly. . . ." (Italics mine.) Dan was, of course, Suu's vice-presidential running mate, not a presidential candidate at all. As for the "ancient" Dr. Suu, Miss FitzGerald elsewhere says that in 1964 Suu was "in his nineties" (p. 257). As a matter of dull fact, Suu was born in 1905, was 62 years old at the time of the 1967 elections, and died in 1970 at the quite ordinary age of 65.

[9] Charles Joiner, "South Vietnam: Political, Military and Constitutional Arenas in Nation Building," *Asian Survey,* January 1968, p. 62.

Some military leaders were annoyed and some downright dismayed by Ky's excess of campaigning zeal prior to the official start of the campaign—and, perhaps more to the point, before the top military leadership had formally decided whom it would support for president.

General Thieu announced on June 14 that he planned to run for the presidency but did not file his formal candidacy application until June 27; he listed his running mate as Trinh Quoc Khanh, leader of the Hoa Hao Social Democratic party. On the same day, Marshal Ky announced that his vice-presidential candidate would be Nguyen Van Loc, another prominent general.

At this point the leading generals, including both Thieu and Ky, met in a three-day secret session to determine who would be the official candidate of the military. On June 30, it was announced that Thieu would be the presidential candidate and that Ky would join the ticket as vice president.[10] This forced political marriage appeared to be exactly that even during the campaign. General Thieu immediately made it clear that he was not only technically but actually the head of the ticket. Ky sulked—sometimes even failing to appear on the platform or at a reception with Thieu.

The other general whose name was bruited about during June and July was Duong Van Minh, who was then living in exile in Bangkok. Premier Ky had asserted in May that neither General Minh nor General Nguyen Chanh Thi, an exile in the U.S. because of his cooperation with the antigovernment Buddhist leaders in 1966, would be allowed to return in the immediate future. In spite of military opposition to his candidacy, General Minh's name was filed by his proposed running mate Tran Ngoc Lieng, a former social welfare commissioner.

By the end of the filing period, June 30, 1967, 18 presidential slates and 64 ten-member senatorial lists had been filed. The slates represented virtually every non-Communist political position in Vietnam. On July 1, the National Assembly approved 17 of the 18 presidential slates for the first posting—omitting only that of two relative unknowns whose documents the assembly found to be not in order.

The next week, during which complaints against the presidential slates were accepted, objections were filed against three of the most

---

[10] Joiner, "Arenas in Nation Building," pp. 62–63. For a colorful story of what presumably took place during those three days, see Robert Shaplen, *The Road From War: Vietnam, 1965–1970* (New York: Harper and Row, 1970), pp. 155–157.

prominent. The Minh-Lieng slate was criticized on grounds of "national security" and because Lieng had once been a French citizen and was, therefore, ineligible under the constitution to hold the office. Complaints filed against the Thanh-Huyen slate (Vu Van Huyen was a Saigon lawyer) claimed that Au Truong Thanh, former minister of finance, was "pro-Communist and pro-neutralist." Finally, there were complaints against the Thieu-Ky slate for their refusal to leave their government positions during the campaign.

**Decisions on Eligibility.** All 18 lists, as required by law, were sent to the Central Election Council on July 7 along with the complaints lodged against them. The council included the presiding judge of the Supreme Court of Appeals (chairman), the dean of the Lawyers Corps, a National Assembly deputy, the chairman of the State Council (the highest administrative court), and the special commissioner for administration as voting members.[11]

The Central Election Council's report to the National Assembly recommended that General Minh's slate be excluded because of Lieng's former French citizenship. The council also recommended disapproval of the Thanh slate because of his "pro-Communist and pro-neutralist activities." Five lesser candidates were also opposed by the council on various grounds. The Thieu-Ky ticket was recommended for approval. The council report went to the Special Committee created by the National Assembly "to report to the National Assembly on matters of establishing lists of candidates, controlling the propriety of the election and announcing the results of the election for the first President and Vice President." The committee consisted of 16 members and its chairman was deputy Nguyen Thanh Vinh. By September, when it acted on the election returns, it had become a 19-member committee appointed by Suu, but it is not clear whether his selections were approved by the assembly or not.[12]

The Special Committee offered candidates the opportunity to defend themselves against the original challenges or against disapproval by the Central Election Council. After the hearings, the committee recommended that the assembly approve six slates against which there had

---

[11] See Article 16 of the election law, Law No. 001/67, in *Public Administration Bulletin*, no. 39, p. 7.

[12] Howard R. Penniman, *Decision in South Vietnam* (Washington, D. C.: Free Society Association, Inc., 1967), pp. 47–48.

been no complaints and four more against which only minor complaints had been registered. It recommended the rejection of the Thanh-Huyen slate and three others. It made no recommendation concerning four slates, including those of Minh-Lieng and Thieu-Ky. As to the latter two, a majority supported the Minh-Lieng slate and opposed approval of the Thieu-Ky slate. Because the committee was unable to reach unanimous agreement about either of these slates, it made no formal recommendation.

The National Assembly supported the formal recommendations of the committee. It then approved the Thieu-Ky slate and rejected the Minh-Lieng and the other two slates concerning which the committee had made no formal recommendation.

The issue in the case of the Thieu-Ky slate revolved around the meaning of Article 17 of the election law, which provided that military officers and civil servants must request leave without pay from the date of the deadline for applications through election day. The same article explicitly exempted "persons holding popularly elected positions." The article covered Suu as an elected member of the National Assembly, but it left in limbo Thieu and Ky who held the highest policy-making positions in the country but had never been elected to these offices. The assembly voted 56–19 to approve the Thieu-Ky slate on the ground that positions of the level of chief of state and prime minister were not intended to be included among those from which candidates must take leave of absence to run for public office. Some dissenters argued against allowing them to run because they feared that Thieu and Ky "would take advantage of their position to ensure their election." [13] It was this fear, not the language of the law, that almost certainly motivated the opposition.

**Criticism of the Decisions.** Critics of the assembly's decisions focused on the handling of three slates—Thieu-Ky, Minh-Lieng, and Thanh-Huyen. Curiously, the argument sometimes seemed to denounce the assembly for overturning the Special Committee's unofficial decisions on Thieu-Ky and Minh-Lieng, while objecting to the assembly's failure to overturn the Thanh-Huyen ruling that had been unanimously agreed to and formally recommended by the committee.

[13] *Keesing's,* November 11–18, 1967, pp. 22351–22352.

Some critics argued that to use Lieng's former French citizenship as a reason for rejecting the Minh-Lieng slate was to rely on a "technicality." [14] It is, of course, the same kind of technicality that was written into the United States Constitution (Article 2): "No person except a natural born citizen, or a citizen of the United States, at the time of the adoption of this Constitution, shall be eligible to the office of President." It is also the same kind of provision that is to be found in the constitutions of most democratic societies and one that may be crucial to a developing society searching for self-identity. Particularly abhorrent under these circumstances is allegiance to the former colonial power. Robert Devereux says that the constitutional wording "Vietnamese citizenship from day of birth" was "chosen deliberately to disqualify those Vietnamese who at some point in their life acquired French citizenship and then reverted to Vietnamese citizenship after the French withdrawal in 1954." [15] In any event, if General Minh had been serious about being a candidate, he could always have chosen a running mate whose former citizenship would not have provided such an obvious ground for exclusion.

Critics were also quick to denounce the assembly for barring the Thanh-Huyen slate—this time, in effect, for supporting the decision of its Special Committee. The slate was excluded first by the Central Election Council and then by the Special Committee on grounds of Thanh's "pro-Communism and pro-neutralism in favor of Communism." While the council was hearing complaints and reviewing the qualifications of the candidates, the national police announced the break up of the Viet Cong Saigon-Gia Dinh Intellectual Proselytizing Committee and linked Thanh with that committee. Some opponents of the decision to exclude the slate were particularly critical of the allegation that Thanh had con-

[14] See Penniman, *Decision,* p. 34. In a generally excellent article ("Restructuring Government in South Vietnam," *Asian Survey,* August 1967, p. 625), I. Milton Sacks speaks of the disqualification of the Minh slate *"on the technical ground* that his running mate was ineligible due to possession of French citizenship." (Italics mine.) FitzGerald (*Fire in the Lake,* p. 335) mistakenly asserts that "the once popular General Duong Van Minh, now living in exile, is eliminated on the technicality that he was residing out of the country." The ground for the exclusion of Minh, as noted, was the former French citizenship of his vice-presidential candidate and had nothing to do with Minh's residence. In fact, the law stated—after the requirement that candidates must have lived in Vietnam territory for ten years immediately preceding the election—that "time spent abroad on official mission or in political exile is considered time spent in Vietnam."

[15] Robert Devereux, "South Vietnam's New Constitutional Structure," *Asian Survey,* August 1968, p. 628, footnote 5.

fessed in 1960 that he had Communist connections. If this confession had been made in 1960, how could he then have been accepted as the commissioner for economy and finance in the Ky government? They also criticized the government's rejection of Thanh's slogan, "No more bombs," and of the slate's symbol, a bomb with a big "X" through it.[16]

Professor Joiner, discussing the exclusion of the Thanh ticket, says that "the NLF planned to support at least one non-Communist peace candidate, possibly as a ruse for pre-election urban violence. However, this was never tied to Thanh, whose error appeared to be timing in announcing a peace platform." [17] Shaplen notes only that Au Truong Thanh "was disqualified as a Presidential candidate on the ground that he was 'pro-Communist.' " [18] Professor Sacks criticized the exclusion of General Minh, but made no comment on Thanh's.[19]

Five lesser slates were also excluded from the campaign by the National Assembly. None of them involved public figures of any stature

---

[16] One of those critics, David Wurfel, in his "Dr. David Wurfel Reports on Vietnam" (Preliminary Report of Vietnam Election Observer for Methodist Peace Division, SANE, Friends Committee on National Legislation, and Unitarian Universalist Association, Washington, D. C., September 21, 1967), states that the charges of Communist connections "were sustained in the Constituent Assembly partly by supporters of Tran Van Huong who expected Thanh to support Huong and were dismayed at his last minute candidacy. Nevertheless, it was government pressure that rounded up the necessary majority for his disqualification." Wurfel does not mention the prior decisions by the Central Election Council or the Special Committee of the assembly. Wurfel, incidentally, also denounces the decision against General Minh and says his "sins" consisted of his popularity with various groups. He neglects in this instance to mention the former French citizenship of Minh's running mate.

George M. Kahin and John W. Lewis, *The United States in Vietnam,* rev. ed. (New York: Dial Press, 1969), pp. 352–354, are also highly critical of the decision. They raise the question (as in fact Wurfel did also) whether the murder of the secretary of its "most independent minded" member may not have determined the council's action; and they find it ominous that the murder was unsolved late in October. As for the decision to bar Thanh's candidacy, they say that in spite of government pressures "it appeared that a majority of the Constituent Assembly would approve Thanh's candidacy and that he would benefit in the upcoming campaign from the widespread sentiment for peace." When the head of the police and two armed guards walked into the balcony, according to this thesis, the assembly lost its nerve and voted Thanh down.

Kahin and Lewis offer no proof of any connection between the murder and the decision of the council. They make no mention of the unanimous decision of the Special Committee against Thanh.

[17] Joiner, "Arenas in Nation Building," p. 63.

[18] Shaplen, *Road From War,* p. 159.

[19] Sacks, "Restructuring Government," pp. 625–626.

nor did their exclusion conflict with the decisions of the Central Election Council—or have any appreciable impact on the outcome of the election in September.

Professor Joiner sums up the matter by saying that "the eleven slates approved in mid-July present an impressive list despite disqualification of seven tickets." [20]

**The Final List.** The 11 slates included three already identified—Nguyen Van Thieu and Nguyen Cao Ky, Phan Khac Suu and Phan Quang Dan, and Tran Van Huong and Mai Tho Truyen.

The candidates on the remaining eight slates were less well-known. Nguyen Dinh Quat and his vice-presidential candidate Tran Cuu Chan (1) were both minor national figures. Quat was the industrialist who had run for the presidency against Diem in 1961 and received about 4 percent of the vote. Professor Chan had been minister of education for a time. Ha Thuc Ky and Dr. Nguyen Van Dinh (2) had some recognition in the country. Ky was general secretary of the conservative Revolutionary Dai Viet party and had been minister of interior in 1964. Dinh was an educator. Nguyen Hoa Hiep (3) had been minister of interior two years earlier. His vice-presidential candidate, Nguyen The Truyen, had also been the running mate of Ho Nhat Tan in 1961 on a ticket that received 8 percent of the vote. Tran Van Ly (4) had once been governor of Central Vietnam in the period of French control. His running mate was a wealthy landowner from the Mekong Delta, Huynh Cong Duong. The "surprise" candidate who ended up running far ahead of some of his better known rivals was Truong Dinh Dzu (5), a Saigon lawyer from Central Vietnam. His vice-presidential candidate was Tran Van Chieu who had once been chairman of the Saigon Chamber of Commerce.

The last three—Vu Hong Khanh and Duong Trung Dong (6), Hoang Co Binh and Lieu Quang Khinh (7), and Pham Huy Co and Ly Quoc Sinh (8)—were almost totally without prior national or political experience. Their presence points up the fact that it was relatively easy to become approved candidates for the highest offices in the country. These three slates and that of Tran Van Ly won a combined total of fewer than half a million votes.

[20] Joiner, "Arenas in Nation Building," p. 63.

## The Campaign

The campaign officially opened on August 3 and ended at noon, September 2, 1967.

Some general rules were laid down in the election law for the conduct of the campaign, including the regulation of campaign financing. A Central Election Campaign Committee was established for the whole country, composed of one principal and one alternate representative for each slate. A similar committee, named by the central committee, was established in each province and autonomous municipality.

All candidates received equal assistance. The campaign committees fixed the number and nature of the posters to be put up by all candidates and arranged for their printing and distribution. They arranged for "organizing talks between electors and candidates or their representatives." Equal time was guaranteed to presidential candidates on radio and television, both publicly controlled in Vietnam. The Central Election Campaign Committee was empowered to determine the procedures for press conferences and the modes of broadcasting and televising.[21] It also had to approve the symbols, photographs, and texts of the posters and leaflets. Within broad limits the candidates faced no problems in choosing their texts and symbols. The best known of the symbols was the "white pigeon," as the translation in the press release called it, of the Dzu-Chieu slate.

The government bore the full costs for administering the elections and for observers at the polls. In addition, it covered campaign costs up to a maximum of two piasters per elector per slate, except that the government would pay out no more than 12 piasters even though the number of slates went beyond six. Since there were 11 in 1967, the government expenditure amounted to roughly 1.15 piasters per voter per slate.

The law required that each presidential slate deposit 200,000 piasters—about $1,700—with the treasury. If a slate withdrew after the posting of the list of candidates or if it received fewer than 10 percent of the total valid votes cast, the deposit was forfeit and the candidates would have to reimburse the government "the sum of money expended

[21] Law No. 001/67, Articles 18–23, reprinted in *Public Administration Bulletin*, no. 39, pp. 7–10.

on their behalf by the Electoral [sic] Campaign Committee for printing leaflets and posters." [22]

Nothing further was said in the law about the matter of campaign expenditures except for one ambiguous provision that any candidate could be fined who exceeded "the amounts, modes and time limits prescribed by the Election Campaign Committee." [23] The meaning of the phrase is not immediately clear, but the experience of the campaign suggests that it was not intended to limit—nor did it in fact limit—individual spending to the amount granted by the government or authorized by the campaign committee (on a showing of "need" by a particular slate). The government allocated 60,239,012 piasters—about $510,000—to the campaign. Divided 11 ways, that amounted to about $46,400 per slate.

The law contained no provision for reporting campaign expenditures, so there is no official evidence of further spending. Denis Warner reported that Truong Dinh Dzu claimed to have spent $350,000 for organizing and conducting his campaign. Warner expressed doubt that Dzu had actually raised and spent that amount of money, but Dzu felt perfectly free to make the claim.[24] Robert Shaplen, while not commenting on the size of the Dzu campaign budget, noted that "it has been said on good authority that Dzu received funds from the French—his six point peace plan closely resembled French Foreign Minister Couve de Murville's program." [25]

The government, under the law, was not obligated to provide transportation for the candidates. But it was soon obvious that if the candidates were to speak throughout the country, the government would have to supply air transportation: private transportation was virtually nonexistent, and surface travel was not safe for much of the country. As a result, the government accepted responsibility for transportation in areas where the only feasible means of travel was by air.

The first multi-candidate trip under these arrangements was on August 8 to Quang Tri in the north. The plane landed some nine miles from Quang Tri. Trucks were the only available means of transport into

[22] Ibid., Article 21.

[23] Ibid., Article 36. This article is similar to Article 23 which referred to use of posters, TV, radio, et cetera, as prescribed by law and the campaign committee. In this instance the law seemed clearly not to refer to expenditure of funds.

[24] See Warner, "South Vietnam Exists," *The Reporter,* September 21, 1967, p. 18.

[25] Shaplen, *Road From War,* p. 168.

the city. The candidates—Thieu and Ky were not among them—refused the trucks (one candidate said they were recently retired garbage trucks) and insisted that they be flown back to Saigon. The province chief who had failed to meet the plane said he had been told nothing about the flight. Two days later, Tran Van Huong and Phan Khac Suu announced they would stop campaigning unless they had assurances of no more "irregularities." After sitting out the campaign for a couple of days, they reversed themselves and resumed campaigning. There were no further serious complaints about transportation.[26]

A solution to the transportation problem did not end the disputes between the rest of the candidates and the Thieu-Ky slate. The latter assumed the role of busy leaders directing the affairs of the country in the midst of war—unable, as a consequence, to take time away from the nation's business for political activities. As it has been for other incumbents in other countries at other times—and Thieu and Ky were, in effect, incumbents—the affairs of state included the dedication of new national buildings, new markets, and also periodic nationwide reports of progress in the war.

Thieu and Ky simply ignored the other 10 slates, which brought cries of outrage from their opponents who argued that all candidates should appear together to debate the issues so that citizens could hear all of them respond to the same questions. Transcripts of the meetings indicate that not all the other candidates attended the officially sponsored discussions. Lieu Quang Khinh, for example, apologized for the inability of the head of his ticket, Hoang Co Binh, to attend the session in My Tho: he "was busy campaigning in Central Vietnam."

When General Thieu did participate in the public discussions in My Tho, other candidates then objected that Thieu drew all the attention of the crowds and the press. When Thieu arrived late, the crowd became so noisy—both applauding and booing—that the candidate then speaking had difficulty making himself heard. Besides, "foreign correspondents, mainly American," sought to interview Thieu on the platform itself and further disturbed the proceedings. Finally, when Thieu left

[26] See Penniman, *Decision,* pp. 16–17. FitzGerald (*Fire in the Lake,* p. 335) incorrectly suggests that the Quang Tri episode was one of a continuing series of transportation problems when she says: "if the candidates organized a meeting in Quang Tri, the airplane *would tend to fly them to Dong Ha or some other provincial town where no one was expecting them* and where they would face the totally unacceptable choice of taking a lift from the Americans or braving a bus ride on Front controlled highways." (Italics mine.)

early, after speaking sixth on the program, most of the audience drifted away, leaving the last speakers with almost no one to talk to.[27] The complaints, with minor variations, are common to those made against incumbents seeking reelection in any society.

Reports of the public discussions are interesting, however, in the information they provide about the spectrum of opinion presented, the nature of the questions asked of the various candidates, and the reactions of segments of the public to the candidates and their platforms. To get some sense of the meetings, a complete running account of one such meeting on August 26 in My Tho, the second largest city in the Mekong Delta, is reproduced in the appendix.[28] The reader will note that Ky was not present. Thieu's presence marked the first time that either member of the slate had attended a candidate meeting. While most presidential candidates carried the brunt of the debate, vice-presidential candidate Phan Quang Dan, rather than the much older Phan Khac Suu, used most of the time allotted to their ticket. Finally, the reader will note the variety of the positions argued on the most important issue—that of the war and relations with the National Liberation Front and the Democratic Republic of Vietnam (DRV). The arguments presented at My Tho differed little from the arguments presented elsewhere in the country.

The audiences, in any case, were not intimidated by the candidates—even those in office. In one public appearance during the campaign, in Hue, Premier Ky was hooted off the platform with cries from the audience, "Lanh Dao Cowboy [Down with the cowboy]!" [29]

The final meeting of all the candidates was held two days before election day in the big square in front of the National Assembly building (formerly the Saigon opera house). Neither Thieu nor Ky attended the meeting. With the star attractions missing, the listeners did not fill the large area cordoned off for the meeting. Still, it was a respectable crowd

---

[27] FitzGerald (*Fire in the Lake,* p. 335) errs when she asserts that Thieu "would insist on speaking in ninth place" at candidate meetings because "nine" is the "lucky number for the Vietnamese." As noted, he spoke sixth at My Tho and I have found no record of a meeting where he did in fact speak ninth. (Incidentally, some who claim a more thorough knowledge of Vietnamese numerology than I have insist that "three" is the most lucky of numbers and that "six" is the most unlucky.)

[28] See Appendix B.

[29] Richard Critchfield, *The Long Charade: Political Subversion in the Vietnam War* (New York: Harcourt, Brace and World, Inc., 1968), pp. 350–351.

of several thousand, including the inevitable young men who hung from the arms and legs of the huge statue commemorating the Vietnamese marines. The candidates made their last appeals to the voters. The meeting broke up in less than two hours.[30] The Viet Cong had fired rockets into crowds in the square in previous years, and some observers suggested that the relatively small crowd and the short duration of the meeting resulted at least in part from the fear of rockets. There were none.

General Thieu, in an election eve radio and television appearance, called on all citizens to come out and vote the next day. On Sunday morning, just as the polls were opening, planes flew over Saigon dropping small leaflets reminding the voters one more time to cast their ballots.

## The Election

There was little violence during the presidential campaign until the last days before voting. Records of acts of terrorism for 1967 showed an average of 478 per week for the first eight months of the year. During the first three days of September (election day and the two days before), there were 579 acts of terror which translates into a weekly rate of 1351, or almost three times the normal rate. Sixty-two civilians were killed on election day alone. Senator George Murphy (R., Calif.) and Governor William Guy (D., N.D.) of the U.S. observer team arrived at a polling place in Phy Lam, a district capital in Phu Yen province, behind schedule. Had they not been late they would have been present when a grenade exploded, killing three and injuring 11.[31]

The election was watched by hundreds of persons from non-Communist countries. Some 574 American reporters were there, as were newsmen from most western European and many Asian countries. President Lyndon B. Johnson appointed a team of distinguished Ameri-

[30] The team of American observers watched the proceedings from the top of the hotel at the edge of the square. Virtually the whole American news corps was more concerned with the politically important members of the observer team than with the meeting below. In retrospect, an interesting aspect of the whole situation was the running debate carried on between newsmen and some observers. Governor Richard Hughes of New Jersey was involved in continuing arguments with journalists who attacked his defense of the elections. The debates also involved Governor Thomas McCall of Oregon and the three senators on the team—Edmund Muskie, Bourke Hickenlooper, and George Murphy.

[31] Penniman, *Decision*, p. 28.

cans to observe the election. The team included three senators, three governors, two mayors and a county commissioner, four representatives of the news media, and others representing various segments of the society. Three political scientists accompanied the team as consultants.[32] Former Ambassador Henry Cabot Lodge served as the leader and coordinator of the group. Official observer teams came from other countries, but none was as large as the American group. Probably no national election in so small a country has been observed by so many people. That part of South Vietnam in which elections could be held was smaller than the state of Florida and had a population of perhaps 12 to 13 million.[33]

There were very few reports of problems at the polls. Ballots were said to be in short supply at occasional polling places, but that was no major problem. The registration lists at all the voting places in a district included the names of all the qualified voters in the district. The identification system made it possible for a voter to vote in any polling place in

---

[32] The American observers were: Senators Bourke B. Hickenlooper (R., Iowa), George L. Murphy (R., Calif.), and Edmund S. Muskie (D., Maine), Governors William L. Guy (D., N. D.), Richard J. Hughes (D., N. J.), and Thomas L. McCall (R., Ore.); Ed Munro, president of the National Association of Counties; and Mayors Joseph M. Barr (D., Pittsburgh) and Theodore R. McKeldin (R., Baltimore). Representing the news media were John S. Knight, president of Knight Newspapers; Donald H. McGannon, president of Westinghouse Broadcasting Company; Eugene C. Patterson, editor of the *Atlanta Constitution;* and Stanford Smith, general manager of the American Newspaper Publishers Association. The three clergymen were Dr. Edward L. R. Elson, pastor of the National Presbyterian Church in Washington, D. C.; Archbishop Robert E. Lucey of the Diocese of San Antonio; and Rabbi Jacob P. Rudin, president of the Synagogue Council of America. Also present as observers were Eldon James, former national commander of the American Legion; Joseph Scerra, incoming commander of the Veterans of Foreign Wars; James B. Antell, president of the U.S. Junior Chamber of Commerce; Werner P. Gullander, president of the National Association of Manufacturers; David Sullivan, vice president of the AFL-CIO; and Whitney M. Young, Jr., president of the Urban League.

The electoral specialists who accompanied the observers as special advisers were Richard M. Scammon, director of the Elections Research Center, Professor Donald G. Herzberg, director of the Eagleton Institute of Politics at Rutgers University, and the author of this book.

[33] *Public Administration Bulletin,* no. 38 (June 1967), pp. 68–69, noted that "the population of South Vietnam has not been clearly established. Information provided in statistical statements has no guarantee." There are differences between local authorities and the central government and between agencies in the central government. Still, using a complex formula, an estimate of 10,390,731 is given (not including another 1,700,000 anti-Communist refugees) as the figure for persons under government control. The number undoubtedly increased somewhat between May, when these figures were developed, and early August, when the final registration for the presidential and senatorial elections was completed.

his district without danger of duplicate voting. (Once the corner had been cut off his voter card, he could no longer gain access to ballots or ballot boxes.) The opportunity to vote anywhere in the district meant that, unless ballots were in short supply throughout the district, no one had to lose his vote. In Saigon in 1967, there were 315 polling places in the three districts. The polling places within each district were not far apart. In other words, ignoring the inconvenience, the voter had ample opportunity to vote even if one polling place ran short of ballots.[34] In a hamlet with a single polling place there obviously would have been a problem, but no such difficulties were reported.

The ballots were counted in most places immediately after the polls closed.[35] The rules for reporting the results of the election, however, meant that these results were relatively slow in arriving in Saigon. Unlike the arrangement in the United States where local areas report each precinct as the votes are counted, the reports from each Vietnamese unit were not made to the next higher unit until the full return for the whole unit was available. Thus, the village made its report to the district only after all hamlet results had been received. The district sent its report to the province only when all village reports were tabulated. The same held true for the provinces. Few province returns reached Saigon, therefore, until late election evening, September 3. By noon of the next day, virtually all unofficial figures had been received and posted.

**The Results.** The returns brought several surprises. First, the vote for the Thieu-Ky slate was considerably lower than had been predicted by the candidates themselves and by most commentators. Ky had predicted the slate would win more than 50 percent of the vote. Thieu had estimated more than 40 percent. In fact they received 34.8 percent.

---

[34] Variations on the Vietnam arrangement have operated in other jurisdictions. Until recent years Atlanta, Georgia, for example, allowed citizens to vote in their precincts or at city hall.

[35] See T. E. Smith, E.B.E., *Elections in Developing Countries: A Study of Electoral Procedures Used in Tropical Africa, Southeast Asia and the British Caribbean* (London: Macmillan and Co., Ltd., 1956), pp. 252–254, for a description of "Counting Procedures When There Are Separate Ballot Papers for Each Candidate or Party List." Although this description refers to practice in France and in former French colonies and does not mention Vietnam, it describes the Vietnamese system precisely. Smith's comment on the merits of the system are useful: "Moreover, the counting of votes immediately after the closure of the polls rules out the possibility of tampering with the ballot box *en route* from the polling station to the count and it contributes to the speedy announcement of the result of the election."

Even more surprising was the identity of the runner-up slate. Neither member of the Truong Dinh Dzu-Tran Van Chieu slate was well known. Dzu was a Saigon lawyer with a somewhat shady reputation as one who dealt casually with his tax payments and deposited funds outside the country in violation of national law. He was the only candidate who ran on a strong peace platform. (The symbol for the slate was that "white pigeon.") In spite of his handicap as one of the relatively unknown candidates, Dzu received 17.2 percent of the vote.

Running third was one of the two best known of the civilian slates. Phan Khac Suu and Phan Quang Dan were long-time nationalists, both open opponents of the late Ngo Dinh Diem, and both very well known in the cities and the countryside. The Suu-Dan slate finished third with 10.8 percent of the vote. In fourth place with 10.01 percent was the Tran Van Huong-Mai Tho Truyen slate. The former had been prime minister, mayor of Saigon, a professor, and a popular intellectual in the capital city. Truyen was a less well known national civil servant.

Two other slates received more than 5 percent of the popular vote. Ha Thuc Ky and Phan Van Dinh, both teachers, finished fifth with 7.3 percent of the vote. Nguyen Dinh Quat, a candidate for president in 1961 against Diem, and his vice-presidential running mate Tran Cuu Chan, a former cabinet minister, finished sixth with 6.2 percent.

The official nationwide tabulations are listed below. (The official results by province and autonomous city are given in Appendix C.)

| | *Votes* | *Percent of total* |
|---|---|---|
| Thieu/Ky | 1,649,552 | 34.8 |
| Dzu/Chieu | 817,120 | 17.2 |
| Suu/Dan | 513,374 | 10.8 |
| Huong/Truyen | 474,100 | 10.0 |
| Ky/Dinh | 349,473 | 7.3 |
| Quat/Chan | 291,754 | 6.2 |
| Hiep/Truyen | 160,800 | 3.5 |
| Khanh/Dang | 149,276 | 3.2 |
| Binh/Kinh | 131,069 | 2.9 |
| Co/Sinh | 106,317 | 2.2 |
| Ly/Duong | 92,604 | 1.9 |
| Total (valid votes) | 4,735,449 | 100.0 |

The number of registered voters for the presidential-senatorial election was 5,853,384 as compared with 5,288,572 who were registered for the election to the Constituent Assembly almost exactly a year earlier. This increase of 564,872 provides a rough index to the level of pacification during the intervening year. Since the population of South Vietnam had been rising, perhaps 50,000 could be attributed to population increase, leaving more than half-a-million new voters who lived in areas liberated from Viet Cong control or who had left disputed areas and moved to the district towns or capital cities.

The turnout for the September 3 election was 4,902,748, or 83.7 percent of the electorate—up by about three percentage points over 1966. The number of spoiled ballots was 167,299, or 3.14 percent of the ballots cast.

**The Vote by Province.** Regionally, Thieu carried the most jurisdictions in the second and fourth Corps areas. In the second he carried all provinces and both the autonomous cities. In IV Corps he lost but one province. In III Corps he carried eight provinces and the little city of Vung Tau, while losing three provinces to Dzu, and the capital, Saigon, to Huong. In I Corps he won three provinces, while Suu won one province and the two autonomous cities, and Dzu won the province of Quang Ngai. Of the six autonomous cities in the country, Thieu lost the three largest: Saigon, Danang, and Hue, where 678,840 votes were cast. His share was 24.81 percent in Saigon, 25.03 percent in Danang, and 18.94 percent in Hue. He won a plurality in the other three: Dalat, Cam Ranh, and Vung Tau, which together cast only 77,393 valid ballots. His share of the vote was 45.12 percent in Vung Tau, 36.56 percent in Dalat, and 34.59 percent in Cam Ranh. For all six cities his share was 26.41 percent, or about eight points below his national average. These cities contributed only 11.92 percent of Thieu's nationwide vote although together they accounted for 16 percent of the valid national vote.

In the six cities Huong received 20.52 percent of the votes, or about twice his national average, and 32.73 percent of his total vote. These cities gave Dzu 12.95 percent of their votes, which amounted to 12.01 percent of his national total. Suu won 16.28 percent of this city vote, or 23.97 percent of all his votes. These figures point up the sharp difference between the urban and rural votes. Thieu and Dzu did much

# ADMINISTRATIVE DIVISIONS OF SOUTH VIETNAM, 1967

better outside the cities, while Suu and especially Huong were much more successful in the cities than in the countryside.

Thieu finished second in eight of the nine jurisdictions won by other candidates. (In Thua Thien the slate of Ha Thuc Ky, leader of the Revolutionary Dai Viet party, finished second behind Suu, and Thieu finished third.) He finished second in the other three provinces he lost in I Corps. In III Corps he was second behind Huong in Saigon and second in the three provinces won by Dzu. In IV Corps he was second to Dzu in the one province he lost. In the 41 provinces carried by Thieu, Dzu finished second in 28; Suu in eight; Huong in four; and Ky in one.

It is interesting to note the distribution of provinces carried by Thieu and the others with respect to categories of pacification. All provinces were classified in six broad categories ranging downward from five to zero.[36] Categories five through three indicated secure or relatively secure areas. Categories two and one were contested areas, and zero meant VC control. Since there were no provinces or autonomous cities rated 5 or 0, and only one rated less than 1, the table below shows only four general categories:

| | *Below 2* | *2–3* | *3–4* | *4–5* |
|---|---|---|---|---|
| Dzu | 1 | 3 | 1 | . . . |
| Huong | . . . | . . . | 1 | . . . |
| Suu | . . . | 1 | 2 | . . . |
| Thieu | 8 | 21 | 10 | 2 |
| Totals | 9 | 25 | 14 | 2 |

The chart reveals no clear pattern—which doubtless results from the fact that Thieu won 41 of the 50 jurisdictions with which we are dealing. Still, it is suggestive: four of the five provinces carried by Dzu were rated as contested areas, and he finished second in all six of the least secure districts outside the I Corps area (where Suu ran second in the two least secure provinces). *Keesing's* notes that Dzu finished second in five western provinces "in all of which heavy fighting had recently taken place."

A clearer pattern may emerge by describing the conditions of some of the areas Thieu lost and comparing them with prior expectations and

[36] According to the Level of Pacification index developed by the U.S. Military Assistance Command (Saigon), Civil Operations and Revolutionary Development Supports (CORDS).

predictions about voter response. In the first place, as already noted, Thieu did least well in the north, in I Corps. A long succession of governments had run up against militant Buddhist leadership in Danang and Hue and also in the largest of the northern provinces, Thua Thien, which surrounds the city of Hue. These three jurisdictions all went rather heavily for Suu who also finished second in two other provinces in I Corps. Suu was a Cao Dai member himself (some sources classified him as Buddhist in 1967),[37] but he had worked closely with the Buddhists in the recent past. By contrast, Thieu and Ky had been in open conflict with the Buddhists in 1966 and 1967. Tran Van Huong as prime minister three years earlier had threatened to use force to stop the continuing antigovernment activities of the northern Buddhists. Dzu was simply an unknown so far as the Buddhist issue was concerned. Contrary to most predictions, the presence of large numbers of troops (generally termed ARVN) in the area did not produce a large vote for Thieu and Ky.

Thieu and Ky won all provinces in the more sparsely settled II Corps area, and ran particularly well in the highlands where there are large numbers of ethnic voters. The government had made an effort in the months before the elections to assist and give recognition to the Montagnards, and this may have paid dividends in voter support.[38] Most of the other presidential candidates did not even bother to campaign in the Montagnard areas. Their lack of effort may have been a recognition of Thieu-Ky strength, or possibly they simply preferred to concentrate on the provinces with larger populations. The U.S. presence was important in the great expansion of the coastal city of Cam Ranh and the sharply increased prosperity of the area. These factors probably helped the Thieu-Ky slate.

Tran Van Huong, the one identified Confucian, carried the city of Saigon by the narrow margin of 2,400 votes—137,962 to 135,527 for Thieu. The two together won just over 50 percent of the Saigon valid

[37] The 22 presidential and vice-presidential candidates in 1967 were not all clearly identified as to religion. Eight were listed as Buddhists with no breakdown as to faction, four as Catholics, one as Confucian, two as Cao Dai followers, one as a member of the Hoa Hao sect, and six were unclassified. Ky did not identify himself, saying, "My parents were both Buddhists, but at age 36 I'm too young to make up my mind on so important a question as religion." See Penniman, *Decision,* pp. 37–38.

[38] Joiner, "Arenas in Nation Building," p. 65, suggests that corruption was a factor in the Thieu-Ky vote in II Corps.

vote. Candidates Suu and Dzu won half the remaining votes, while the rest were scattered among the other seven candidates. Considering his background, it was not surprising that Huong won. Some suggested that he should have won by more. The Saigon elections were not, however, a significant source of complaints of fraud. Saigon had the lowest turnout in the nation (76.1 percent) and the largest number of spoiled ballots (6.3 percent). Both figures may indicate the protest of big city voters against the whole system: abstentionism has long been considered by the French to be a legitimate means of expressing discontent.[39]

The vote for Truong Dinh Dzu is the most interesting to analyze. The five provinces he won were all areas of heavy Viet Cong activity. Three of them—Tay Ninh, Kien Phong, and Hau Nghia—touch on the Cambodian border right at a major point of the 1970 U.S.-South Vietnamese incursions. Tay Ninh, in fact, is within a few miles of COSVN (Central Office for South Vietnam), the headquarters for the whole North Vietnamese effort in the South. And Hau Nghia is at the tip of the Parrot's Beak, the section of Cambodia that pushes farthest into South Vietnam. As noted elsewhere in this volume, 81 of the 150 villages in Hau Nghia were VC-controlled while the control of another 37 was uncertain—in general, controlled by the government during the day and by the VC at night. Binh Duong is bounded on the south and west by Hau Nghia and Tay Ninh provinces and was a major route into II and III Corps for North Vietnamese soldiers and supplies coming down through Laos and Cambodia. The fifth province carried by Dzu was up in I Corps. Quang Ngai had been for some years the VC headquarters for the lower I Corps or Do Xa region of the central highlands. Communist maps showing their administrative divisions and military regions in South Vietnam label Quang Ngai as the "Northern Subregion."

Richard Critchfield, seeking to explain the large vote in the Delta for the virtually unknown Dzu, who ran second to Thieu and won nearly twice as many votes as Huong even in the latter's hometown, had this

---

[39] Books are written on abstentionism in France. One of the best and most recent is by Alain Lancelot, *L'Abstentionisme Electoral en France* (Paris: Armand Colin, 1968). When registration is more or less automatic, as it is in most countries other than the United States, to abstain is much more likely to be an act of will than here where the law may be the cause of one's failure to be registered. Residence requirements, the necessity of going to a central registration place, et cetera, are factors that prevent registration in the United States and may be the major cause of failure to vote, rather than some conscious decision to stay home as a protest against the system or the process.

to say: "that hundreds of thousands of peasants cast ballots for Dzu suggested to many of my friends [Vietnamese] that the Communists were now capable of mobilizing a large minority of the population into massive collusion action." A bit later he states, "but only Viet Cong support could explain Dzu's vote." [40]

The fact that Thieu ran second to Dzu in the four provinces carried by the latter in the south and the further fact that Dzu was second to Thieu in all but one of the other Delta provinces suggest that, in marginal regions, the pressures on voters must have been intense from both sides. The secrecy of the ballot probably prevented even greater polarization.

### Criticisms and Evaluations

**Criticism of the Elections.** Overall, the election was administered in a remarkably efficient manner. While engaged in a war with the armies of North Vietnam and the rebel forces of the South, the government managed to register 5,853,384 voters and to conduct an election in which 4,902,748 cast ballots. The responsible national and provincial campaign committees had established the rules for the campaign, arranged for 14 public meetings for the presidential candidates, set up two press conferences, and prepared for three radio and television broadcasts by all candidates.

The Special Commission for Administration itself noted some shortcomings in the conduct of the elections. It pointed to the fact that some polling places opened late, that elsewhere there was an occasional shortage of ballots or an unnecessary tie-up of voters, that in some places the voter received fewer than the total number of ballots from which to choose, that the checking of registration lists was not always efficient, and so on. When listing these criticisms, Allan E. Goodman, then at Harvard's Center for International Affairs, noted that the failures "involved problems of logistics and lack of familiarity with election procedures." [41]

There were indeed problems during the campaign and on election day. But Richard M. Scammon, director of the Elections Research Center, summed up the elections as "reasonably efficient, reasonably

---

[40] Critchfield, *Political Subversion*, pp. 356–357. Critchfield was reporting for the Washington *Evening Star* while in Vietnam.

[41] Goodman, "Notes on the Administration of Elections in South Vietnam," a paper prepared for delivery to the Southeast Asia Development Advisory Group (SEADAG), December 4, 1967.

honest, and reasonably free." Members of the President's observer team generally agreed. Some members of the team had gone to Vietnam "expect[ing] the elections to be corrupt. Some supported U.S. policy and some did not, but a number really expected to find corruption. All 25 came back with the view that this had been, in fact, a well and fairly and honestly run election. . . ." [42] Individual members of the group were critical of the exclusion of Au Truong Thanh and/or Duong Van Minh. Others concluded that the elections were conducted honestly but continued to object to U.S. policy in Southeast Asia [43]—which is, of course, a perfectly rational distinction between two related but separable facts. Some commentators agreed with the general tenor of the comments by members of the President's observer team; some were more skeptical or even highly critical of the whole process.[44] This last group included

---

[42] Penniman, *Decision,* p. 45. Samples of their comments are reprinted below from *Keesing's,* November 11–18, 1967, pp. 22353–22354:

> Mr. Guy called the elections "as moving and profound an example of the desire for self-determination as can be found anywhere"; Mr. McCall declared that they had been "as good as any election in the United States"; and Senator Murphy asserted that "there is no greater example in all history of a nation striving toward democracy." Mr. Hughes said that he had been "most impressed by efforts to shield the vote," and that the fairness of the election would be "evident to a blind man." Mr. Theodore McKeldin (the Republican Mayor of Baltimore) said that the only irregularity he had seen had been a voting envelope containing three ballots instead of one, and this vote had been disqualified. Mr. Whitney Young (executive director of the National Urban League and a prominent Negro civil rights leader) said that he was "completely satisfied that it was as free an election as possible under the circumstances," and that he had found "vigorous and even vitriolic" criticism of the Government in Vietnamese newspapers. Other members of the party were more reserved in their comments. Senator Muskie said that "fraud is not always evident on the surface," and commented that some "authoritarian instincts" among the South Vietnamese would have to be curbed. Mr. John Knight, a newspaper proprietor, said that the election was "reasonably honest, reasonably fair, and about all one could expect from a developing country."

See also Lyndon Johnson, *The Vantage Point* (New York: Holt, Rinehart and Winston, 1971), p. 265.

[43] See Penniman, *Decision,* pp. 44–45.

[44] See, for example, Joiner, "Arenas in Nation Building" (pp. 62–68):

> Upon analysis, the presidential election permitted freer expression of views than had previous forums. Administration of the election was a tremendous assignment for the Ministry of Administration, a body generally accepted as fair. . . . [At the same time he noted direct and indirect pressures on civil and military administrators.] The large plurality of the military ticket in II Corps, though less than a majority, must be viewed skeptically. Still, other tickets received pluralities in six prov-

members of the United States Senate, some of whom denounced the conduct of the elections even before they were held.[45]

Some of the candidates and elements of the Saigon press also predenounced the elections. Phan Quang Dan, for one, the vice-presidential candidate on the Suu ticket and the former leader of the anti-Diem forces in 1959 and 1961, was perhaps the best known and one of the most outspoken. At a press conference four days before the election, he told reporters how elections can be stolen and sometimes implied that the government would in fact use these devices for assuring victory in September. His charges were really a kind of catalogue of the well-known means of illegally influencing election results. The descriptions were altered, in most instances, to fit the special circumstances of South Vietnam in 1967. He talked of stuffing ballot boxes, multiple voting, the stealing of boxes, and so on, and put special emphasis on the probability of fraud in particularly insecure areas.[46] His remarks were widely reported in the press, sometimes in stories suggesting that Dan was describing actual elections in South Vietnam rather than possible means of subverting elections in general.

His predictions of election day hanky-panky were, in a sense, not unreasonable. Nor were his expectations of influence by virtue of the government's military presence in contested areas. Few nations—perhaps only the United States in 1862 and 1864 and South Vietnam in 1958 and after—have held elections at all while being invaded by a foreign power and/or during civil war. The experience of these two countries further tended to strengthen Dan's expectations. In the border states of the United States in 1864 and in Vietnam during the elections

---

> inces . . . and in three cities . . . , constituencies where there were 1,640,053 registered voters and 1,333,582 votes cast. These pluralities occurred in all Corps areas except General Vinh Loc's Corps II. Irregularities reported by civilian candidates definitely occurred.

Robert Shaplen argued that the election "particularly the Senate election in the opinion of many Vietnamese—in contrast to that of American and foreign observers who briefly watched and hastily praised it—was less free and fair than the election last year for the Constituent Assembly. . . ." Shaplen also quoted some Vietnamese as being skeptical of the value of holding elections at all at that time. Still, Shaplen was by no means wholly critical of the conduct of the elections. See Chapter 12 in his *The Road From War: Vietnam, 1965–1970.*

[45] For example, Senators Robert Kennedy (D., N. Y.), Jacob Javits (R., N. Y.), and Wayne Morse (D., Ore.).

[46] Paraphrased from English-language press release on behalf of the Suu for President National Committee.

of the Diem period, the norms of honest elections were generally thought to have been violated. Close examination of the reports of the 1967 voting suggests that the election results simply did not conform to these expectations—least of all, as noted above (page 74), with respect to low-security areas.[47]

**More Criticism of the Election.** Two other widely circulated charges were made both prior to and after the elections. Both related to the claim that the government was trying to "steal" the elections. The first of these charges was that soldiers would be instructed how to vote and that, by some means, the commander of each unit would know how the soldiers voted. A second charge was that some persons, soldiers in particular, had been given more than one voting card and that these cards had been issued to make possible multiple voting for the Thieu-Ky military ticket.

The returns by province show no obvious relationship between the presence of large military units in areas of conflict and the size of the Thieu-Ky vote. Indeed, as noted earlier, in I Corps and III Corps where there were large numbers of troops, the Thieu-Ky ticket did less well than in other regions, while in the south—with relatively fewer troops—the Thieu-Ky and the Dzu slates normally ran one-two.

The second charge—that extra voter cards were passed out to soldiers and others—is equally hard to substantiate. The best known story was of the soldier in Can Tho who presumably had three electoral cards. Professor Wurfel in his report on the elections spoke of two women with the same address in Gia Dinh, each of whom had two cards. There were a number of other observers who mentioned duplicate cards. A lieutenant colonel in Hau Nghia told a group in my presence that he had two cards. In other words, there seems to be no doubt that an unspecifiable number of persons, often military, had more than one voting

---

[47] Frances FitzGerald (*Fire in the Lake,* pp. 335–336) specifically argues two points. She speaks of the "smallness" of Thieu's victory, although he won by slightly more than a 2-to-1 margin over Dzu. And she inaccurately asserts: the Thieu-Ky ticket's "strongest support [came] from the isolated military districts, where the local commanders kept close watch over the voting, and the Americans did not. In the more politically sophisticated and less militarily controlled urban districts the generals made such a poor showing that at the end of the day their managers, panicky at the low count, stuffed the ballot boxes with thousands of extra votes." Presumably, by Miss FitzGerald's own testimony, this was done with "the Americans" looking on.

card. But there is no evidence that anyone saw a soldier or civilian vote or attempt to vote twice on election day.[48]

It seems unlikely, somehow, that persons who came forward to show that they had more than one card would have made any use of the duplicates. If they were in on a government-initiated fraud, it is unlikely that they would have announced the fact in the first place. If they were not working with the government, then error and not fraud would seem to have been the explanation. Duplicate cards could have been distributed as the result of human or mechanical error. (In 1971, when the whole process was computerized, there also were instances of duplication.) But the *use* of more than one card required deliberate individual action.

The lieutenant colonel in Hau Nghia pointed out some of the problems confronting any soldier who wished to use more than one card. There was no absentee voting. Furthermore, all ARVN soldiers were on duty on election day with responsibility for maintaining the security of the polls. So, while he might have had cards both as a soldier and as a resident of some city or village, the soldier could not vote in his prior residence simply because he had no way of getting there and remaining on duty at the same time.

Multiple voting was by no means easy to carry off even if a soldier had more than one card, could move from his duty station to his home city or hamlet, and had a burning desire to vote more than once. If he had two cards, presumably he could have voted first at one voting place and then at another where his name was registered—all of which would have required considerable dedication to multiple voting. In a village or hamlet, an attempt to cast more than one ballot would normally have meant that the voter had to appear twice before the same voting officials and the same watchers, and he was almost sure to be known either by the officials or the watchers or both. Again it seems unlikely that multiple voting under such circumstances could have happened very often.[49] In fact, if there was the necessary collusion among officials

[48] See Penniman, *Decision,* pp. 21–23, and p. 47. One possible exception to the last statement was the claim made by one reporter for a national news magazine that he had seen a young woman vote twice at the polling place he had observed. The fact that one voted first for the presidential candidates and then for the senatorial candidates may have confused him; at any rate, he did not mention either the incident or the voting procedure in his news reports.

[49] In the United States prior to 1880, the use of another person's name ("personation") or voting at more than one polling place was common enough in some

to allow multiple voting, it would surely have been easier to find some other way to cheat.

Another method of subverting the electoral process, as propounded by a few writers, was that of inflating the voting figures to the advantage of the military ticket. Professor Wurfel suggested that "fraud on election day was extensive, producing 300,000–500,000 votes and inflating the total number of votes by the same number." He went on to state—alone, it seems, among all observers—that

> the manufacture of votes without voters was relatively easy because there was no effective check on whether the voter ever appeared personally at the polling place. The only record which officials could present was a string of voting card corners ostensibly clipped as voters *entered* the polls. But this proved nothing. Officials themselves could have brought dozens of voting cards to the polling place, clipped them, and then deposited an equivalent number of ballots in the box after the polling place closed.

He said he saw two policemen who presented their cards to be clipped without voting.[50] Contrary to Professor Wurfel's description, the cards were clipped only *after* the votes were cast and the names checked against a registration list. No other observer claimed to have seen a sequence of events in any way comparable to the one reported by Wurfel.

Elsewhere on the vote inflation front, Lieutenant Colonel William Corson—a physicist, a onetime Marine tank corps officer, and a frequent critic of U.S. policy in Vietnam—gave registration and voting figures for Kien Hoa province that purported to show a padding of votes well beyond the number of registered voters. He claimed that while there were only 120,000 registered voters in the province, there were 150,000 votes recorded.[51] The charge would indeed be a serious one—but for the fact that his figures are at variance with all other figures for the province published by the provincial or national government, either at

---

machine-controlled cities, but the circumstances were entirely different. Until the introduction of the Australian ballot system, there was no registration of eligible voters and no way to check the claims of potential voters that they lived in the district and that this was their only attempt to vote. With the introduction of the registration system, which required that the name be on the list at only one polling place and that the name be checked off as the voter cast his ballot, the number of cases of multiple voting dropped precipitously.

[50] Wurfel, "Wurfel Reports on Vietnam," p. 3; italics added.

[51] William R. Corson, *The Betrayal* (New York: W. W. Norton, 1968), p. 112.

the time of the election or in the official tally, up to and including the voting results now reposing in the National Archives in Saigon. The actual numbers for Kien Hoa province, which have always been available, show the following: 118,345 registered, 102,715 voting (for an 86.4 percent turnout), and 101,345 valid ballots—with the Thieu-Ky ticket receiving 40,845 or 40 percent of the valid votes. Compounding the misconceptions conveyed by Colonel Corson is the fact that Professors Kahin and Lewis have uncritically accepted his report.[52]

**Approval of the Election Results.** By the time the last returns came in from the provinces, Dzu had taken the lead in trying to discredit the results. He charged that two-thirds of Thieu's votes had been obtained by fraud and that in a free election the military would have received no more than 10 percent of the vote. He argued, and soon was joined by other critics in South Vietnam and the United States, that the elections should be declared void and the National Assembly should call for new ones. (The scheduling of new elections was mandatory under the law if the votes voided by the National Assembly involved election units where the total vote that might have been cast was more than the number of votes separating the two leading candidates.)

Buddhists and students took to the street to demand an end to the Thieu-Ky government. Demonstrations occurred regularly in Saigon and in the strongholds of the United Buddhist Church in Hue and Danang.

---

[52] Kahin and Lewis (*United States in Vietnam,* p. 408, footnote 16), repeat Corson's figures and continue: "Although according to *The New York Times,* NLF control was considered so widespread in this province [Kien Hoa] that it had been possible previously for Saigon to hold elections in only six out of the 115 villages, in the presidential election Thieu and Ky were reported to have carried it by a margin of 26,000 votes." Professors Kahin and Lewis do not point out that the government quite sensibly required a higher degree of security for village council elections than for national elections. Thus the latter were held in many semi-secure villages where province chiefs were still appointing the local officials. In other words, no correspondence between the number of villages electing their officials in the spring and the number where voters cast ballots in the fall elections should be expected.

Elsewhere they lament that "both the Saigon government and the U.S. Department of State have refused to make public the district-by-district breakdown of votes. *Presumably this is because of the widely made charge that there were a number of serious discrepancies between the statistics for provincial election totals and the district returns*" (p. 356, second footnote, italics mine). First, district returns, although not *published,* were posted on election day and are readily available in the National Archives, as are hamlet, village and province returns. Second, Professors Kahin and Lewis present no evidence that the charges were "widely made" or the discrepancies "serious." And third, a thorough check on any discrepancies would have to begin at the hamlet, not district level.

Signs carried by the demonstrators were frequently in English, thus emphasizing a point made by William Tuohy of the *Los Angeles Times* that candidates and demonstrators in South Vietnam were often directing their demands to Americans in Saigon and to television viewers in the United States rather than to Vietnamese in or out of the National Assembly.[53] It was widely accepted that Dzu was responsible for whipping up student demonstrations in the frantic nights just before the National Assembly handed down its formal decision.

Phan Khac Suu, who finished third, joined the critics, along with six other defeated candidates. He became a secondary hero of the demonstrators because of his denunciations of the elections. On one occasion, demonstrators were so delighted with his fervor that they carried Suu, who was also president of the National Assembly, about the chamber and into the streets. The demonstrations increased in intensity during the final week before the assembly's decision. With the decision handed down, they stopped abruptly.[54]

The charges of corruption, fraud, and error in the balloting went first to the National Assembly and then were passed on to the Central Election Council. The latter body was made up of distinguished persons from the assembly, the courts, the administrative branch, and the public. The council considered charges that involved roughly a quarter of all the voting places in the country and 1,444,647 of the 5,853,251 votes cast.[55] These figures greatly exaggerate the magnitude of the charges because any claim of irregularity, even if it went to only a single voter or ballot, automatically affected all ballots cast at the polling place where the alleged irregularity occurred. By unanimous decision, the council reported in its recommendation to the assembly that most of the charges made against the administration of the elections were not supported by

---

[53] See Penniman, *Decision,* p. 17.

[54] It is probably true that in any society where there have been charges of irregularities and there is a reasonable degree of freedom, there will be criticism and threats of action—violent or nonviolent—until the last of the formal processes involved in the decision has taken place. At that point the demonstrations subside unless revolution is actually imminent. Our own experience during the dispute over the outcome of the Hayes-Tilden contest in 1876 is instructive. Until the night before the decision by a special commission, demonstrators in New York marched under the slogan "Tilden or Blood." When the commission's decision went against him, and even though the decision was highly partisan, Tilden accepted it as final and the demonstrations ceased.

[55] Lester A. Sobel, ed., *South Vietnam: U.S.-Communist Confrontation in Southeast Asia, 1966–67,* vol. 2 (New York: Facts on File, Inc., 1969), p. 463.

evidence and that such irregularities as did take place were not of sufficient importance to have any bearing on the outcome.

The report was next referred by the National Assembly to its Special Committee—the same committee whose informal decisions on slates the assembly had rejected in July. It was headed by Nguyen Thanh Vinh who later succeeded Suu, after his death in 1970, as the head of the oppositionist National Salvation Front. Vinh was also a member of a losing senatorial slate. The committee reversed the recommendations of the Central Election Council and recommended that the elections be annulled and new ones called. The vote was 16 to 2 with one abstention. The committee reached its decision on September 30 and sent its report to the assembly. The assembly was required to take final action by October 3.

The assembly has been described as bedlam during those hours when the reports of the Special Committee and the council were being considered. Late on the evening of October 3, just before the deadline, the National Assembly voted 58–43, with one abstention and four spoiled ballots, to follow the recommendation of the Central Election Council rather than the advice of the Special Committee. Commenting on the decision, James D. Rosenthal said that the action of the assembly supported the view of election observers that the elections had been conducted in a generally fair manner. He went on to say that the judgment of the assembly's members about the legitimacy of the outcome was even more positive than the vote indicated because the vote reflected some political considerations unrelated to the main issue.[56]

The political considerations that influenced the votes of some deputies could have included their own public status. Robert Erlandson reported in the *Baltimore Sun* that 59 of the 117 deputies in the National Assembly sought election to the new Senate—and only 11 of them had been elected.[57] It has already been pointed out that the chairman of the Special Committee was second in command of a political coalition headed by Suu, one of the candidates whose fate was directly under consideration. A number of the members of the committee were also among the losers in the Senate races. The senatorial elections technically

---

[56] James D. Rosenthal, "Analysis of Election Results in South Vietnam," a paper prepared for delivery at the Southeast Asia Development Advisory Group (SEADAG), December 4, 1967.

[57] *Baltimore Sun,* October 3, 1967.

would not have been affected by throwing out the presidential results, but that action certainly would have cast doubt all across the board.

**"Reasonably Honest and Reasonably Free."** By the time the matter reached the assembly, questions about the elections had been reduced to six general categories:

1. Had there been discrepancies between the number of votes recorded on the tally sheet and the number of people who actually voted? In other words, the tally sheet might have added up to one number while the number of clipped corners of electoral cards or the number checked off the voting list might have been very different.

2. Were there "illegal erasures" on the tally sheets—erasures, that is to say, that were not properly initialed?

3. Were ballot boxes illegally removed from the polling place? (The most widely discussed case was in Long An, a low-security province, where the police had removed some ballot boxes but had not allowed all the observers to follow along to watch the counting and where fewer than 100 votes separated Dzu from Thieu. It was 15,608 for Thieu and 15,535 for Dzu. The same sort of charge cropped up in Binh Tuy province—a small province where only 23,000 persons voted. There the Thieu-Ky ticket received 11,237 votes, and Dzu was second with 5,143.)

4. Were tally sheets from widely separated areas written in the same handwriting?

5. Had there been intentionally incorrect additions on the tally sheets?

6. Had any tally sheets been turned in after the September 10 deadline? [58]

Had all the charges been upheld, Dzu and not Thieu would have been the big loser. Thieu's vote would have dropped from 1,649,552 to 1,216,390, while Dzu's vote would have gone down from 817,120 to 228,309. Thieu's margin over Dzu would have increased from 832,432 to 988,081, or a net increase of 155,469—and Dzu would have dropped to fourth, behind Suu and Huong. Thieu's winning margin would have been very slightly reduced. Obviously, the charges came primarily from the regions carried by Dzu; most of them were from the provinces in the Delta and along the Cambodian border. (The ultimate in "conspiracy"

[58] Penniman, *Decision,* p. 51.

theories, to be sure, might see in this a ploy on the part of the military leadership to put the burden on Dzu—by rigging the vote in the areas of his greatest strength and, if caught, throwing out most of *his* vote. The only trouble with such a theory is the total absence of supporting evidence.) None of this would have mattered, anyway, because if all the charges had been accepted, a new election would have been mandatory.

Phan Khac Suu, who had refused to step down as president of the assembly the night before—saying that "he would be impartial" because he had "withdrawn the complaints he had originally made against the election's honesty" [59]—was so angered by the decision of the assembly that he abstained from voting, refused to announce the final tally, denounced the whole proceeding, and resigned as president of the National Assembly. His action was strangely different from that of his vice-presidential running mate, Phan Quang Dan. In spite of Dan's strong criticism of the Thieu-Ky ticket and his chalk talk on possible fraud before the elections, he was one of the first to accept the outcome as legitimate. "I'm sure," he said, "there was some tampering, but it was certainly not enough to invalidate the election. The military ticket won and it would have won, though by less, even if the election had been one hundred percent honest. There were just too many civilian candidates." [60]

Reports of the National Assembly's action add some interesting footnotes. The *Baltimore Sun* story observed that Major Nguyen Mong Hung of the national police was watching from the balcony as the deputies voted "secretly" in a booth below. The story implied that his presence amounted to coercion in favor of Thieu-Ky. By contrast, Lee Lescaze of the *Washington Post* asserted that voting out of public sight automatically *helped* the Thieu-Ky ticket because many deputies who would vote secretly for the military candidates would have been reluctant to make their support public.[61]

---

[59] *Washington Post,* October 2, 1967.

[60] See Denis Warner, "South Vietnam Exists," p. 19. David Wurfel, "Wurfel Reports on Vietnam," p. 4, asserted that Dan estimated the fraud at about 10 percent of the total. But he said Dan "was unwilling to associate himself with any public charge of fraud. He is running for the premiership." None of the others reporting on post-election developments made such an allegation and, of course, Dan was not named premier and never has been.

[61] *Washington Post,* October 3, 1967, and *Baltimore Sun,* October 3, 1967. To support the Thieu ticket publicly, said the *Post* story, "is bravery of a sort. It is not likely to help a political career and this situation indicates how far South Vietnam is from forming a government built on significant cooperation between the generals and their opponents."

The suggestion that politicians hesitated to be publicly associated with the Thieu government has often appeared in the South Vietnam and American press. The assumption of an either/or division between the military and civilian lists was almost universal. Dan, as quoted above, spoke of the inability to defeat the military ticket because there "were just too many civilian candidates." The strongest statement of the extent and degree of dislike of the military was made by Wesley R. Fishel. After agreeing with the general conclusions that the elections were relatively free of corruption and that there were not enough irregularities to affect the outcome, Professor Fishel concluded:

> Finally, the election results, examined in restrospect, showed a vigorous public dislike—even detestation—of the military regime. They showed also, however, that the Vietnamese nationalist leaders, however strong their dislike of a military regime, could not bring themselves to unite even when they recognized that their disunity (reflected in the fact that 10 civilian slates competed with the single military slate for the Presidency) made a military victory inevitable.[62]

Many activists in Saigon and elsewhere obviously disapproved of the military candidates. Some students of Vietnam speak of the contempt held for the military by members of the urban mandarin class, who regard military officers as simply a lesser breed, unworthy of intellectual leadership. It is difficult to ignore a set of propositions so vigorously and widely stated: (1) civilians dislike or "detest" military leaders; and (2) the contest at the polls is between military and civilian candidates and, because the presence of ten civilian candidates divides the civilian vote, the victory of military candidates is made certain. It is asserted that General Duong Van Minh's candidacy was blocked because the military did not want to divide its vote and make it possible for a civilian to slip in. Curiously, however, when discussing the exclusion of Au Truong Thanh, no point is made of the fact that the military could further have fragmented the civilian vote precisely by letting him run. Rather, the suggestion is that Thanh was a threat to Thieu as the only credible "peace" candidate. (Wurfel came up with the novel idea that Dzu's campaign, by contrast, was "believed by many to be possible only because he had the backing of the CIA.")[63]

---

[62] Wesley Fishel, ed., *Vietnam: Anatomy of Conflict* (Itasca, Illinois: Peacock Press, 1968). See Professor Fishel's editorial comments, pp. 675–676.
[63] Wurfel, "Wurfel Reports on Vietnam," p. 7.

Both military and civilian candidates spoke in passing of this division. Premier Ky commented early in the campaign that "if a civilian were elected and found unsatisfactory, the military had the democratic right to rectify the situation." [64] When a questioner asked General Thieu about another alleged Ky remark that he would lead a coup if a civilian were elected, Thieu "replied that Ky had said something like that but he, Thieu, had just recently said that he would respect the election results and that the army would serve any elected regime." [65] Remarks such as those attributed to Ky certainly could have deepened any existing cleavage. It is difficult to estimate the impact of Thieu's response. The vote throughout the country, while reflecting religious affiliations, rural-urban differences, and the pressures of immediate conflict, showed little evidence of a "military" or "anti-military" vote.[66] The vote in Saigon may have been partially anti-military but, except for the vocal intellectuals and activists, this would be virtually impossible—in the absence of survey data—to demonstrate. The actual vote in areas of major military presence simply did not reflect solid military backing for Thieu.

Whatever the polarity may or may not have been within the electorate, the issues pushed by the candidates during the campaign did not reveal any such clean-cut policy differences between most of the civilian candidates and General Thieu. If the voters were issue-oriented and if the issue of greatest importance to them was the war and the circumstances for bringing about peace, then the sharp division was between candidate Dzu and *all* the remaining candidates—military as well as civilian. Denis Warner put the point well:

---

[64] Sacks, "Restructuring Government," p. 625.

[65] Quoted in the report of the meeting of the presidential candidates at My Tho, August 26, 1967. See Appendix B.

[66] The account of the My Tho meeting, which tells of sharp questions to Thieu, offers some slight evidence on the matter of attitudes toward the "military ticket." It also notes that at the conclusion there was "a burst of cheers and applause. Most but not all of the soldiers in the crowd joined in the cheers as did numbers of civilians."

Curiously, most of Vietnam's heroes seem to be persons whose reputations are based primarily on their military exploits. A reading of any history of Vietnam will confirm this statement. A casual survey of a half dozen experts on Vietnam who were asked to list the five most widely accepted heroes or heroines yielded five names, all persons whose reputations were based on military exploits. Only one of the experts deviated from the five names. He named four persons of military background and one poet.

Against this perhaps romanticized background [i.e., Dzu's own description of how he had worked under an alias for years before the elections to establish his political network], Dzu's performance merits further analysis. Of eleven tickets running for office (including that of the military), nine, with varying degrees of emphasis had similar views on the conduct of war. They favored attempts to persuade Hanoi to negotiate, but failing any response, all nine were prepared to continue hostilities. Among them they got nearly eighty percent of the vote. The solitary hawk who was bent on liberation of the North, whether by ground invasion or by bombing, found that only about two percent of the South Vietnamese voters supported his stand.

Dzu advocated among other things an unconditional end to the bombing, both in the North and in Vietcong areas of the South. Yet despite his platform and efforts, only nineteen [sic] percent of the voters supported him, and without the support of the National Liberation Front his tally would have been much smaller. His Senate ticket running under the white dove emblem ran unimpressively in all but the provinces under strong NLF influence. . . .

. . . . No doubt a genuine National Liberation Front candidate or even a more respected advocate of peace at any price would have won many more votes. Moreover some of the Communist vote in central Vietnam [67] and elsewhere went to opposition candidates who were running with Buddhist or other support. The fact remains, however, that neither by the ineffective NLF boycott, nor by votes cast for Dzu, nor by attempts to disrupt the polls did the Vietcong enhance its prestige or give any indication that it has majority support among the South Vietnamese people.[68]

---

[67] Here the term "central Vietnam" is used to refer to the divisions recognized for the whole of Vietnam prior to the Geneva agreements of 1954. In modern South Vietnam the area included in "central Vietnam" is primarily that of the northern provinces below the 17th parallel and above the III and IV Corps areas—formerly known as Cochinchina.

[68] Warner, "South Vietnam Exists," pp. 18–19. There were differences in degree among the nine candidates other than Dzu and Pham Huy Co who advocated invasion of North Vietnam. These nine spoke of a willingness to stop the bombing for specified periods if the North Vietnamese were prepared to make reciprocal concessions when peace discussions started. Reports in the last two weeks of the campaign suggested that Thieu modified his own position, making it more conciliatory and therefore more like the positions of most of the civilian slates. In the last candidate broadcast on September 1, Thieu advocated a bombing halt to test the sincerity of Hanoi's peace proposals.

Just prior to the election, the prestigious London-based publication, *The Economist,* reported:

> Basically the Americans are uneasy lest the result "go sour" on them, either way. If their protégés Thieu and Ky get huge majorities, critics will say that the election has been rigged. If Thieu and Ky get only a narrow majority, the charge will be that they do not really have the support of the mass of the people.[69]

What the Americans of whom *The Economist* spoke did not appear to realize was that a 35 percent vote for Thieu, more than twice that of his nearest competitor, would be denounced on both counts—(a) it was rigged *and* (b) it showed he had no support.

[69] September 2, 1967, p. 781. The same issue noted that "many sophisticated observers are already debunking the whole exercise as an American-engineered charade with overtones of farce; their credibility would be greater if they were not the very people who would be protesting vehemently if the Americans had not insisted on elections but had chosen to go on supporting a puppet, quasi-dictatorial regime. . . ."

# 5

# National Assembly Elections of 1967

### Senate Elections

Elections for the 60 members of the Senate were held the same day as the presidential election, September 3. Six 10-member slates were to be elected.

The electoral law added some candidate qualifications to those set out in the constitution: residence in Vietnam for the three years immediately prior to election day except for those on official mission or in political exile; and the exclusion of those who had been convicted of certain criminal offenses,[1] the insane, the bankrupt who were not yet rehabilitated, military or government officials who had resigned or been dismissed for disciplinary reasons, and "those who have directly or indirectly worked for communism and pro-communist neutralism or worked in the interests of communism."[2] Civil servants or military personnel had to take leave of absence to run.

Each member of each slate was required to submit documents showing that he met all the constitutional and legal qualifications. If one member of a slate failed to meet these requirements, no substitute would be accepted and the entire list was excluded. Applications for candidacy had to be filed with the special commissioner for administration or the minister of interior by June 30. They then went to the Central Election Council and the lists were to be posted by July 1.

---

[1] For all elective national offices, not only were felonies disqualifying but no one who had been "guilty of deserting the scene of a traffic accident" could be a candidate.

[2] Election of Senators Law No. 002/67, Article 11, in U.S. Agency for International Development (Saigon), *Public Administration Bulletin,* no. 39 (August 1, 1967), pp. 20–37. All citations for the Senate election rules are from this source.

Following a period for receiving complaints and a decision by the council concerning eligibility, the second and final posting was to take place in Saigon on July 22 and elsewhere no later than July 26—i.e., five weeks before election day.

As in the case of the presidential election, a Central Election Campaign Committee with representatives from all eligible slates was set up in the capital, and similar committees in each province and municipality. The central committee was responsible for setting the rules for posters, broadcasts, schedules of public meetings, and circumstances of press conferences.

The government was authorized to spend one piaster per voter per slate up to a maximum of 18 slates. Each slate was required to deposit 180,000 piasters, or about $1,500. If a slate received less than 3 percent of the vote, the deposit was forfeited. Further, such a slate also had to reimburse the treasury for any amount spent above 180,000 piasters for its share of the campaign costs.

Each slate could choose its own symbol (except that "queer, international, and religious symbols are forbidden"), prepare a text on its program, and include pictures of all the candidates. All these appeared on the government-financed posters, and the names and symbol on the ballot as well.

The campaign officially began August 3 and ended at noon, September 2. The six slates winning the most votes would be elected. In case two or more slates tied for the winning positions, "the list with the highest aggregate age [was to be] declared elected." [3]

Unofficial results would be sent by the provinces and autonomous municipalities to the Central Election Council which would immediately announce them. The final reports had to be in by September 13. The council was to review these results, check invalid and contested ballots, and announce the official results of the elections on September 18, 1967. The report and documents were to be filed with the Senate "as documents of proof in future validation of Senators." If the council found irregularities "sufficiently serious to affect the honesty and the results of the election, then it will declare the entire election invalid." In such a case, a new election law and a new election would be required.[4]

---

[3] This provision reflects the Vietnamese veneration of age and also follows the French mode of breaking ties.

[4] Election of Senators Law No. 002/67, Article 38.

The reader will note that, in nearly every detail, the format of the senatorial elections was parallel to that of the presidential.

**The Campaign and the Outcome.** Originally 64 slates sought approval to campaign for Senate seats. Of that number, 48 slates or 480 candidates were approved. Several of the 16 slates that did not make the second posting had withdrawn without waiting for action by the Central Election Council. Most of the slates that were disqualified were made up of persons who were little known in the country. The disqualified slates, however, did include two that were close to or backed by Thich Tri Quang, the antigovernment Buddhist leader. One of these was led by Ho Huu Tuong, "a writer often accused of pro-neutralism and pro-communism who was sentenced to death during the regime of Ngo Dinh Diem in 1962." The second Buddhist-supported slate was led by Tuong's son.[5] A slate with trade union backing was disqualified because of the failure of one of its members to provide all the necessary certification papers. All lists that were loosely identified with the leading presidential candidates won council approval.

Included among the 480 approved candidates were more than half the members of the National Assembly. Many more were members of provincial and autonomous city councils who were seeking to move up to roles at the national level. A disproportionately high percentage of all candidates were residents of Saigon.

The senatorial campaign went almost unnoticed both in the United States and in Vietnam. All attention, both press and public, was drawn to the presidential candidates. And the number of slates and candidates created a bewildering sorting-out problem for both the voter and the foreign observer.

If the contests for the upper house were not widely reported, it was not because the candidates were afforded no opportunity to make their appeals public. All slates were given four opportunities to appear on radio and two shots at television. Meetings were set up for representatives of the slates in seven of the eight districts in Saigon. In addition each slate could, of course, make its independent arrangements for meetings.[6]

---

[5] *New York Times,* July 22, 1967.

[6] Allan E. Goodman, "Notes on the Administration of Elections in South Vietnam," a paper presented before the Southeast Asia Development Advisory Group (SEADAG), December 4, 1967, p. 8.

The results showed high public support for the Farmer-Worker-Soldier slate of former General Tran Van Don. It won 980,474 votes and led in 17 of the 44 provinces and in all six of the autonomous cities. No other slate came close to matching that record, and all the rest were closely bunched. The sixth and last winning ticket won with 553,632 votes. Seven more tickets received between half-a-million and 551,000 votes. The lowest of the 48 slates was the only one to fall below the 300,000 level. The spread between the sixth and forty-seventh slate was only about five percentage points—from 11.7 percent of the total vote to 6.5 percent.

In addition to the Farmer-Worker-Soldier slate, the five other winners in order were: second (with 631,616), the Lily list, a Catholic slate under the leadership of Nguyen Van Huyen; third (with 600,720), the Bright Star ticket, headed by Nguyen Gia Hien with the backing again of Catholics, especially refugee Catholics; fourth (with 569,975), the Vietnamese Sun ticket, led by Huynh Van Cao who had been identified with the Diem regime in spite of his opposition to the suppression of the Buddhist demonstrations; fifth (with 553,720), the Solidarity for Progress list headed by Tran Van Lam, now minister of foreign affairs, who had by then served as an ambassador; and the last of the winners (with 553,632) was the Revolutionary Dai Viet called the Rice Sheaf slate, under Nguyen Ngoc Ky.

The election results were very close. Indeed, the question of which slate finished sixth was a matter of some debate. The order of finish as first announced was ultimately accepted as the correct one. In the interim between that first announcement on September 5 and the posting of the official order by the Central Election Council on September 18, there was a period when another list made up primarily of Hoa Hao and Cao Dai adherents was unofficially listed as the winner.

Two slates that were predominantly Catholic were among the six winners, and there were Catholics on two others. Between 25 and 30 Catholics were elected all told. While their margin of victory was slight, their victories were a tribute to the relatively effective organization of the Catholics, who constitute only about 10 percent of the voting population of South Vietnam.

The front-running slate included among its candidates Tring Quang Guy who was deputy president of the Vietnamese Labor Federation (CVT) and so had the backing of its president, Tran Quoc Buu. The

CVT was the only large membership organization to support the Farmer-Worker-Soldier slate.

The slate supported by the moderate Buddhists fared badly, winning only 365,000 votes and placing 34th. The Hoa Hao slate finished just out of the running in seventh place.

The Farmer-Worker-Soldier slate was perhaps the one certain independent among the winners. The slate headed by Tran Van Lam might also have been classified as part of the "loyal opposition." In general, the Thieu regime could expect to receive support for the war effort from most new senators, and particularly from the two slates that were dominated by Catholic members and the other two that included Catholics. No slate associated with Premier Nguyen Cao Ky or with Truong Dinh Dzu was elected.

The senators elected in 1967 were overwhelmingly Vietnamese. One Montagnard and one North Vietnamese refugee Montagnard were elected to the 60-member body. Women fared no better, also winning only two seats. While the oldest member was 71 and the youngest 30, the bulk of the seats (44) went to persons between the ages of 36 and 55. The winners' profile, by profession or occupation, was as follows:[7]

| | |
|---|---|
| Liberal professions (lawyers, chemists and physicians) | 15 |
| Military | 9 |
| Teachers | 8 |
| Trade and businessmen | 8 |
| Deputies, Constituent Assembly | 7 |
| Technicians | 6 |
| Civil servants | 5 |
| Farmers | 1 |
| Notables | 1 |
| | 60 |

**Criticism of the Senate Elections.** The Senate elections were criticized on several counts. First, there were objections to the exclusion of the two militant Buddhist slates; thus, it was claimed, the elections did not provide a free, wide-ranging choice to the voters. Second, critics objected to the fact that voters had to choose an entire 10-member slate,

[7] *Public Administration Bulletin*, no. 41 (November 30, 1967), p. 87.

not just those members they preferred.[8] A related objection was the fact that below the top two or three names, most of the members of most slates were nonentities. Third, critics objected to the counting, as noted above, since the unofficial results at one time showed a winning slate that ultimately lost.

The most telling criticism is the one that objected to the number of names (10) on each ballot and to the total number of ballots (48) among which the voter was forced to choose. The first problem might be solved simply by reducing the number of members on a slate. The second is of a very different order because it goes to the whole matter of limiting the number of persons who can qualify for election, which in turn drives the lawmaker back to the old problem of who can be eliminated from candidacy without seriously reducing freedom of action and choice.

Whatever the solution to the second problem of choosing six slates from among so many, there can be little doubt that the large number of slates was confusing for voters. The law required that the ballots be shuffled around so that no one ballot gained advantage from being regularly at the top or bottom of the pile of 48 that was handed to each voter. To that end, the official distributing the ballots moved a small stone from list to list to show him where to start the next group of 48 that he put together for the voters.

The relatively minor difference in the number of persons who supported the top lists and the number who supported the bottom list strongly suggests that, beyond perhaps a few voters who could recognize and deliberately choose the six slates they preferred and a few more who could select one, two, or three slates where they recognized the leading name, most voters may well have made their selections more or less randomly or voted for fewer than the six slates they were entitled to select. The latter could have been a deliberate choice by sophisticated voters who voted only for their real favorites while withholding votes from others in order not to jeopardize their first choices. It was equally likely that some voters simply quit when they ran out of names that they knew. The total vote for all slates was 21,884,602. If all the 4,902,748 persons who cast ballots for the presidency voted also for senators, then

[8] The voter is equally restricted when casting a ballot under a proportional representation scheme. Then, whatever the view of the voters about the merits of the various candidates on the list, they are elected in the order in which their names are listed by party leaders.

they cast an average of only 4.46 ballots instead of six as allowed. To turn it the other way around, if all those who voted for president cast their six ballots, then only 3,647,434 bothered to vote for senatorial slates.

The explanation doubtless falls somewhere in between but almost certainly closer to the first alternative—namely, that many voters failed to cast the six they were legally allowed. The voting arrangement provided for the voter to get in a line where his identity and voter cards were checked. He then received his presidential ballots which he took into a booth to cast. When he came out of the booth, he was still inside the general voting enclosure and could make his way out only by going past the table where he would receive his 48 Senate ballots, then to a voting booth for senators where he made his choice, then past the ballot box for Senate only, and finally past the official who clipped the corner off his card. It seems unlikely that many voters who had cast their presidential ballot would then deliberately walk through the whole senatorial voting process but refuse to take or cast ballots. A few perhaps. But, more likely, they picked up senatorial ballots and then did not cast all of them—either deliberately or because of ignorance of the process or of the candidates.

## House Elections

**Election Rules.** Membership in the House of Representatives, or lower house, was constitutionally established at 100 to 200—the precise number being based on the voting population in the country. Each autonomous city and province received at least one seat, but the number of seats for the 50 jurisdictions equalled one for every 50,000 voters or major fraction of that number. By way of illustration, Quang Tri received two seats for its 107,281 registered voters while Hue received only one seat for its 54,827 registered voters. Large population dictated that Saigon be divided into three districts, with four, five, and six seats respectively. Saigon's registered voters numbered 765,340. Suburban Gia Dinh, with 562,190 registered voters, was divided into two districts, one with six seats and the other with five. All candidates ran at-large in their province or city (or district in Saigon and Gia Dinh). Voters could cast as many votes as there were seats assigned to their constituency. To return to our examples: in Quang Tri, then, the two candidates receiving the most votes would win, and in Hue it would be winner-take-all. In Saigon the top four candidates in one district, the top five in another, and the top six in the third district would win. A plurality, not a majority, of the valid votes was all that was required.

Sixteen seats were set aside for various minority ethnic groups in the country—six for Vietnamese of Cambodian descent were assigned to six Delta provinces, five Montagnards were to be elected from provinces in II Corps and one from Quang Ngai in I Corps, two Chams from Binh Thuan and Ninh Thuan provinces, and two North Vietnamese Montagnard refugees from Tuyen Duc and Ninh Thuan. The 16 "ethnic" seats were in 14 different provinces. They did not depend on the number of qualified voters in any one province, although there was a rough correspondence between the total nationwide membership of each ethnic group and the number of seats assigned to them overall. The constituency for some of these seats was less than the 50,000 required for regular competitive seats. Only voters of the particular ethnic group could vote for these candidates, and the balloting was also kept separate.

Basic control of the elections rested with the election councils that were established in each province and autonomous city. Each seven-member council was broadly representative. The chairman was the presiding judge of the Court of First Instance (or of the local Conciliation Court or the Conciliation Court with Extended Jurisdiction) or, if there were no court in the locality, a magistrate nominated by the Ministry of Justice. The other six were three members of the provincial or municipal council (not candidates for the House) chosen by lot; two voter representatives chosen by lot from a list drawn up by the provincial or municipal council; and one representative of the city, town, or province administrative office who also served as reporter. The election councils received applications for candidacy and screened them. Their decisions could be appealed to the Central Election Council to which they sent the names and dossiers of all persons whose eligibility had been challenged.

Each constituency created an electoral campaign committee made up of one representative from each of the candidates. The committee, like its presidential and senatorial counterparts, determined the character of the posters, and laid down the rules for use of sound trucks, press conferences, and other media.

The cost of the campaigns was borne largely by the treasury, but each candidate was required to deposit 10,000 piasters (about $85.00). The deposit was returned if the candidate received as much as 5 percent of the vote. He forfeited the deposit if his percentage dropped below

5 percent and had to pay the difference between 10,000 piasters and the actual amount spent by the government in his behalf.

The local councils were responsible for the honesty of the elections. They inquired into complaints about the conduct of voting, checked the tally sheets, and announced the official results.

Complaints were to be filed with the Court of First Instance or the Court of Conciliation with Extended Jurisdiction. If a winning candidate was found to have violated the provisions of any one of four articles of the law, "the courts can rule that he will not be allowed to take his seat." In fact the House itself was the judge of its own members, because the same law provided that "in deciding on the validation of deputies the Lower House will take into account definitive court rulings" (Article 42).[9]

**The Campaign and the Outcome.** The campaign began on October 6 and ended at noon on October 21. The election was held on Sunday, October 22, 1967. The second posting had named 1,235 candidates seeking 137 seats. Sixty-eight dropped out before election day, so the final figure was 1,172, of which 47 were ethnic candidates running for the 16 seats set aside for them. The remaining 1,125 candidates campaigned for 121 seats—for an average of 9.2 candidates per seat. There were provinces where ethnic candidates exactly matched the number of seats, but only in Kien Tuong province was there an unopposed candidate for a regular Vietnamese seat. In Phu Bon two candidates sought one seat and in Chuong Tien three candidates contested another. In most constituencies, however, the number of contenders was much higher.

There was no obvious pattern of difference in the ratio of candidates to seats between regions or provinces, or between rural and urban areas. In Dalat, 17 candidates campaigned for one seat. In Saigon, 236 candidates were listed in the second posting, but by election day the number had dropped to 211, for an average of 15.5 competing for each of the 15 seats from the capital. In suburban Gia Dinh, the numbers were almost as great: 162 seeking 11 seats, for an average of 14.7 per seat. Bac Lieu, a rural province in the Delta, attracted 11 candidates for the single seat. In Long Khanh in III Corps, it was 15 candidates for one seat; in mountainous Darlac in II Corps, it was 16 for two seats; in the city of Danang to the north in I Corps, it was 19 candidates seeking two

[9] See *Public Administration Bulletin,* no. 41 (November 30, 1967), pp. 88–106 for full translation of the law. So far as I know, court cases involving winning candidates did not arise in 1967.

seats, while in the nearby province of Quang Ngai, 26 candidates sought four seats.

In view of the large number of candidates and the almost total lack of party organization, it is not surprising that only seven candidates won contested seats with a majority of the votes—and five of the seven were ethnic candidates faced with less than the usual competition. No more than one majority winner turned up in any province. No city gave any candidate a majority of its votes. Indeed, in Saigon no winning candidate received more than 20 percent of the votes cast in his district, and half the winners received 10 percent or less. The same general picture held for Gia Dinh's 11 seats. Over half the successful candidates nationally received less than 25 percent of the total vote. The House elections were similar to nonpartisan elections in some U.S. cities or some primary elections in one-party states where large numbers vie for election and no one wins more than a handful of votes.

Name recognition seems to have played a role in the results. Of the 40 National Assembly deputies seeking election, 19 were successful. Teachers, civil servants, and servicemen (a term that covered ex-servicemen and officers or enlisted men)—professions in which people are likely to be well known in Vietnam—constituted just over half the candidates but won 85 of the 137 seats. By contrast, four of the occupational categories in which people are not widely known—farmers, businessmen, professionals other than teachers, and a miscellaneous grouping—included 445 candidates but returned only 22 winners. One category that seems somewhat out of line is the one for elected officials below the level of the National Assembly, of which there were 102 candidates and only nine winners. To be sure, executive officials at the district and province levels—the presidentially appointed province and district chiefs and their deputies—were forbidden to run in their provinces. Council members at the province and village levels could run in their home provinces, but they were much less well known. The breakdown of the assembly, by profession or occupation, was as follows:[10]

| | |
|---|---|
| Servicemen and ex-servicemen | 30 |
| Civil servants and ex-civil servants | 29 |
| Teachers | 26 |
| Deputies, Constituent Assembly | 19 |

[10] Ibid., p. 125.

| | |
|---|---|
| Other elected officials (prefecture, province, city and village levels) | 9 |
| Liberal professions | 10 |
| Industrialists, businessmen | 6 |
| Farmers | 4 |
| Journalists | 2 |
| Other | 2 |
| | 137 |

The registration lists posted for the presidential and senatorial elections were used again for the House elections. The turnout was down (since September) from 83.7 to 73 percent. The drop in Saigon was from 76.1 to 57.8 percent and in Gia Dinh, from 79.5 to 64.5 percent. Elsewhere in the country, the drop in turnout generally was about six to eight percentage points.

In his review of the House members elected in 1967, Professor Joiner says that "32 of the Representatives [originally] came from North Vietnam, 44 from Central Vietnam, and 59 [were] Southerners," while the origins of the other two were unknown. He lists the religious affiliations of the winners as "46 Buddhists, 35 Catholics, 13 Hoa Hao, 6 Therevada Buddhists (Khmer), 5 Cao Dai, 2 Protestants and 4 Confucianists," leaving 26 whose religious affiliations were unknown. He notes also that "the various South Vietnamese parties, groups and sects were represented." Ten House members were connected with Tran Van Don's party, 12 were from the Southern Renaissance Movement, eight (from Hue, Danang, and Saigon) were pro-Tri Quang militants, and 15 were militant Catholics. "Thus," Professor Joiner concludes, "the Lower House includes voices for each of the religious, regional, ethnic and political interest groups." [11] Which, to be sure, is part of what democratic elections are all about.

[11] Charles Joiner, "South Vietnam: Political, Military and Constitutional Arenas in Nation Building," *Asian Survey,* January 1968, p. 67. When Joiner refers to "North," "Central," and "South" in this context, he is speaking of the divisions of Vietnam prior to independence in 1954.

# Historical Setting: Two

*(In which major policy initiatives and institutional developments are described.)*

The years from 1967 to 1970—bounded, from this volume's perspective, by the first and second round of national elections—were filled with events of fundamental bearing on the evolution of South Vietnam as a nation. The war turned sharply in favor of South Vietnam. The Tet offensive of 1968 was, on balance, a victory for ARVN. The Communists lost large numbers of troops. More important, they lost irreplaceable Viet Cong cadres who were exposed by the attack and literally decimated when the anticipated uprising by the city people against the government failed to materialize.

The allied incursion into Cambodia in the spring of 1970 destroyed North Vietnamese supplies and reduced the Communist capacity to return to the offensive. Once the border of Cambodia ceased to be sacrosanct, a long-time barrier to South Vietnamese counteroffensive action was removed. The myth of Cambodian neutrality was buried for good.

In a curious and ironic sense, however, Tet represented a "defeat" for the United States. The Tet offensive was a severe psychological blow to supporters of President Johnson's program in South Vietnam. In Congress, the doves waxed and the hawks went into hiding. Sometimes Secretary Rusk and the President himself seemed to be the administration's only defenders. To be sure, a majority of the delegates to the Democratic National Convention favored the nomination of Vice President Hubert H. Humphrey and endorsed the President's conduct of the war—but, increasingly, the debate in both parties turned on this or that alternative strategy for "winding down" the U.S. commitment.

These U.S. developments placed new responsibilities on the Saigon regime, as did President Nixon's program of "Vietnamization." Under such forced draft, the government of South Vietnam seemed to gain new confidence in itself.

**Land Reform.** President Thieu moved with increasing vigor into land reform. The government took advantage of laws passed as far back as the Diem period and subsequently secured the enactment of the far-reaching land-to-the-tiller program which authorized a massive transfer of land to the tenants.

Land was given to tenants outright. The government paid former owners at the rate of two-and-a-half times the annual value of the crops. Payments with interest were to be made over a 10-year period. The maximum permissible size of land holdings was reduced from the 100 hectares (250 acres) allowed under the Diem program of 1956 to but 15 hectares (37 acres). The redistributed land was limited to three hectares for recipients in the Delta and one hectare in the central lowlands. Land beyond that needed for tenants was distributed to the families of war dead, ex-soldiers, government workers, and farm laborers. The new land owners were forbidden to sell their holdings for a minimum of 15 years after acquisition. Those who were in the process of acquiring land under earlier purchase programs were relieved of further obligations if they had paid as much as 50 percent of the land price. Peasants who were cultivating land given them by the Viet Cong kept it. The law applied to both rice and secondary crop land. It also expropriated land not directly cultivated by the landowners as well as communal rice lands.[1] By contrast with the VC, the government gave tenants permanent deeds to the land.

Figure 2 shows the increase in the distribution of land under the provisions of earlier programs and the even more impressive increase under the first 10 months of the Land-to-the-Tiller Act. The Thieu regime distributed two-and-a-half times as many hectares of land in

---

[1] See MacDonald Salter, "The Broadening Base of Land Reform in South Vietnam," *Asian Survey,* August 1970, pp. 724–737, for a description of the current program and the provisions of the Land-to-the-Tiller Act. Roy L. Prosterman also has an article on the same topic, pp. 751–754, "Land-to-the-Tiller in South Vietnam: The Tables Turn." There are other related articles in an issue devoted to "Politics, Land Reform and Development in the Countryside." Most of these are concerned with periods prior to the massive changes under the Thieu regime in 1970 but provide excellent background.

**Figure 2**

LAND REDISTRIBUTION IN SOUTH VIETNAM, 1963-70

*(in hectares, cumulative)*

| Year | Distribution of Expropriated Land | Distribution of Former French-owned Land | Land Redistribution at Refugee and Resettlement Centers | Regularization of Squatters' Land | Montagnard Land Identification Program | Land-to-the-Tiller Program | Total |
|---|---|---|---|---|---|---|---|
| 1963 | 246,166<br>(115,321) | | | | | | 246,166<br>(115,321) |
| 1964 | 246,940<br>(115,594) | | | | | | 246,940<br>(115,594) |
| 1965 | 247,774<br>(115,912) | | | | | | 247,774<br>(115,912) |
| 1966 | 248,092<br>(116,051) | 3,990<br>(2,349) | 10,010<br>(4,370) | 1,760<br>(2,516) | | | 263,852<br>(125,286) |
| 1967 | 250,548<br>(116,835) | 4,498<br>(2,729) | 18,759<br>(7,682) | 2,161<br>(2,961) | | | 275,966<br>(130,207) |
| 1968 | 250,972<br>(116,968) | 14,955<br>(5,994) | 22,306<br>(9,846) | 3,449<br>(4,059) | | | 291,682<br>(136,867) |
| 1969 | 281,113<br>(128,228) | 70,270<br>(26,082) | 35,517<br>(24,451) | 7,976<br>(13,325) | | | 394,876<br>(192,086) |
| 1970 | 298,347<br>(135,000) | 87,461<br>(32,352) | 49,863<br>(50,110) | 20,780<br>(30,521) | 38,569<br>(13,891) | 210,371<br>(162,341) | 705,391<br>(424,215) |

**Notes:** The first three columns record the implementation of Ordinance 57 decreed in 1956.
The numbers in parentheses refer to the numbers of farmers receiving land under the various redistribution programs.

**Source:** Republic of Vietnam, Ministry of Land Reform and Agriculture and Fishery Development.

its first three years, 1968 through 1970, as the government had distributed in the preceding 12. Land distributed in 1970 alone amounted to 310,515 hectares, or more than the total distributed during the years 1956 to 1968 inclusive. Furthermore, formerly small Viet Cong taxes had grown larger than the rent demanded by landlords, so that even before the new government land reform, the VC programs were becoming less attractive.[2]

Land distribution paralleled other significant developments at the village and hamlet level. During the period from 1967 through 1970, virtually every locality in the country replaced officials appointed by Saigon with chiefs and councillors elected by and accountable to the villagers themselves. By the end of 1970, some 2,048 of the 2,151 active villages and 9,859 of the 10,506 active hamlets had elected their councils and chiefs.[3] Perhaps most important, beginning in 1969, the government of South Vietnam gave arms not only to village officials but also to those ordinary local citizens who were in the People's Self-Defense Force, which was now under village rather than national control.[4] In other words, the land reform program took place under circumstances that met what Dennis J. Duncanson has elsewhere called an essential prior requirement: "that development aid should only be distributed in places where the police function is covered adequately."[5]

**Supreme Court.** The Supreme Court was provided for in the constitution but was formally created only when the National Assembly enacted legislation in September of 1968. The law gave the new court great power. It was to be the highest court of appeal with authority to pass on the constitutionality of legislation. It was authorized to screen presidential and vice-presidential candidates and be the final judge of presidential

---

[2] Samuel L. Popkin, "Pacification: Politics and the Village," *Asian Survey,* August 1969, pp. 662–671, provides an interesting account of the developments in pacification including the impact of the Tet offensive.

[3] There are, according to the Vietnam embassy's *Viet-Nam Bulletin,* an additional 407 villages and 3,318 hamlets listed as "non-active." Some were abandoned in free-fire zones and others merged with active villages.

[4] John P. Roche, in the *Washington Post,* December 8, 1971, comments on the arming of the citizens and discusses the distribution of land.

[5] Duncanson, "The Police Function and Its Problems," in Frank N. Trager, ed., *Lessons of Vietnam* (New York: American-Asian Educational Exchange, 1971), p. 13. The entire essay is an interesting discussion of important aspects of modernization that are often neglected in other studies.

elections. The power to outlaw political parties that were "pro-Communist or neutralist" was shifted from the executive branch to the new court.

The members of the Supreme Court were chosen by the National Assembly, meeting in joint session, following a complex screening process. The position of chief justice was to be determined by election within the court for a term of one year.

In 1968, some 54 lawyers, public prosecutors, and presiding judges applied for the nine Supreme Court posts. An Electoral Commission made up of the president of the Senate and one other senator, the speaker of the House of Representatives and another representative, and a judge, a prosecutor, and a practicing lawyer screened the applicants. The commission rejected nine candidates for failing to meet the constitutional and legal requirements—essentially the same as those for other high national office, with the additional requirement of 10 years of legal experience. Next, three 50-man panels—one chosen by the Bar Association, one by the Association of Judges, and one by the Association of Public Prosecutors—were to reduce the number of candidates to 30: 10 judges, 10 prosecutors, and 10 lawyers. In fact, they cut the number to 24 because too few private lawyers—whose business was good and incomes were high—applied for consideration. Only then did the National Assembly finally make its choice of four judges, four prosecutors, and one practicing lawyer.

The new judges were men of high reputation in their profession and in the country generally. Tran Minh Tiet, who was later chosen by his colleagues as chief justice, had been openly critical of President Thieu and his administration. He was one of three persons who received more than 100 assembly votes. Both Tiet and Nguyen Van Si had served as ministers of the interior, Tiet during the Diem years. All the judges were between 43 and 56 years old.

The Supreme Court, according to Professor Charles Joiner, "staked out a thoroughly non-Confucianist role as an independent judiciary." [6] Professor Joiner specifically referred to the case of a member of the House of Representatives, Tran Ngoc Chau, whose brother Captain Tran Ngoc Hien was a North Vietnamese agent. Deputy Chau was found guilty by a military court of having Communist affiliations—in spite of his claim that the U.S. embassy had been aware of and approved

[6] Joiner, "Political Processes in the Two Vietnams," *Current History,* vol. 59 (December 1970), pp. 358–359.

his relations with his brother—and was sentenced to 20 years hard labor. Later a new trial reduced his term to 10 years. "The Supreme Court ruled that the sentence was illegal, but it did not order his release. [The decision did not keep Chau out of prison] but his case resulted in the supremacy of the civil over the military judiciary." [7]

In the late spring of 1970, the court overruled several decisions of lower courts. In one appeal, it rejected the government's handling of student strikers protesting the arrest of a student leader who had campaigned against increased university fees. In another, it declared Thieu's tax program unconstitutional, thus forcing a change of economic policy. It also ruled unconstitutional the field military courts. Professor Joiner, after noting these cases, concluded that the court was not a "serious block to executive misuse of power. . . . But this transplanted American-style institution provided an avenue of redress in the face of governmental transgressions against the Constitution. . . ." [8]

**The National Assembly and the President.** The early years of any government are difficult. They are especially difficult for a new government in a war-divided country. Most observers were skeptical in 1967 about the possible evolution of a national legislature that would be in any real sense independent of the executive. The record from then to 1970 certainly did not suggest legislative dominance, but during its annual sessions—at least four months in duration—the National Assembly debated significant issues and was freely critical of the Thieu regime. It forced the executive to change its course of action in some matters, amended some legislative requests, and wrote some legislation of its own. The record was one of great executive influence but not of absolute executive control.

[7] Ibid., p. 359. The reader may be reminded of the inability of the United States Supreme Court to provide a complete check on executive excesses in this country during the Civil War and either of the World Wars. Indeed, the Court in this country has been careful not to order the President to act during wartime and thus face a losing showdown. In *Ex Parte Merryman,* an appeals court did order the executive to release a prisoner in 1862, but President Lincoln simply ignored the order.

[8] Ibid.

# 6
# National Assembly Elections: 1970-1971

## Senate Elections: 1970

Elections for 30 members of the Senate who had drawn three-year terms were scheduled for August 30, 1970. Under the 1970 election law, the rules for candidacy remained essentially unchanged from 1967 except for one new article: candidates in earlier elections who had failed to win the minimum number of votes required and who had failed to repay the treasury for the cost of their campaigns over and above their deposit were barred. Minimum vote requirements were raised from 1967's 3 percent of those voting, which had clearly not deterred frivolous candidacies, to 5 percent. Further, any candidate failing to win the basic 5 percent had to repay the government within three months.

Membership on the Central Election Council was modified to include two senators who were not themselves candidates. Deposits required of candidates went up from 180,000 to 500,000 piasters, in large part to reflect the inflation during the intervening years. The 1970 law also provided that candidates running for reelection were "entitled to use their old symbols and appellations. If there is any contention about symbols, the candidate who headed the former list has the deciding voice."

The courts were given increased authority in cases involving alleged electoral violations. Parliamentary immunity could not be invoked to prevent judicial action. The Senate had the final voice in deciding on the validity of its own elections but was admonished to take the courts' "advisory" decisions into account.

The election law was proposed by the executive and "debated and modified by both houses and does not appear to favor any side excessively." [1] This was the judgment of the *New York Times* a week before the election.

The 1970 senatorial campaign was largely uneventful. Eighteen 10-member slates filed for candidacy. Sixteen eventually made the second posting, but no serious criticism developed over the elimination of the other two. The slates were generally representative of the principal interest groups. Five were led by men of varying shades of Catholic opinion. Five were led by Buddhists—four with An Quang support and the other "headed by an eccentric monk." The other six included one slate that had appropriated the name and symbol of the leading 1967 list, the Farmer-Worker-Soldier slate with its symbol of the bull on a star. (Former General Tran Van Don, leader of this slate in 1967, had temporarily retired from politics.) The remaining slates included civil servants, university faculty, and diverse intellectuals drawn largely from the Saigon area.

The campaign was somewhat different from earlier ones because the Central Election Council prohibited mass rallies and meetings, on the ground that they were vulnerable to Communist attack. Each slate received 20 minutes of television time and 30 minutes of radio time, all of it free. The political programs were broadcast each evening for the two weeks of the campaign, with the slates taking their turns. The posters—as usual, paid for by the government—were more striking than in 1967. Some called for instant peace. Others demanded the resignation of President Thieu. Some candidates, apparently to the surprise of the public, went from door-to-door describing the merits of their slates to housewives or devoted time in the cafes talking to prospective voters.

Two slates led all the others by nearly a quarter of a million votes. The Lotus Flower slate, headed by Vu Van Mau and backed by the An Quang Buddhists, led with 1,149,597 votes. Professor Mau had served as minister of foreign affairs under Diem but resigned in 1963 in protest against Diem's handling of Buddhist issues. His slate included seven Buddhists, one Hoa Hao, one Animist, and one Moslem; two of its members were incumbents. The slate led by comfortable margins in the Buddhist strongholds in both I Corps and II Corps. It managed a good vote in the other two regions as well but did not lead the balloting.

The Sun slate ran a strong second, with 1,106,288 votes, well ahead of the remaining 14. Former General Huynh Van Cao who had led a

[1] *New York Times,* August 23, 1970.

similar slate in 1967 was again head of the ticket. Five members of the slate were incumbent senators. Half the members of the slate were Catholics, and the others included Hoa Hao and Cao Dai sect members and an ethnic Cambodian. Not surprisingly, this slate led in the Delta where Catholics, Hoa Hao, Cao Dai, and ethnic Cambodians are numerous. It also carried the Cao Dai province of Tay Ninh in III Corps and did well in Catholic areas near Saigon.

The Lily slate, as in 1967, was led by Catholic Nguyen Van Huyen. It received 882,274 votes. Four of its members were incumbent senators. Half were Catholic, four were Buddhists, and one a Confucian. Its most prominent member was Tran Van Huong, prime minister in 1964–1965 and 1968–1969. This slate won large pluralities in Saigon and its suburb Gia Dinh and so also carried the III Corps area.

In 1970, some 4,299,516—a low 65.13 percent of the 6,578,082 voters who were registered—cast ballots. The registration was an increase of 724,678 over that of 1967, most of it attributable to the pacification of areas where registration had been impossible three years earlier. There were new voters in the growing cities of Hue and Danang, but the number of voters in metropolitan Saigon area actually dropped. In III Corps, Hau Nghia and Long An, both of which had very low security ratings in 1967, showed the largest increases in 1970—43 and 88 percent, respectively. In IV Corps, the greatest gains were in Kien Hoa (57 percent), Dinh Tuong (61 percent), and An Xuyen (55 percent); all were rural provinces in the Delta with very low security ratings in 1967.

For whatever reason, but possibly because the number of slates—16—was a good deal smaller and because of the presence of an easily identifiable slate with An Quang support, the results suggested a more discriminating vote in 1970 than in 1967. There was a considerably wider spread between the leaders and the also-rans. In addition to the three winning slates, one other reached the 800,000 level. The fifth slate received 146,000 fewer votes. The votes of the others fell off sharply, so that six slates received less than half as many votes as the lowest winning slate. The three winning slates received 26.74, 25.72, and 20.51 percent of the possible vote. By contrast, the three lowest slates received but 9.30, 7.95, and 7.44 percent of the vote. Voters still failed to cast all the votes they were allowed. The total cast for all slates was 9,817,738—which means that the 4,299,516 persons who voted cast an average of only 2.28 votes out of a possible three.

The breakdown by primary occupation of the 30 senators elected in 1970 was as follows, according to a press release (undated) of the Republic of Vietnam:

| | |
|---|---|
| Educators | 7 |
| Lawyers | 7 |
| Military | 3 |
| Businessmen | 4 |
| Engineers | 3 |
| Physicians | 2 |
| Pharmacists | 1 |
| Civil servants | 2 |
| Labor leaders | 1 |
| | 30 |

### House Elections: 1971

**Election Rules.** The rules governing the conduct of elections to the House of Representatives were changed only slightly from those of 1967. In 1967, candidacy was denied to those who were Communists or pro-Communist neutralists or had "worked in the interests of communism." The latter phrase was dropped in 1971. The new law extended from six months to one year the period in which province or district executive officials and other civil servants and military officials above a certain level were prohibited from running in provinces where they had held power.

Membership on the Central Election Council was changed to reflect changes in government structure. The 1970 council was headed by the chief justice or deputy chief justice of the Supreme Court, and included one judge appointed by the Supreme Court, one senator who was not a candidate for the House, one House member who was not seeking reelection (if any), the prosecutor or deputy prosecutor of the Saigon Court of Appeals, and the vice minister or secretary general of the Ministry of Interior.

The deposit required of all candidates was increased to 50,000 piasters—the equivalent of about $143.00. The minimum vote required to avoid loss of deposit was increased from 5 to 10 percent of the "total number of voters who go to the polls in his constituency."

Safeguards against cheating were written into the law. First, if there was a shortage of ballots for any candidate or candidates at any polling place, no ballots could be given out there until a new and complete supply had been received. Second—a rule apparently more for American consumption than for honest elections—no unused ballots could be removed from the voting place. This latter rule had little relevance because only one ballot is counted for any one candidate in any one envelope. A ballot all by itself is just a piece of paper. Therefore, unless an equal number of envelopes was also stolen or counterfeited, and unless the number of envelopes was somehow made to equal the number of corner blocks cut from the voting cards (see Figure 3), it would make no difference how many people had how many ballots. If an envelope contained ballots for more candidates than the number of seats allotted to the particular jurisdiction, then all the ballots in that envelope were invalid.

The number of seats for each province and autonomous city (or subdivision of Saigon and Gia Dinh) remained one for each 50,000 registered voters. The total originally announced was 152, an increase of 15 over the number in 1967. Then, on August 16, Prime Minister Tran Thien Khiem announced that the registration figures listed in the second posting of August 9 required the creation of new seats in several provinces. The new seats were assigned to An Xuyen, Chau Doc, Kien Hoa, and Phong Dinh provinces in the Delta, Gia Dinh province just outside Saigon, and Quang Ngai and Quang Tri provinces in I Corps in the north. As in the case of the earlier apportionment of seats, it was not so much a total population increase as an increase in the population under government rather than VC control—largely a function, in other words, of pacification. The reapportionment showed Saigon down by two seats, I Corps up by five, II Corps up by one, III Corps up by three outside of Saigon, and 15 new seats in IV Corps where Viet Cong strength had been very sharply reduced.

The government recognized the importance of growing urbanization by creating five new autonomous cities—Qui Nhon and Nha Trang in II Corps, and My Tho, Can Tho, and Rach Gia in IV Corps. The total number of autonomous cities thus rose to 11.

**The Election.** The number of persons originally seeking candidacy in 1971 was 1,404. Local election committees rejected 118 of this number. Following appeals to the Central Election Council, 65 of those rejected

**Figure 3**

VOTING CARD ISSUED IN 1971 AND ITS ENGLISH TRANSLATION

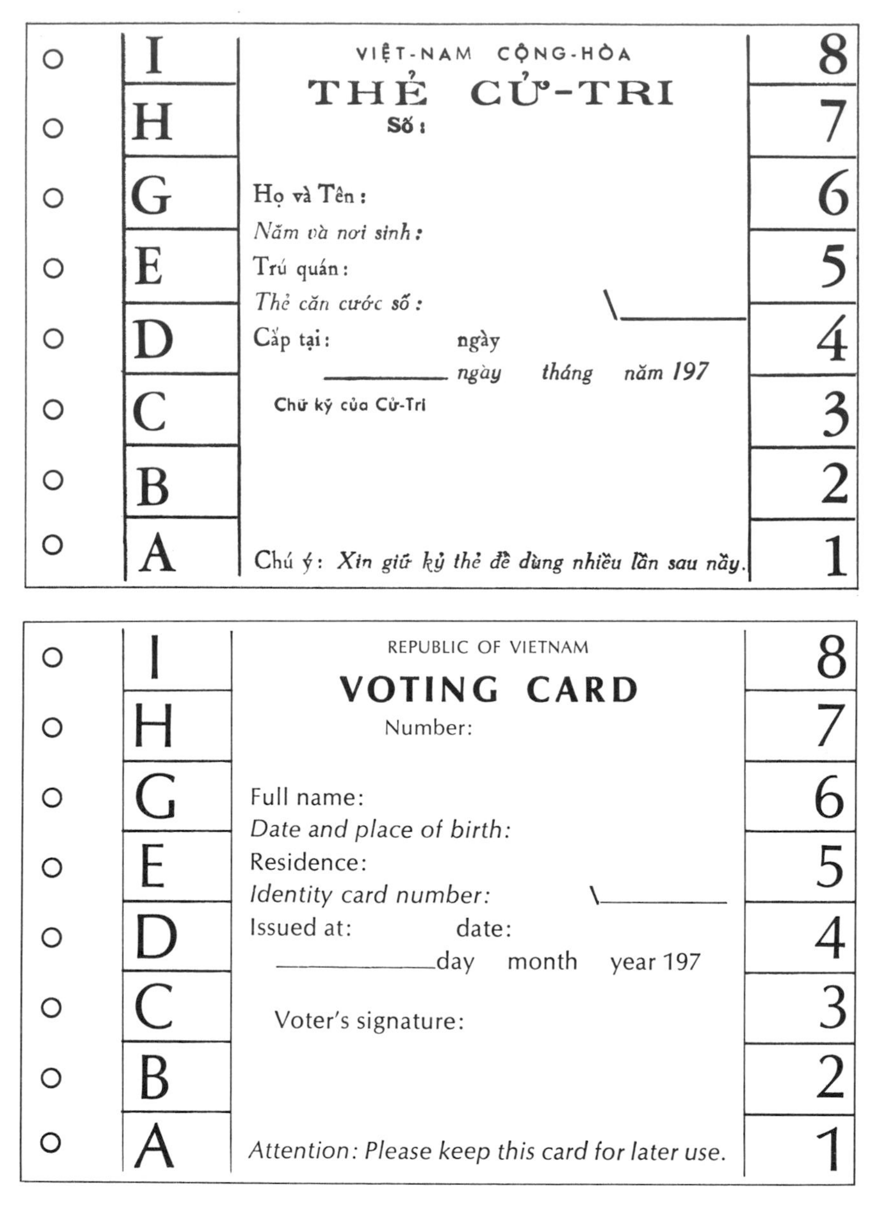

I H G E D C B A

VIỆT-NAM CỘNG-HÒA

THẺ CỬ-TRI

Số:

Họ và Tên:

*Năm và nơi sinh:*

Trú quán:

*Thẻ căn cước số:* \\

Cấp tại: ngày

________ *ngày tháng năm 197*

Chữ ký của Cử-Tri

Chú ý: *Xin giữ kỹ thẻ để dùng nhiều lần sau này.*

8 7 6 5 4 3 2 1

I H G E D C B A

REPUBLIC OF VIETNAM

VOTING CARD

Number:

Full name:

*Date and place of birth:*

Residence:

*Identity card number:* \\

Issued at: date:

________day month year 197

Voter's signature:

*Attention: Please keep this card for later use.*

8 7 6 5 4 3 2 1

**Note:** On this currently valid voting card, the lettered blocks are for use in national elections, the numbered blocks for subnational elections. Block "A" applied to the House elections of August 29, 1971 and block "B" to the presidential election of October 3, 1971. See page 53 for the voting card issued in 1967.

were reinstated. The best known candidate to win his appeal for reinstatement was Ngo Cong Duc—of whom more to follow—a deputy and an editor of a vigorously antigovernment newspaper, who had been rejected by his local committee as pro-Communist and pro-neutralist. Another incumbent, Nguyen Van Dau of My Tho, was excluded on the ground that he had given money to the Viet Cong. He, too, was reinstated. In most other cases, appeals from exclusion based on charges of pro-Communist activities were turned down by the Central Election Council.

In Saigon, 11 would-be candidates were rejected by the local council. The appeals of 10 of the 11 were rejected by the Central Election Council because their military papers were not in order. The appeal of a much publicized Buddhist student leader, Phan Hoa Quang, was rejected because he had not fulfilled his draft obligations. Among the members of the Central Election Council was Tran Quang Thuan, a strong Buddhist who had been elected to the Senate in 1970 on the An Quang slate. The council reinstated most Buddhist candidates who had been rejected by local councils and was generally considered to have enforced the law fairly.

There were 1,332 candidates for 159 seats on the second posting; by election day, that number had dropped to 1,242. The ratio of candidates to seats was 7.8, down slightly from 1967.

Registration for the election was 7,086,146 and the turnout was 5,582,411 or 78.7 percent, up 4.8 percentage points from the 1967 vote.[2] As usual, the turnout was heavier in the countryside than in Saigon where only 59.9 percent of the voters came out. The entire III Corps area (which includes Saigon and its suburbs) had a turnout of 72.3 percent, well below the national average. By contrast, the turnout in I Corps (which includes Hue and Danang), usually low, was a surprising 82.4 percent, the record for the country that year. The presence of An Quang Buddhist candidates on the ballot was almost certainly a factor in this higher than usual vote.

In some provinces and cities where the vote was split among a large number of candidates, the winners carried with only a small percentage of the total vote. In Gia Dinh province, eight winning candidates re-

[2] U.S. Agency for International Development, *Public Administration Bulletin*, no. 57 (December 1, 1971), pp. 46–61, provides turnout figures and the votes for winning candidates.

ceived less than 10 percent of the vote [3]—and one of them, Duong Minh Kinh, received only 6.6 percent. Only one of the 11 winners from Gia Dinh received as much as 12 percent of the vote: he received 30 percent. The Saigon picture was somewhat better. Even with 172 candidates for 13 seats, no winner fell below 12 percent and six received more than 20 percent. Only six winners received a majority of the votes of their province—four in the Delta and two from Phu Bon province in II Corps. A majority of the deputies (81 of 159) were elected with less than 25 percent of the votes of their constituencies.

Incumbents generally fared badly. Of the 119 who sought reelection, only 40 were successful. Of that number, half were classified as oppositionist (i.e., antigovernment) candidates. In Saigon, 10 of the 13 winners were incumbents and four of these were members of the opposition. Ho Van Minh, who was scheduled to be Duong Van Minh's running mate until the latter dropped out of the 1971 presidential race, led all Saigon candidates with 30.2 percent of the vote in his district. Nationwide, of the 28 members of the House who endorsed General Minh's presidential candidacy, 18 won reelection—most of them from the larger urban centers.[4]

While only 20 of the large number of progovernment incumbent-candidates were reelected, those who lost were often beaten by other candidates with government backing. The government's reason for switching support was not always clear, but U.S. embassy officials ascribed some changes to the government's desire to rid itself of hacks and hangers-on in favor of younger, abler supporters.

The largest successful delegation for any single political group was the An Quang Buddhists with 25. Next came the Progressive Nationalist Movement, a coalition of moderate groups that won 19 seats, and the Worker-Farmer party, which had trade union backing and won 14 seats. No other party or group won as many as 10 seats. Any figures on the division between supporters and opponents of the government are necessarily approximations, but a month after the election the best available estimate was 84 progovernment, 60 antigovernment, and 15 indepen-

---

[3] Technically, by failing to meet the 10 percent legal standard, these eight winners were obligated—together with all the losing candidates in Gia Dinh—to forfeit their deposits. One presumes they were excused from that obligation. After all, the 10 percent standard was set to prevent "frivolous" candidates and, almost by definition, winners are not "frivolous."

[4] *New York Times,* August 31, 1971.

dent. Observers point out, however, that members in each category have supported the government on some issues and opposed it on others.

Over half the members of the new House were under 40 years of age (83 of 159). Only 17 were over 50. By occupational grouping, the winners' profile was as follows: [5]

| | |
|---|---|
| Servicemen and ex-servicemen | 44 |
| Incumbent representatives | 40 |
| Civil servants and ex-civil servants | 15 |
| Provincial council members | 13 |
| Physicians, pharmacists | 13 |
| Teachers | 11 |
| Farmers and landowners | 7 |
| Tradesmen | 5 |
| Lawyers | 4 |
| Notables | 2 |
| Miscellaneous | 5 |
| | 159 |

Among both the winners and the losers were some well-known and some notorious types. Former Senator (and General) Tran Van Don, who did not seek reelection to the Senate after heading the most popular slate in 1967, ran for the House in 1971. He chose to campaign in Quang Ngai (although it is not his home) and led all six winners in that province with 30.6 percent of the vote. One report states that according to "American officials in the area, the Government made little effort to defeat him. . . ." [6]—in spite of the fact that he had been a strong critic of the regime while in the Senate. The speaker of the House during the first four years, Nguyen Ba Luong, carried Phuoc Long with 43.3 percent of the vote. In Binh Long, both Duong Van Thuy, the incumbent, and Nguyen Quang Luyen, sometimes known as the "solid gold deputy" because he had once been caught in the airport at Bangkok with a suitcase full of it, were defeated by a highly respected doctor with government support, Pham Ke Toai, who received 28.7 percent of the vote. Two of the government's most vigorous critics, Ngo Cong Duc and Duong Van Ba, were defeated in controversial contests in the Delta.

[5] *Public Administration Bulletin,* no. 57 (December 1, 1971), p. 63.

[6] *New York Times,* August 31, 1971.

**Election Honesty.** As in the case of other South Vietnamese elections, charges of fraud preceded even the nominations. As early as June, before anyone had yet applied for candidacy, there were assertions that "if Duc loses . . . it will be because the government stole it from him." [7] This statement allegedly was made at least three weeks before the candidacies were approved (as Duc's was) and six weeks before the campaign began. Nor did the pressure let up thereafter. General Minh made not untypical charges against the conduct of the elections, and 100 Buddhist monks seized and destroyed a ballot box before the election in Bac Lieu, charging that Duong Van Ba would be cheated out of a deserved victory by the province chief.

Two days before the election, an oppositionist Senate committee (the People's Anti-Fraud Election Committee) headed by Senator Vu Van Mau, who had led the victorious An Quang Buddhist slate in 1970, made a series of charges against the government. The committee denounced the Kien Phong election where the brother of the province chief was seeking a seat. The brother withdrew from the race and the committee took full credit.[8] The committee charged that in Tuyen Duc province, the province chief had ordered the hamlet chiefs to work for government candidates. In Bac Lieu, the committee charged that the government had destroyed opponents' leaflets and that soldiers were under orders from the province chief when they pelted oppositionists with eggs. Further, the committee charged that in Danang the oppositionists were harassed by the police and arrested on vague charges, and that the radio "broke down" as they were broadcasting their campaign speeches. (Whatever the facts in this instance, An Quang candidates won all three seats in Danang and 22 of 24 in the I Corps area as a whole.)

The Senate, spurred on by oppositionist leaders, passed a resolution on September 22 charging that there were irregularities in 12 provinces where elections "were not held in a free and democratic spirit." Their recommendation for action against the province chiefs was restricted to five provinces, however—Bac Lieu, Vinh Binh, Phuoc Long, Phu Bon, and Binh Thuan—two in the Delta, two in II Corps, and one in III Corps.

---

[7] The *Washington Post,* August 27, 1971, quoted "an American advisor" as making this statement two months before the story was written.

[8] According to a knowledgeable U.S. embassy official, a similar case arose in An Xuyen. But here both the province chief and his brother were popular, and the brother won by a comfortable margin.

For his part, General Minh charged irregularities in four provinces —Vinh Binh, Bac Lieu, Phuoc Long, and Binh Tuy. The first three were on both the long and short lists of the Senate resolution, but Binh Tuy was on neither.

In most of the country, the campaign and the election itself were uneventful. Obvious exceptions were the campaigns of Ngo Cong Duc, who sought reelection from Vinh Binh province, and of Duong Van Ba, who campaigned for reelection in nearby Bac Lieu province. Both were vigorous critics of government policies, and both were among the few antigovernment candidates whom the government seriously sought to defeat. A U.S. embassy official noted that "Duc and Ba are clever publicists." Predictably, any allegations of fraud involving these two men would be headline grabbers—and they were.[9]

Duc was described by the *Washington Post* as a "35-year-old deputy [who] has probably been President Thieu's noisiest critic, although by no means the most respected. . . . His lively newspaper, *Tin Sang,* is Vietnam's second largest." [10] He had been jailed earlier in the summer for striking the chairman of the Vinh Binh provincial council, and he was released on demand of the House. On election day, Duc brought more than a hundred people with him from Saigon as election observers. Only 14 were accepted. Whether the others had the required certificates is not known. In any case, his observers agreed with his charges that corners of voter cards were improperly cut off, that many peasants were sent away from the polls without voting, and that voting officials were ordered by the provincial government to hold Duc's vote to no more than 10 percent of the total.

Duc lost. When his case was taken to court, the charges were thrown out because they lacked specificity. The Supreme Court upheld the lower court but at the same time asserted that the province chief should be removed by the president. Thieu did not follow the court's suggestion. Duc was later notified, as were 21 other losing incumbents of draft age (20 of them progovernment), that he could not leave the country because he was eligible for the draft. Duc fled the country anyway to join the Vietnamese exiles in Paris and later went to Sweden.[11]

---

[9] *Washington Post,* August 30, 1971.

[10] Ibid.

[11] Much of this story is based on a report in the *Washington Post,* November 9, 1971, and on interviews with U.S. embassy personnel.

Another though less spectacular case arose in Vinh Binh involving a colleague of Duc, incumbent deputy Nguyen Van Thanh. He also lost. Thanh was involved in a fight at the polls when he charged that forms were being incorrectly filled out. During the struggle, a gun fell out of his pocket. He was arrested and convicted for carrying a deadly weapon in a voting place, but an appeals court reversed his conviction.

Duong Van Ba encountered no precampaigning problems comparable to those of Duc, but he sought to withdraw the day before the elections, alleging that they were sure to be rigged. On election day he was involved in a full quota of difficulties. In Hunghoi village in Bac Lieu province, Buddhist monks seized the official ballot box and smashed it to pieces to prevent what they charged would be an unfair election. The police replaced the ballot box. Next, 100 monks dashed out of their pagoda, captured the ballot box, and threw it into the river. The police then laid siege to the pagoda into which the monks had retreated. Ba, accompanied by two national senators, arrived in a helicopter furnished by Vice President Ky. The helicopter was driven off by rifle fire from the provincial police when it first sought to land. On a second effort it was forced to leave by tear gas. Police arrested the monks and Ba and charged them with seeking to prevent citizens from voting, under a provision of the law originally written to apply to Viet Cong attackers. They also charged Ba with violating the election law by distributing large quantities of his election literature before the official opening of the campaign as a "special supplement" to a Saigon paper. The tension in Bac Lieu was heightened by the fact that the province chief was a cousin of President Thieu and the brother of his personal secretary.

Ba brought charges against the provincial administration in the courts. The local prosecutor refused to prosecute. Ba then brought the case directly to the House, as the law allows, appealing the outcome of the election as certified by Bac Lieu officials. The House refused to reverse the election results.[12]

Another case, this one reaching the Supreme Court, involved the election of Vu Van Quy in Phuoc Tuy province. Election officials there had first sent word to Saigon that Huynh Van Nguyen was the winner by a margin of 268 votes. Later in the evening, the officials telegraphed to say that there had been an error of 100 in the count for each of three

[12] The Ba episode description is based on interviews, as well as the *New York Times,* August 30, 1971, and the *Washington Post,* November 7, 1971.

voting boxes. Under the new count, Quy was the winner by 32 votes. Both the contenders in this instance were antigovernment. In fact, the allegedly misapplied 300 votes were taken from the government-supported candidate who, in any case, was running third. The Supreme Court upheld sentences against Quy and six election officials for election irregularities and recommended against seating Quy.

Suits involving another 19 candidates reached the courts. Either candidates or their supporters could bring suit, and either could appeal a lower court judgment to the Supreme Court—which heard nine appeals in all. In general, the Supreme Court upheld fines and prison sentences against polling officials; in three cases it upheld fines against winning candidates even as it affirmed election in two of the three cases. The court seemed to make no distinction between pro- and antigovernment candidates or between winners and losers. In addition to deciding these nine cases, the Supreme Court also advised President Thieu to fire three province chiefs for violations of the election rules.

The House was the final arbiter of the election results. Some cases were considered by the House that had gone up through the Supreme Court, but some cases had bypassed the courts altogether. The Ba case fell in the latter category. The House, while critical of some provincial officials and some successful candidates, seated all winners certified by local officials. In addition to the Ba decision, the House rejected appeals by losing candidates from Tuyen Duc province who alleged that poll watchers had not been allowed to observe the count of ballots brought to the provincial capital from remote hamlets. The local election council had denied the allegation. The House also rejected the charge from Kien Giang province that the government had transported only progovernment voters to the polls. And it rejected the Supreme Court's recommendation that the election of oppositionist Vu Van Quy be nullified.

There was clearly a basis for some charges of corruption. The provinces where the charges seemed best supported were largely confined to newly recontrolled areas of the southern Delta—Bac Lieu and Vinh Binh—plus only a few constituencies in other regions. The constituencies where there seemed to be the widest agreement as to irregularities were those in which the winners gained substantial pluralities. Four of the six instances where candidates received a clear majority were targets of special condemnation. In other cases where fraud was generally thought to have occurred, the winning candidates received more than 36 percent and usually more than 45 percent of the vote. The one exception was in Phuoc Tuy where oppositionist winner Vu Van Quy received only 10.4 percent. Which is not to say that all races won by 36 percent or more were subjected to serious fraud charges; but, except for Phuoc Tuy, in all instances in which fraud was widely believed to have occurred the winning candidate did receive 36 percent or more of the vote.

**Possible Lessons.** The level of voter participation was higher than in previous nonpresidential elections. The number of candidates remained very high. Only 53 potential candidates were excluded from seeking office and most of these for failure to meet clear constitutional and legal requirements relating to their military obligation. A handful were excluded on ideological grounds. Action by the Central Election Council in sustaining appeals was an important factor in holding this number down. A very few candidates were excluded by the council for supporting North Vietnam. The evidence in these instances appeared to be massive.

In the long run, the development of an independent role for the courts in policing the elections may have had the greatest significance for increasing electoral integrity. In 1971, the Supreme Court showed an independence of the executive branch nationally and, often enough, so did the local courts. The fact that both government-supported and oppositionist candidates were both convicted and acquitted in the local courts and that the higher courts acted on appeals without obvious bias provided a foundation for strengthening the court system. And a reputation for judicial integrity improves the chances for more nearly fraud-free elections in the future.

The problem in most areas, in 1970-1971 as in 1967, remained lack of political organization—not excessive organizational control. Professor Goodman has suggested that during this period

> the development of political organization *did* continue. Pro-government groups tended to purge themselves of ineffective and inactive members. Incumbents who made little effort to become involved with their constituencies were defeated, as were those who contributed little to the workings of the Assembly. At first, the government tended to move corrupt and inefficient incumbents to remote constituencies. But there, public pressure usually proved so great that government support of these incumbents was withdrawn in favor of more qualified

> candidates. Opposition groups returned to both Houses of the National Assembly with more adherents, and the prospect of greater cooperation with more independent-minded pro-government Deputies and Senators. The rash of statements that appeared in 1967 denouncing the elections was absent in 1970 and 1971. Even militant An Quang Buddhist leaders acknowledged the importance of the elections to their efforts at political mobilization and the necessity to participate in politics within the framework of the Constitution.[13]

Professor Goodman's assessment strikes one as correct. There are other evidences of encouraging organizational development and of increasing independence of both legislature and judiciary from executive dominance. Nonetheless, the movement toward more competent and effective political organization may remain slower than the needs of Vietnamese society demand.

[13] Allan Goodman, "What Went Wrong In Saigon?", *Freedom at Issue,* January-February 1972, p. 14.

# 7
# Presidential Election of 1971

The outcome of the 1967 presidential election in some sense beclouded President Thieu's entire first term. His failure to win more than 34.8 percent of the vote was a boon to his critics and a constant irritant to the president. The press in Saigon and in the United States and anti-Thieu politicians in Vietnam and Washington never let him forget his minority mandate. To some it was evidence of his lack of personal popularity, his coldness, his introverted and secretive character, his lack of charisma.[1] They insisted that his policies, especially his war policies in conjunction with those of the United States, were no more popular with the Vietnamese people than was Thieu himself.

These allegations of a "flawed" mandate were, at the very least, arguable—and on two distinct levels. With respect to performance, Thieu had provided the country a stable government for the first time since the middle years of the Diem regime; he had made impressive strides toward fundamental land reform; and he had brought pacification to substantial areas of the countryside. And if he was not charismatic, he was also not conspicuously unpopular with any large segment of the population aside from some Buddhists in the north and some of the intellectuals, students, and veterans in Saigon. On the level of institutional process, the voters in 1967 gave the extreme left as represented by Truong Dinh Dzu, who called for immediate cessation of fighting, only 17.2 percent of the vote. They gave the extreme right as represented

[1] There are some who question the widespread view that Thieu lacks charisma. Some persons who have followed him on speech-making tours into the countryside and who understand the language insist that he inspires his audience. They say they have seen him move an audience to tears with his speeches.

by Pham Huy Co, who called for five million U.S. soldiers and the invasion of North Vietnam, a mere 2.2 percent of the vote. Voters cast 80.4 percent of their ballots for the remaining nine candidates, all of them centrists who supported the continuation of the fighting while searching for a peace formula that would leave South Vietnam free to choose its own course—and Thieu was a centrist among centrists.[2] He may have fallen short of some ideal personification of the Good, the True, and the Beautiful—but he was no illogical product of an evolving political-governmental system that might, one day, produce another national leader more nearly attuned to the model of the Saigon-Washington-New York intellectual establishment. The first order of business, clearly, had to be the institutionalization of the system itself.

Press reports suggested that President Thieu was acutely sensitive to the interpretation given the election results by his critics. Alvin Shuster said that being a minority president "has been gnawing at him. . . . He feels it has weakened his authority and provided valuable ammunition to his opponents in their frequent charges that he does not represent the South Vietnamese people." [3] Thieu obviously was of a mind to recommend an election law in 1971 that would prevent a repetition of the 11-way race of 1967. The question was, what kind of an election law?

## Election Preliminaries

To solve the problem, Thieu at first toyed with the possibility of a run-off system, as he had in 1967. He dropped the idea in December of 1970 and the National Assembly never seriously considered it when writing the 1971 presidential election law. Instead, the House passed and sent

---

[2] It is worth reminding U.S. critics in particular that a 34.8 percent vote is not that unimpressive, least of all in a field of 11 candidates, and even less so in the absence of a highly structured party system. Minority U.S. presidents have been more the rule than the exception. Indeed, in very recent years—1948 and 1968, for example—when there have been just one or two "major" minor parties in the field, a winning vote of about 45 percent seems to be regarded as perfectly acceptable in the United States. In 1860, Abraham Lincoln received only 39.8 percent of the vote in a four-man race. Woodrow Wilson received 41.9 percent in 1912 in a race in which four candidates each received more than 5 percent. And, of course, President Nixon won with 43.4 percent in 1968 in a three-man contest. The analogy is even more obvious in primaries with multiple candidates where much lower winning percentages are commonplace. Senator George McGovern, for example, won in a field of 12 candidates in the 1972 Wisconsin presidential primary with only 30 percent of the Democratic vote.

[3] *New York Times,* June 7, 1971.

on to the Senate a bill that would have the effect of limiting the number of candidates by requiring the endorsement of either 40 members of the National Assembly (out of 197) *or* 100 members of provincial or autonomous municipal councils (out of 554). No endorser could sign more than one petition without nullifying all his signatures, and all endorsements for any one candidate had to come from one source *or* the other. These rules would allow a maximum of nine candidates, assuming that no aspirant secured more than roughly the minimum required.

The bill encountered stiff opposition in the Senate. The restrictive clause was removed by a vote of 30-14, thus leaving the nomination process more or less as it had been in 1967. The measure was returned to the House where a two-thirds vote was required to override the Senate deletion. More than the usual uproar developed during the House debate on the issue. Nguyen Dac Dan, an ardent supporter of Vice President Ky, terrorized the other members of the House when he threatened to toss a live grenade among his colleagues. Eventually, the House adjourned and Dan was subdued. On June 3, the House re-passed the bill—with the restrictive endorsement clause—by a vote of 101 to 21; it was signed by the president on June 23.

The new law made other changes as well. The Supreme Court, not the National Assembly, now had the responsibility for receiving nomination petitions and for approving or disapproving the tickets. Candidate deposits went up from 1.5 to 2 million piasters ($7,300), and the amount the government was obligated to spend went up from two to three piasters per voter per slate with a limit of 18 piasters for all candidates—a limit of negligible significance in view of the restrictions on candidacy built into the law. (Because of inflation, both increases were more apparent than real.) Candidates who received less than 20 percent of the votes cast would lose their deposit and would have to pay the treasury for any money spent by the government in their behalf in excess of the deposit. The election was scheduled "on a Sunday, four weeks before the term of the incumbent ends." (President Thieu's first term was scheduled to end October 31, 1971.) Finally, it was the Supreme Court that was to be the ultimate judge of the election's validity. It could confirm the outcome or nullify the election and call for a new one.

None of the new provisions caused any problems—except the one requiring endorsements. General Duong Van Minh among others challenged the constitutionality of this provision. They alleged that the law contravened Article 13 of the constitution which states that "every citizen has the right to vote, run for office, and participate in public affairs on an equal basis and in accordance with conditions and procedures prescribed by law." The restrictions clearly made it impossible for some citizens to "run for office," but equally clearly these were "conditions and procedures prescribed by law."

On July 13, 1971, the Supreme Court upheld the constitutionality of the law, including its limitations on candidacy.

**The Candidates.** For more than a year it had seemed probable that there would be only three strong candidates, General Minh, Vice President Nguyen Cao Ky, and President Thieu. The first to make a public move was General Minh, who had returned on November 4, 1968, after four years of exile and who, on October 30, 1970, announced his decision to run for the presidency. He made his announcement at the home of Senator Tran Van Don. Two weeks later he added the qualification that he would be a candidate in the election "if it takes place." [4] A little later he further qualified his announcement of candidacy by asserting that he would run if the elections were not "rigged." He stuck by this latter phraseology until his actual withdrawal on August 20, 1971, six weeks before the scheduled election.

As soon as it became clear that the law would require endorsements for candidacy, Minh and Ky laid plans to assure that they would not compete for signatures and thus inadvertently prevent one or both from qualifying. Minh restricted his efforts to get endorsements to members of the National Assembly. Ky sought his from council members in the provinces and autonomous cities.

President Thieu went after signatures wherever he could find them. He secured 104 from the National Assembly and 452 from an estimated 550 councillors.[5]

Minh picked up his quota from the National Assembly. Ky, however, could not get enough endorsements from council members to meet the legal requirements: Thieu had virtually preempted the remaining supply both in the National Assembly and in the provincial and city councils. Barring an unexpected move by the Supreme Court, then, it seemed that Ky would not be able to get on the ballot.

---

[4] From an interview with Agence France-Presse as quoted in *Keesing's*, December 26–31, 1970, p. 24359.

[5] Some 554 were elected to the councils in 1970 but the number still in office a year later was slightly lower.

President Thieu formally filed on July 24, 1971. His vice-presidential running mate was Senator Tran Van Huong who had twice served as prime minister and finished fourth in the presidential election of 1967. After he had retired as prime minister (or been dropped by Thieu) in 1969, he ran for the Senate in 1970 and won. He was also a former mayor of Saigon and, before that, had been a college professor of botany. Huong was 67 years old. He was generally respected in Saigon; in fact he carried the city in 1967.

Under the new election law, there could be an alternate vice-presidential candidate named who would replace the first candidate in the event the latter dropped out of the race. President Thieu picked 46-year-old Tran Thien Khiem, the then current prime minister who had replaced Huong in 1969. He was a general prior to moving into politics. Khiem went on leave of absence as prime minister when the campaign was officially under way, as required by the election law.

Two days after the president filed for reelection, General Minh—misgivings and all—filed his own slate with the certified endorsements of 44 members of the assembly. His regular candidate for vice president was Ho Van Minh who had been elected to the lower house from a Saigon constituency in 1967 and had served as first deputy speaker of that body, where he was regarded as one of the ablest of the opposition leaders. He was Catholic, a medical doctor, and 34 years old. General Minh's alternate candidate for vice president was Senator Hong Son Don. He had been elected on the Farmer-Worker-Soldier slate that led the senatorial voting in 1967. He was a wealthy businessman and a member of the Cao Dai religious sect. In the Senate, he was a member of the economic and defense committees.

Vice President Ky, who had been the first to assert his firm candidacy in June, was the last of the big three to file. He waited until the final filing date, August 4, and even then filed incomplete papers: they bore only 61 properly certified endorsements by provincial and municipal councillors. He presented another 41 signatures that did not have the required certification of the province chief or mayor: the 41 had already endorsed President Thieu and could not therefore legally endorse any other candidate.

Ky's vice-presidential candidate was Truong Vinh Le who had been chairman of the National Assembly back in the Diem government but had held no public office since. He was a Catholic. He had led a slate of candidates in the 1970 Senate election that was believed to have

Thieu's support. It finished fourth, just out of the money. (Ky picked no back-up candidate.)

The Office of the Supreme Court (i.e., three members only) posted the list of slates on August 5. The list included the Thieu-Huong-Khiem and the Minh-Minh-Dong slates. Provisionally, it refused to post Vice President Ky's slate because of his failure to provide the necessary 100 certified signatures. The court made it clear, however, that this was a preliminary decision and that Ky could appeal the decision to the full court. The full court, under the law, had to decide on the final posting at least 40 days before the election—on or before August 21.

During the period between the first posting and the Supreme Court's final ruling, General Minh and Vice President Ky continued to issue periodic denunciations of the president and of the probable "rigging" of the election. General Minh made public what he charged were orders to the provincial leaders under the title of "Instructions for Presidential Election Campaign Strategy." General Minh insisted that the document proved his point that the elections were going to be rigged. The letter was addressed to no one and signed by no one. It was marked "Top Secret." [6]

No one denied that such a letter might have been sent to the province chiefs. One U.S. embassy official suggested to me that the letter might also have had some material added to it, but he thought much of it was authentic. Professor Allan E. Goodman apparently accepted the document as authentic but refused to take it seriously:

> The most striking aspect of the document that General Duong Van Minh released to the press—the document containing Thieu's detailed plans for rigging the election—is the similarity it bore to the campaign plans advanced by almost every group that ran a candidate in the 1967 presidential election. The document called for analysis of the chances of the slate in each province, assessments of the opposition it would face, and specified the level and kind of harassment that should be employed to discourage opponents. It, like others I have seen, was a sophisticated war plan.[7]

---

[6] For a copy, see the extension of remarks by Representative Charles B. Rangel (D., N. Y.), *Congressional Record,* October 5, 1971, p. E10427.

[7] Goodman, "What Went Wrong in Saigon?" *Freedom at Issue,* January-February 1972, p. 15. Some Americans with experience in U.S. political campaigns agreed, on reading the document, that it was not to be taken seriously but disagreed with the assessment that it was "a sophisticated war plan." Rather, they regarded it simply as an example of the "dirty tricks" genre.

General Minh withdrew from the race on August 20. He had hinted earlier that he would do just that because, on his showing, the barring of Ky was another indication that the election was rigged. At the time, however, one of his associates was quoted as saying that "even if Thieu steals 20 percent of our vote we can still win." [8] Reporters speculated during the two weeks between the first posting and Minh's withdrawal that he might drop out, but some thought it unlikely that he would do so until after the House elections on August 29 when he would be better able to judge the probable honesty of the whole process.[9] In any case he did withdraw, blasting the process as "a contemptible farce which will make the people lose all hope of a democratic regime and prevent a reconciliation among the Vietnamese people." [10]

Almost before the U.S. embassy could express its regret over General Minh's withdrawal, the Supreme Court handed down a surprise decision putting Vice President Ky back in the race. The full court reversed the earlier decision of the three-judge panel against Ky's candidacy by upholding the validity of a challenge by a councillor from Saigon who argued that Thieu could not properly secure signatures from both council members at the provincial and municipal level *and* from members of the National Assembly. The court accepted Thieu's National Assembly endorsements but revoked his 452 endorsements by council members. The court then validated enough signatures of the councillors who endorsed Ky after first supporting Thieu to give Ky his necessary 100 signatures.

At the same session, the Supreme Court accepted Minh's withdrawal. It then immediately posted the second and final list with two slates—Ky's and Thieu's. According to the law, this posting prevented Ky from withdrawing.

But Ky, after discussions with General Minh and various antigovernment peace groups, withdrew anyway on August 23. He alleged that the election was indeed rigged by the Thieu administration. And in spite of the legal technicalities, the Supreme Court, after several days of hesitation, removed Ky's name from the final list.

At the time he withdrew, Ky demanded that new elections be called. He proposed that both he and President Thieu resign their positions and

[8] *Washington Post,* August 6, 1971.

[9] Ibid., August 16, 1971.

[10] Quoted in *Keesing's,* November 20–27, 1971, p. 24946.

turn power over to the president of the Senate under the provisions of Article 56 of the constitution. The National Assembly would then provide for new elections during the next 90 days.[11]

President Thieu announced that he would continue to campaign and that the election would go on as scheduled. During the course of the next weeks, he redefined the coming election as a referendum in which the people could vote to endorse or repudiate his presidency. If they repudiated it, he would step down. He detailed ways in which voters could express their opposition: they could drop empty envelopes into the ballot box, or they could destroy or deface the ballot itself. In any such cases the ballot was to be counted against the regime. Thieu announced that if he received less than 50 percent support (presumably of votes cast), he would quit after first arranging for new elections. This election/referendum clearly satisfied no one—except perhaps those who wished to discredit the whole South Vietnamese enterprise.

Ambassador Ellsworth Bunker had worked hard during the late spring and early summer to assure that elections acceptable to the American constituency would take place. He wanted the result, however it came out, to be credible. Initially, he sought to persuade Thieu to make the law itself less restrictive and, failing that, urged him not to act in a manner that would drive other candidates out of the race. Some credit his pleas with the turnabout of the court on Ky's eligibility. He urged both Minh and Ky to stay in the race. Specifically, he was reported to have talked to Minh about the importance of a "loyal opposition" in a democratic society, where even the loser plays a significant role in the preservation of the system. General Minh rejected the argument and publicly asserted that Ambassador Bunker had offered to contribute to the cost of his campaign if only he would run. Most reporters, American and Vietnamese, tended to accept Bunker's denial that he had made any such offer.

**Alternative Solutions to the Election Problem.** The most widely discussed alternative was the one proposed by Vice President Ky: postponement, following the resignation of both Thieu and himself. A variant of this proposal was pressed for a time by U.S. Senator Henry Jackson (D., Wash.) who had long been identified as a liberal in domes-

[11] Article 56 clearly was not intended as a device for arranging caretaker governments preparatory to regular elections. There were other problems with using the article in the 1971 situation that will be noted later.

tic matters but a hawk on Vietnam. Indeed, Senator Jackson suggested that unless a "real" election and not a referendum were held, he personally would have to look again at the whole question of U.S. aid to South Vietnam.

Actually, there were a number of difficulties associated with the Ky proposal or most any variant of it. The Supreme Court could not reopen the candidate list nor could it postpone the election. Under the law, which it had earlier held to be constitutional, the court was authorized only to establish the list of candidates and this it had done with the first and second posting. It could even be argued that the court had gone beyond its powers in allowing Ky to withdraw in the first place, but it all happened so fast that Ky had no real chance to withdraw before the second and final posting. The whole episode certainly had a heavy-handed quality about it. But that did not affect the limitations on the court's power to cancel and reschedule elections.

The election had been scheduled as late as possible to comply with the constitutional provision that it be held one month before the expiration of the president's term. If the election were postponed, action would have to be taken by the National Assembly—not only to postpone but also to amend the constitution to cover the period after the president's term had expired: the constitution makes no provision for a "caretaker" executive. To delay the election and to provide for a successor would thus require constitutional amendments which in turn would require the support of "two-thirds of the total number of Representatives and Senators."

There remained the question of who *were* the members of the lower house. Some 159 members had just been elected or reelected on August 29. The terms of the lame-duck members of the House did not expire until the end of October. There was discussion at the time, however, of beginning the terms of the newly elected members on October 4 (which did in fact occur)—but, even then, no decision on a new presidential election could be made until after the difficult process of organizing the House had taken place. Because only 40 members had served in the first National Assembly, organizing the new House would be doubly difficult. If, on the other hand, the lame-duck House were to make the decision, then, obviously, fewer than one-third of the members who would pass on so important an issue would be persons in whom the electorate had expressed the confidence of the ballot box.

Topping even this one was the problem of who would be the candidates in such a new election. Most of those who talked of postponement seemed confident that both General Minh and Vice President Ky would enter the race along with President Thieu. There clearly could be no such assurance. These were the three men most likely to gain widespread support, to be sure, but that had been just as true for the election that now (in this scenario) was to be called off. Nothing could be written into the law that would guarantee the presence of either Ky or Minh in the proposed new election. After all, both men had already voluntarily withdrawn. They apparently did so because of the endorsement procedure, but the evidence is rather compelling that this was largely subterfuge. It is probable that Minh and possible that Ky would have refused to run next time, just as they had refused to run in the regularly scheduled election. As Professor Goodman put the matter:

> Of all the commentary about the presidential election, none has taken so much space and time as the debate over its fairness. Prior to the election, the principal candidates themselves focused public attention on this issue and declared that they would not run if they believed the elections rigged. *This, in fact, must be taken as a statement that the candidates would not run if they expected to lose. . . .*[12] (Italics mine.)

The law could hardly assure all candidates that they would win.

**The Problem of the Law.** President Thieu's responsibility for the debacle goes farther back than the decisions of the summer. The law was written in a manner acceptable to Thieu, but he soon found himself less and less able to control the ultimate nature of the presidential contest. Every step he took led him almost inevitably to become hostage to the vagaries of General Minh.[13]

Minh had laid the groundwork for his entrance *and* exit as far back as November of 1970. He rarely spoke of the upcoming election and his own role without asserting that he would be a candidate only if he felt certain that the election was not "rigged." Also, as Peter Osnos

---

[12] Goodman, "What Went Wrong," p. 15.

[13] The interpretation in this section is based on what seems to be the logic of a situation in which Thieu found himself when he was trying to force his will on a set of circumstances that was not under his control: General Minh, whom Thieu most wanted to meet and defeat, simply did not feel bound to make the race and could not be forced to do so. A long report and analysis by Alvin Shuster presents at least a partially parallel argument based on his discussions with "informed sources" in Saigon. See the *New York Times,* August 29, 1971.

pointed out in the *Washington Post,* General Minh addressed his remarks not to the Vietnamese but to the foreign press. Osnos wrote, "Minh has been granting long and rambling interviews to one foreign journalist after another, but has yet to see the local press. . . ." [14] It was the U.S., not Vietnam, that might force the kind of election that would make a Minh victory possible. If it did not and he withdrew, it would be American "influentials" who would lead the attack on Thieu.

Crucial to Minh's chances of winning was the candidacy of Vice President Ky in a three-man race. According to the Minh analysts, Ky would draw most of his votes from the same sources as President Thieu. And if these two divided more or less evenly the votes of about 60 percent of the electorate, Minh could win his needed plurality. If, on the other hand, Minh faced Thieu alone, he might be beaten rather badly.

The case is comparable to a number of recent American elections where the winner represented the minority on one side of the only divisive issue in the campaign, while several candidates on the other side divided the majority vote. Mayor John V. Lindsay managed to win in New York City in 1969 with less than 42 percent of the vote while his two "conservative" opponents, Mario A. Procaccino and John A. Marchi, together divided just over 58 percent. In 1966, George P. Mahoney, representing fewer than one-third of the Democratic voters of Maryland, won the gubernatorial nomination by defeating two major and several minor opponents who divided more than 68 percent of the vote. In both cases, a majority of the voters supported positions on key issues that were contrary to those of the winner. An obvious recent case, of course, is that of George C. Wallace in the 1972 Democratic primaries. His opponents, as many as a dozen of them, shared the bulk of the votes in Florida and Maryland, but it was he who won pluralities.[15]

If it was clear to Minh, it was equally clear to President Thieu that the presence or absence of the vice president in the election was the key to the outcome. Thieu, who most observers conceded could win easily in any head-to-head contest,[16] wanted Ky out of the race for two

[14] *Washington Post,* July 25, 1971.

[15] In Michigan, North Carolina, and Tennessee he won by clear majorities.

[16] One young member of the U.S. embassy staff did suggest to me that he felt "Minh could win against Thieu if the President would resign and if the country did not fall apart during the month of a campaign." Relatively few would have joined in that estimate of the situation. More representative of generally informed opinion was the belief expressed to me by the chief of a village a few kilometers from Saigon. He argued that Thieu could have won by a majority even if both

reasons. First, he wanted to avoid even an outside possibility of losing to Minh because the majority was divided between Ky and himself. Second, he wanted to win by an impressive margin.

Thieu's "solution" to the problem was to push Ky out of the race by denying him access to the required endorsements. But pushing Ky out jeopardized Minh's candidacy at the same time. Minh and Ky were so conscious of their importance to one another that they coordinated plans throughout the summer. They agreed on the most effective way of seeking endorsements and later consulted each other before either of them announced his withdrawal. Thieu rid himself of Ky. But, in the process, he also lost Minh whose presence he badly needed to bolster his political reputation.

Thieu made two crucial errors—unless, of course, one is prepared to believe that he always intended to run alone. First, he seems to have expected Minh to stay in the contest. An Associated Press story from Saigon in early August described the president as being "unconcerned about Vice-President Nguyen Cao Ky's failure to qualify for the presidential election" because he expected Minh to continue running—and this in spite of the latter's statement that "because of this critical situation, we feel it is necessary for us to reconsider our candidacy." [17]

Some extremist advisers to both Minh and Ky apparently wished to see the election, and possibly even the nation, collapse. Newsmen filed a spate of stories in July and August about the influence of the advisers on the principals but in general doubted they would ultimately persuade Minh or Ky to withdraw. Among those friends on the left who often urged such advice on Minh was Tran Ngoc Lieng, who had been Minh's running mate during his abortive race for the presidency in 1967.[18]

Thieu's second mistake grew in part out of his view about Minh's willingness to stay in the race. Chronologically, this mistake occurred early. It was Thieu's decision to allow a law to be written that did not provide for a runoff. As noted earlier, the very idea of a second round

---

Minh and Ky had remained in the race. Thieu would have peasant support "because he gave us the land, the fertilizer, the pigs and the chickens, and provided a school for our children. Few people on the land know General Minh and fewer know who Ky is. The peasants would cooperate with President Thieu."

[17] Washington *Evening Star,* August 8, 1971.

[18] *New York Times,* July 17, 1971 and August 11, 1971; *Washington Post,* August 10, 1971.

between the two top candidates received little support from any Vietnamese. Further, a multiple-candidate race might have forced Thieu into a runoff—perhaps after finishing second in the first round, with whatever psychological damage that eventuality might have caused for him. It was, of course, remotely possible that he would have failed to make the runoff even though he might have been able to win a head-to-head contest against each candidate individually.[19] From the vantage point of post-election analysis, however, the runoff was one way of securing a *contested election* and a very solid victory, possibly in the first round and certainly in the second. It is, of course, by no means certain that Minh would have found the runoff formula acceptable since his best chance of victory was in a simple plurality election with multiple candidates. The runoff arrangement might not have been any more attractive to him than an initial head-to-head contest.

A few columnists—like Crosby S. Noyes of the *Evening Star,* for example—pointed out that it was General Minh and later Vice President Ky who withdrew from the election, not Thieu, and that Thieu had no power to prevent them from doing so. And even if new elections were to be scheduled, there was no assurance that either or both of them would enter the contest. But for most analysts the simple fact remained that Thieu was the sole candidate, and this had to mean, as a *Washington Post* editorial expressed it, that Thieu had "euchred" both Minh and Ky out of the race.[20]

---

[19] In the 1966 Georgia Democratic primary, for example, three candidates seriously vied for the gubernatorial nomination—Lester Maddox representing the right wing of Georgia politics, Ellis Arnall the left, and James Carter the center. In the first primary, Arnall led the voting while Maddox barely defeated Carter for the second position. In the runoff the conservative Maddox defeated the liberal Arnall. Most observers felt that Carter could have defeated either of them in a two-man race since the Maddox voters would have preferred him to Arnall and the Arnall voters would have preferred him to Maddox. So strong was the anti-Maddox feeling among the pro-Arnall voters, in fact, and so many of them voted for the Republican "Bo" Calloway, that he won a plurality of the vote in the general election. Only the quirk in Georgia law giving the state legislature power to name the governor if no one receives a majority prevented Calloway from being the first Republican governor in the history of the state. Other states have witnessed this same phenomenon of multiple candidates resulting in the selection in a primary of a nominee who later lost the voters of at least one wing of the party to the opposition in the general election. While the example chosen is an American primary, any single-round or runoff may result in the defeat of the candidate of the center who could have defeated each of the others in a head-to-head contest but could not muster a plurality in a multiple-candidate race.

[20] *Washington Post,* September 7, 1971.

**General Duong Van Minh.** To have put his political reputation at the mercy of General Minh was clearly Thieu's monumental misjudgment. For Minh, as described by newsmen and long-time students of Vietnam, simply had too little interest in politics and power to work at being a candidate, *particularly if it appeared he might lose.*

Alvin Shuster frequently referred to his "reticence," noting on one occasion that Minh had "built an image of respectability on [this] . . . foundation" and that he had spent most of his time since returning from exile in 1968 "merely tending his orchids, playing tennis, seeing his old army friends and allowing the people to wonder whether he would ever try again to step into the limelight." [21] General Minh once told a U.S. official, well before the campaign, that if he were free to choose a profession he would be neither general nor politician: he would be a monk. Shuster also noted that "many observers found [Minh's political views] vague" and that he "usually asks his visitors for their reaction to his statement." But Shuster pointed out that those who wish change, "who believe he represents the early path to peace, who find charm in his reticence, who dislike President Thieu for a host of reasons, agree that General Minh may not be the ideal candidate to lead the opposition. But as one of his supporters said today: 'You cannot love what you do not have. You must learn to love what you have.' " [22]

Peter Jay observed that it was as a peace candidate "that most Vietnamese see him. But his plans for peace have been cloaked in the vaguest of generalities. . . ." Minh "opposes any coalition with the communists and supports a strong South Vietnamese army" [23]—not generally considered to be "peace plans" in the Vietnam context. Jay suggested that "being out of power and out of public view may have been beneficial to Minh." He then quoted a Vietnamese journalist to the effect that "Vietnamese automatically dislike the person in power," which is a very commonplace phenomenon indeed.[24]

Before General Minh withdrew from the race he continually denounced the "rigging" of the election. According to Jay, a South

---

[21] *New York Times,* August 1, 1971.
[22] Ibid., November 11, 1970.
[23] *New York Times,* June 15, 1971. For an example of Minh's vagueness in his own words, see "Vietnam: A Question of Confidence," *Foreign Affairs,* vol. 47 (October 1968), pp. 84–91.
[24] *Washington Post,* July 11, 1971.

Vietnamese newsman said some 10 days before Minh's withdrawal: "If he withdraws he has a reason. If he loses he has the same reason. And if he wins, fraud is forgotten." [25]

General Minh did not quit the presidential race without some knowledge of his public strength. His vice-presidential candidate stated that the slate would withdraw "only if it became apparent that the elections were hopelessly rigged for Thieu"—and then added that a poll was "being taken to see what the voters think." [26] The interviews were actually going on in the field just 10 days before the final date for withdrawal, so that Minh must have received up-to-date information on his public support before he decided to throw it all over. When he quit, Henry Bradsher of the Washington *Evening Star* commented: "The 6-foot-1-inch 'Big' Minh was never very sure of himself as he edged into the presidential race. His withdrawal last Friday was the most decisive step he took in the whole situation." [27]

Robert Shaplen's picture of General Minh has varied a good deal over the years. This long-time student of Vietnam was less than favorably disposed toward Minh at the time of the anti-Diem coup. In 1966, he described Minh as the coup's front man while General Tran Van Don did the actual planning.[28] Of the period immediately following the coup, Shaplen stated that if there was a "single leader, it was General Minh . . . , but he proved sadly incapable of the task." He was "the inactive and sulky Chief of State" that summer of 1964.[29]

Subsequently, Shaplen seemed to find Minh more worthy. In mid-1969, he spoke of the need for President Thieu to "bring into the government men like General Duong Van Minh (Big Minh), who headed the junta that overthrew Diem; he could rally important Buddhist support, and he is standing by in Saigon. . . ." [30] He referred to Minh as "a still popular man who has been frequently mentioned as the logical

---

[25] Ibid., August 10, 1971.

[26] Ibid., August 10, 1971.

[27] Washington *Evening Star,* August 27, 1971.

[28] Robert Shaplen, *The Lost Revolution: The U.S. in Vietnam, 1946–1966* (New York: Harper and Row, 1966), p. 202.

[29] Ibid., p. 271.

[30] Robert Shaplen, *The Road From War: Vietnam, 1965–1970* (New York: Harper and Row, 1970), pp. 298–299.

choice to head a special advisory body that could create the broader consensus everybody admits is needed." [31]

In November 1971, Shaplen reported that while Marshal Ky had tried to organize the opposition forces, Minh had said that the "solid American support of Thieu made it futile to attempt anything in the way of opposition." [32] Minh's attitude led Shaplen to comment that "where Ky moves quickly, Big Minh weighs his options carefully—too carefully, some friends believe. He has withdrawn his head at the moment, but he has an objective still in mind—to wait to be summoned at the right moment to save the country from falling apart." Some of his supporters "have lost their faith in him as an opposition leader . . . [but] he cannot be written off, if only because he is the potential compromise leader of an interim government if Thieu should stumble and fall." [33]

Ambassador Bunker's reported appeal to Minh to continue in the race because of the need for a "loyal opposition" was apparently as unavailing as it was compelling from a system-building perspective. Minh, like Ky and Thieu, represented a position, vague as it may have been. But beyond that he was just a personality. He did not represent a party. If he lost he went down as an individual, more or less without a trace. "Loyal opposition," by contrast, implies a continuing party effort so that today's defeat may become tomorrow's victory for some organization more durable than the candidate himself. He is running for a point of view held not only by himself but by his organized cohorts, and for the organization's future prospects. In Vietnam there was and is no such party. Minh was an individual who had the support of other individuals and newspapers at home—and in the United States [34]—all of whom saw in him the best chance of defeating Thieu. Minh was the instrument of

---

[31] Ibid., p. 307. It is striking how often those opposed to the regime in power see the need for that regime to "broaden its base" to secure a "wider consensus." I was impressed by the number of persons in Saigon who offered this suggestion in 1971 and by the fact that always the people who should be brought in were their friends.

[32] Robert Shaplen, "Letter from Saigon," *The New Yorker,* November 13, 1971, p. 84.

[33] Ibid., p. 88.

[34] The American press became involved in the contest as they recommended candidates who might forward their view of America's best interests. *The Economist* made light of this American press custom. After mentioning that Minh and Ky were the probable challengers of President Thieu, *The Economist* (August 29, 1970) noted parenthetically that "Senator Tran Van Don, the probable candidate of the *New York Times,* is ineligible because he was born in France."

their hopes. If he failed, they would look for a new candidate next time—and Minh might not even have the satisfaction of being a part of that ad hoc effort.

A strong man (and one committed to the evolution of democratic processes) might have made the run and, by his own personal effort, continued to have an impact on policy and politics. He might have been offered a position in the government where his opportunities for influence would have increased. Others have followed such a course, even in Vietnam. Tran Van Huong is a leading case in point. But not Minh.

On the bulk of the evidence now available, he is in a profound sense politically frivolous. In 1967, Minh chose a running mate who he knew, presuming he had read the constitution, was not eligible; he almost literally forced the National Assembly to bar his candidacy. He appears always to be less anxious for political power than for public plaudits, and never seems quite prepared to make the extra effort that might get him into electoral contests and possibly win him victories. He has remained in the public arena, issued vague statements, been reassured by the supporting press that he is the popular man of the hour. But then he drops out of the contest, and thus he has never had to put the question of his actual popularity to the test. He retires as the man of principle because the opposition has "rigged" the outcome. He has been, in short, a kind of inarticulate and ineffective figure, the leader of a vague crusade whose supporters sometimes seemed more certain than the candidate what his goals and purposes might be.

General Minh has received his share of the front pages of the Saigon press. He may even continue to do so for another election. (He is 55 years old.) But unless he actually becomes a contestant, he is likely to end as only a footnote to history. Politically serious candidates may lose and find no place in history. But some of them win, and it is they of whom the historians write. For his part, Minh ceased to have any importance in the Vietnam election of 1971 after his withdrawal. Vice President Ky moved back into the headlines while General Minh, after a last-gasp effort to blame Ambassador Bunker for his plight, rapidly faded from public view.

## The Campaign

An election campaign with only one contestant is, for want of a better term, unusual. In countries where this is the norm, the campaigns at least are mercifully brief. But not so in South Vietnam in 1971. The constitutional and legal script called for a campaign of at least four weeks, and a four-week campaign there was. In fact, a precampaign campaign had been going on since the fall of 1970 when Big Minh had made his qualified announcement of candidacy and when almost every observer was certain that Vice President Ky would also joint the lists.[35]

All the excitement fizzled out by late August when only President Thieu was left seeking the presidency. He said he would continue to campaign for a vote that would measure support of his regime. So, for 30 days prior to October 2, 1971, there was a campaign of one man against an "opposition slate" of negative votes or abstensions.

Thieu began his campaign with a brief television address, pressing the point that both Minh and Ky had been qualified by the Supreme Court to contest the election but both had chosen not to run. It was their free decision, he said, and in no way affected his own responsibility to continue to seek election in the manner prescribed by the constitution. The two slates that had withdrawn chose now to talk about "rigged elections" but their arguments were not convincing. He rejected Ky's proposal that both resign, saying he could not thus avoid the responsibilities of his office. Only the Communists would gain from the unavoidable disruptions. So the election must be held and he would carry out his constitutional duty. The people would have an opportunity to express confidence or lack of it in his administration and, he promised, he would abide by their decision.

In the first of four formal campaign speeches, he reiterated his will to continue and explained how the people could express their opposition. Most of all he asked them to vote and called on provincial and municipal governments to assist in producing a big turnout.

His second speech was a statement of platform with heavy emphasis on his "Four Noes." Peace must be restored to South Vietnam, but (1) no concessions of territory to the Communists, (2) no coalition with the Communists, (3) no neutralism of the kind proposed by the Communists, and (4) no Communist party and no Communist ideology freely operating in South Vietnam.

His third speech outlined the accomplishments of the regime. He described the success of pacification and subsequent elections in the

[35] Subsequent reports have suggested, however, that Ky really wanted to be asked by President Thieu to continue as vice president (*Washington Post,* March 28, 1971).

villages and hamlets, the various social welfare programs for the benefit of orphans, veterans, the aged, et cetera, health programs, and education, and he put particular emphasis on the extent of land reform in the preceding 15 months.

The final speech was a summary of the first three and again appealed to the people to come out and vote.

On three of the four occasions, his running mate Tran Van Huong was introduced by the president and spoke briefly prior to Thieu's main speech. His most interesting speech was the first one in which he acknowledged the criticism of those who insisted that he had "defiled" his ethics, his honor, and his reputation by running at all. Huong said that, precisely to the contrary, he was working for his country. He was too old to seek the demanding job of president and, further, could not finance such a campaign. He had come to know General Thieu in the years since 1965, and he joined Thieu in his campaign in behalf of "the survival of South Vietnam." It was for this same reason that he had served two years earlier as prime minister. If this was to "defile" his honor, Huong said, then he must do it willingly for the sake of the nation.

Opposition to the Thieu campaign took the form not only of criticism from opponents who had dropped out of the race and their supporters but also of demonstrations directed at the regime and sometimes at Americans in Saigon and in Danang and Hue. There was some violence, but its extent was grossly exaggerated in media reports to the United States. Near the end of the campaign, Peter Osnos filed a long article from Saigon that commented on this point. Under the subhead "City in Flames," he wrote:

> When there was a rash of fire bombings of U.S. vehicles the week before last, some news agency accounts made it sound as if the city was in flames.
>
> [Taking into account the breaking up of a George McGovern meeting and the bombing of a nightclub] . . . one news magazine called it "the most violent week in Saigon since the 1968 Tet offensive"—an assertion scoffed at by long time residents.
>
> One indication of the way Saigon must have seemed from afar was a telegram sent to an American firm here from its home office carrying this desperate-sounding message:

"Recent reports suggest street violence may be factor re continuation of office stop Please send immediately complete and objective analysis of potential danger to staff resident in Saigon stop Is relief after elections foreseeable your advice will control stop."

The Saigon office said there was no reason to close. This is not a city in flames nor even more than the usual amount of uproar. It is—at least for today—the same crowded, noisy and smelly capital of a country at war that it has been for years.[36]

While the evidence suggests that the magnitude of the rioting and violence was greatly exaggerated, nonetheless there were parades with chanting, speeches, and some violence—which usually took the form of clashes between students or disabled veterans and the police, and some burning of American and Saigon police cars. Even this latter was much exaggerated by the nightly repetition on television. Three days before the election, the Associated Press reported that "more than two dozen vehicles have been hit by fire bombs in recent weeks. The majority were American military or civilian vehicles. Police jeeps also have been a frequent target of the fire bombers."[37] The same article reported that there had been only one known fatality—"a U.S. sailor burned September 14 when youths firebombed his truck."

Meanwhile, Vice President Ky's supporters set up an anti-election committee, the People's Coordinating Committee Against Dictatorship.[38] It was headed by Ky's ally, the Hoa Hao leader Trinh Quoc Khanh. The organizing group included veterans, students, Buddhists, and Catholics. Senator Nguyen Phuoc Dai who claimed to be representing General Minh was also present. But her presence and ambiguous status

[36] *Washington Post,* September 27, 1971. In large measure because of reports in the press and TV footage of riots and fires, friends urged me to check with the U.S. embassy as soon as I arrived in Saigon in order to discuss areas of high security risk in the city. The response of officials at the embassy was, "You can walk anywhere in the city. Saigon is safer than either Washington or New York." It was a situation in striking contrast with that of four years earlier when the city was by no means quiet and safe everywhere and no one would have advised a visitor that it was.

[37] Washington *Evening Star,* September 29, 1971. These figures were far below the impression left by TV news shows, on which it is rather hard to distinguish one evening's burning car from another's.

[38] The committee went under various labels. Sometimes it was just the People Against Dictatorship, some called it the People's Force Against Dictatorship, and still others referred to it as the Committee Against Dictatorship.

were not enough to satisfy some other leaders. One Ky associate said of Minh after the latter failed to sign an anti-Thieu resolution, "We keep inviting him and hoping he will join us, but so far he has not. He may think it is too early yet to commit himself." [39] Earlier a Ky aide had asserted of Minh, "He wants us to bring him his victory on a platter." This remark had been made when Minh refused to attend an anti-Thieu gathering even after a contingent of disabled veterans headed by another Ky supporter, Dinh Truong Thu, had held a rally in front of Minh's downtown villa in an attempt to force him to come out and join the organized opponents of the election.[40]

With only three days to go, Big Minh finally broke his silence and spoke out against the election. He said that, as a consequence of an election held under the current circumstances, the regime "will cease to have a democratic and legal basis, will lose all credit in the eyes of the world and will be completely alienated from the people." Peter Osnos, in reporting the statement, suggested that Minh was trying to "reassert his position as the most prominent opposition figure." At this same time, Minh also was offered the chairmanship of the People's Committee to Struggle for Democracy and Peace, a rival of the committee established by Ky supporters four days earlier.[41]

A "convention" of the Ky organization was held in Saigon to urge the Supreme Court to call off the whole affair in order "to avoid serious consequences following the unconstitutional and unlawful election." It asked the National Assembly to resolve the crisis and called on the people to boycott the election. Further, it asked Thieu to recognize the danger of dictatorship and cease to run alone.[42]

Trade union leader and head of the Vietnam Workers and Peasants party, Tran Quoc Buu, charged that these demonstrations "usually give a good opportunity for dishonest traders and the Communists to exploit the situation." The election must be held as stipulated in the constitution "to avoid a political vacuum [that] the Communists always long for to take advantage [of] for themselves." [43] Ten nights before

[39] *New York Times,* September 27, 1971. Minh's spokesman, oppositionist deputy Nguyen Huu Chung, did sign the resolution as did another supporter and recently reelected deputy, Ly Quy Chung. Both were from Saigon.

[40] Ibid., September 26, 1971.

[41] *Washington Post,* September 29, 1971.

[42] *Vietnam Sunday Mirror* (Saigon), October 3, 1971.

[43] *Vietnam Daily Mirror,* October 2, 1971. Buu expressed the same views to me while also pointing out that he disagreed with Thieu on many issues.

the "convention," Buu's home had been bombed, destroying virtually everything in the room where he normally spent the evening with his family. It was generally believed that the Communists were responsible for the bombing.

In the final days before the election, according to Associated Press stories, President Thieu ordered the police to "shoot to kill" rioters who "throw fire bombs or otherwise endanger lives." Some news sources omitted the "shoot to kill" phrase.[44] Whatever the president's words, the police continued to disperse demonstrators with tear gas, not gunfire. No demonstrators were killed by the police during the month of demonstrations and vandalism.

The demonstrations reported to the United States were almost exclusively in Saigon. Only brief references were made to demonstrations in Hue and Danang. One such story spoke of three days of clashes between demonstrators and police in Danang and the fact that schools had been closed in that city for one day.[45] The day before the election another story contained a passing reference to the fact that "between 50 and 150 university students burned election posters and hurled fire bombs at police in a three-hour anti-government demonstration."[46]

## The Election

The preelection demonstrations were followed by a relatively quiet and peaceful election day except in Danang, where street fighting lasted throughout the day and left one dead and 57 injured. A minor, much smaller disturbance occurred down the coast in Nha Trang. In Danang, an American adviser showed police how to fire tear gas canisters into the crowd. The next day, the top U.S. representative in the city apologized to the mayor of Danang for this violation of the U.S. pledge to avoid any intervention in the conduct of the election.

Election morning got under way in Saigon with the explosion of three VC rockets—the first in 10 months to strike the city. One rocket

[44] Washington *Evening Star,* September 29, 1971. The *Washington Post* also reported the "shoot to kill" order in its September 30 edition.

[45] Washington *Evening Star,* September 29 and 30.

[46] Ibid., October 2, 1971.

killed three persons and injured five others. Otherwise the capital was quiet.

Everyone expected the government to receive its strongest support in the rural areas. In developing countries, rural voters have generally followed the village leadership which, in this instance, meant support of the Thieu regime. Peasant support for Thieu was reinforced by stepped up land reform in 1969–1971, improved rice, favorable trade arrangements for the peasants, more pigs and chickens, and improved educational and health facilities. Alvin Shuster predicted a week before the election that perhaps a boycott would have some impact in the cities "which are traditionally anti-government. But the peasants in the countryside, where Thieu-appointed province chiefs call the shots, will undoubtedly be trooping to the polls in large numbers and dropping valid ballots into the boxes." [47]

After the election, Peter Osnos reported that in the Delta "villagers seemed to regard trooping to the polls as an obligation, like paying taxes, and showed little interest in mutilating their ballots since Thieu was certain to be elected anyway." [48]

The results nationally reflected this general reaction. The turnout was 87.9 percent of the registered voters, or 6,327,631 of a possible 7,192,660. Some 5,971,114 supported the Thieu-Huong ticket, while 353,070 spoiled their ballots or deposited empty envelopes in the ballot box to indicate their opposition to the regime. Another 865,029 abstained—most of them in the urban centers.[49] Which is to say that Thieu received 94.3 percent of the actual vote and 83 percent of the potential vote.

---

[47] *New York Times,* September 26, 1971. In some villages and hamlets the chiefs went to great effort to get voters to the polls. In one hamlet in Go Cong, where I arrived less than an hour before the polls were to close, the hamlet chief announced that all citizens had voted except two. He told the province chief that election workers were even then out trying to find the delinquents to bring them in to vote. There was no evidence of fraud in the voting process, and no need for it. It was enough to get the voter there. He could then be expected to cast his vote "correctly" in almost every case. When I departed just before the polls closed, the missing voters still had not been found.

[48] *Washington Post,* October 5, 1971.

[49] All figures used for 1971 are from the returns reported to the Ministry of Interior by the autonomous cities, provinces, and the very small military units in Cambodia. Detailed figures for the 1971, as well as the 1967, presidential election are given in Appendix C.

The vote by regions showed the turnout and pro-Thieu vote as follows:

| | | *Turnout* | | *Valid Votes* | |
|---|---|---|---|---|---|
| | *Registered Voters* | *Number* | *% of registration* | *Number* | *% of turnout* |
| I Corps | 1,130,658 | 972,079 | 85.9 | 886,585 | 91.2 |
| II Corps | 1,282,572 | 1,165,094 | 90.1 | 1,123,823 | 96.5 |
| III Corps | 2,248,122 | 1,847,820 | 82.1 | 1,672,173 | 90.4 |
| IV Corps | 2,531,308 | 2,337,558 | 92.3 | 2,283,691 | 97.6 |
| Polling Stations in Cambodia | | 5,080 | | 4,842 | 95.2 |
| Total | 7,192,660 | 6,327,631 | 87.9 | 5,971,114 | 94.3 |

A breakdown by provinces and cities, comparing 1971 with 1967, provides some interesting figures. In areas (mostly Buddhist) where Phan Khac Suu led all contenders in 1967, the turnout in 1971 was low and the number of spoiled ballots high. In the city of Hue, for example, the number of registered voters had risen from 54,827 to 62,558, but the turnout actually went down from 45,203 to 42,045. In percentage terms, the 1971 turnout was only 67.2 of the registered voters as compared with 82.4 in 1967. There were very few invalid ballots cast in Hue or anywhere else in the country in 1967. In 1971, by contrast, only 64.3 percent of the ballots cast in Hue were valid. If the Thieu support level is defined as the percentage of valid ballots cast for the Thieu-Huong ticket out of the number of possible votes that could have been cast (i.e., the number of registered voters), we find in Hue a support level of only 43.3 percent.

In the city of Danang, also a Suu stronghold in 1967, the turnout was 76.0 percent and the valid ballots only 74.4 percent. The Thieu support level was 56 percent.

Thua Thien, the largest northern province which surrounds Hue, was also carried by Suu in 1967. In 1971, it had the smallest turnout of the provinces in I Corps, 82.6 percent. The valid vote was 85.9 percent, giving a support level of 70.9 percent. This figure was one of the lowest for any province anywhere in the country.

Saigon was the only jurisdiction that was carried by the Tran Van Huong slate in 1967. This time, Saigon had a turnout of 76.5 percent,

ADMINISTRATIVE DIVISIONS OF
SOUTH VIETNAM, 1971

Demarcation line
QUANG TRI
Hué
THUA THIEN
Da Nang
QUANG NAM
I CORPS
QUANG TIN
QUANG NGAI
LAOS
THAILAND
KONTUM
BINH DINH
PLEIKU
Qui Nhon
PHU BON
PHU YEN
DARLAC
CAMBODIA
KHANH HOA
Nha Trang
QUANG DUC
Da Lat
TUYEN DUC
Cam Ranh
PHUOC LONG
BINH LONG
NINH THUAN
LAM DONG
Phnom Penh
TAY NINH
BINH DUONG
LONG KHANH
BINH THUAN
II CORPS
BINH TUY
BIEN HOA
HAU NGHIA
KIEN PHONG
KIEN TUONG
CHAU DOC
LONG AN
Saigon
GIA DINH
PHUOC TUY
III CORPS
DINH TUONG
KIEN GIANG
AN GIANG
SA DEC
My Tho
GO CONG
Vung Tau
VINH LONG
KIEN HOA
Rach Gia
Can Tho
DAO PHU QUOC
(KIEN GIANG)
PHONG DINH
VINH BINH
CHUONG THIEN
BA XUYEN
BAC LIEU
AN XUYEN
IV CORPS
Province boundary
International boundary
Military region boundary
National capital
Da Lat Autonomous municipality
0 50 100 miles
0 100 kilometers
Con Son
(Administered from Saigon)

of which 83.6 percent cast valid votes. The Thieu support level was 64.15 percent.

The two major suburban provinces just outside Saigon—Gia Dinh and Bien Hoa—were also low, both in turnout and support for the regime. Gia Dinh, which included the island of Con Son in 1971, had a turnout of 79.6 percent, a valid vote of 93.6 percent, and an overall support level of 74.30 percent. Bien Hoa's turnout was 76.2 percent, its valid vote 86.0 percent, and its support level 65.4 percent. Both these provinces and the city of Saigon have Catholic populations far outstripping the national total of 10 percent.

The provinces carried by Truong Dinh Dzu in 1967 showed a very different pattern in 1971 from those carried by either Huong or Suu. In 1967, Dzu carried Quang Ngai province in I Corps. In 1971, that province had a turnout of 84.4 percent with valid votes reaching 95.5 percent and gave Thieu a support level of 80.9 percent. In Hau Nghia in III Corps, 91.3 percent of the voters turned out to cast 93.6 percent valid votes for Thieu. The support level was 85.7 percent. In Tay Ninh, the other province in the region carried by Dzu in 1967, there was a 93.0 percent turnout with 95.9 percent voting for Thieu and a support level of 89.4 percent. In Long An, a province just below Hau Nghia, where Thieu had won in 1967 over the protests of the Dzu supporters by fewer than 300 votes, there was a turnout of 93.3 percent, a pro-Thieu vote of 97.9 percent, and a Thieu support level of 91.7 percent.

In 1967, Dzu carried only one province in IV Corps, Kien Phong, although in general he did better in that region than in any other. His strength was in the outlying areas close to those under Viet Cong control. As noted in Chapter 4, the VC or the NLF—allegedly—got out the Dzu vote in 1967. In any case, in 1971, neither the VC nor the NLF were of any consequence politically in the Delta, and the Thieu vote went up sharply. In Kien Phong the turnout was 89.7 percent of whom 96.5 percent voted for Thieu. His support level was 86.6 percent.

The IV Corps area underwent a transformation in the four years after 1967. The number of qualified voters grew by 836,320, or 49.3 percent, which was more than twice the growth rate of any other region. (The rate of increase of qualified voters in the other regions was I Corps, 24.0 percent; II Corps, 5.2 percent; and III Corps, 6.3 percent.) By 1971, more persons were registered to vote in IV

Corps than in any other region. This was directly related to pacification. Many of the villages and hamlets in the Delta were under government protection for the first time in years. It was also in the Delta, of course, that the land reform and other agrarian assistance programs were having their greatest impact.

Curiously, the lowest support for Thieu in the Delta came from An Giang, the province with the highest internal security rating in 1967. There, the 1971 turnout was only 82.5 percent with 93.5 percent valid votes. The support level was a low 76.9 percent. Thieu had carried the province in 1967, although both Dzu and Ha Thuc Ky had received a respectable vote. Perhaps the reason for the atypical vote in An Giang is the large Hoa Hao population in the province which has never given solid support to Thieu. Otherwise in IV Corps, it was the three new autonomous cities that registered the least support for the Thieu slate—no great surprise.

The figures throughout the country for 1967 and 1971 seem to suggest the following: (1) cities and provinces carried by Suu and by Huong in 1967 remained strongholds of anti-Thieu sentiment; (2) areas of Dzu strength in 1967 moved sharply to solid Thieu support in 1971; and (3) areas in the Delta with low security ratings in 1967, which had been areas of conflict and in which the VC and NLF may well have forced support for Dzu, now offered no opposition to the government slate.

## Charges of Fraud

Fraud was most frequently charged in the Delta and in II Corps but some charges were made in all regions. In II and IV Corps, the military was strong and the provincial governments had considerable power, simply because some areas in both regions were still rather more dependent on the military and the police to shield them from the Viet Cong. Both turnout and government support were expected to be high in these same rural provinces.

The Supreme Court twice voted to uphold the validity of the election against charges of unconstitutionality—on grounds that there had been only one candidate, and that the constitution guaranteed the voter freedom to "select" a president. Once the court voted 8–1 and the second time 6–3 to reject various versions of the charge.

The court, after reviewing the provisions of the constitution, the presidential election law, and the developments in the campaign up to the withdrawal of Ky and Minh, made the following point:

> The election with only one ticket has been criticized as unconstitutional and unlawful.
>
> The above criticism is not valid because of the fact that freedom to stand for election is a constitutional right; the candidates may, of their own will, run for election or withdraw their candidature; the barring of the election for the sole reason that only one ticket exists or no other tickets exist or other tickets have withdrawn their candidature, will lead to the consequence that one individual may prevent the implementation of the constitution.[50]

In addition, the court pointed out that after the election "no one filed a complaint on important irregularities that would affect the honesty of the election at one or several voting places."[51]

Most of the furor about the election and its conduct faded away within a week after the Supreme Court handed down its decision. The election was officially over, and President Thieu had won his second term.

---

[50] U.S. Agency for International Development, *Public Administration Bulletin,* no. 57 (December 1, 1971), p. 75.

[51] Ibid., p. 76.

# 8
# Press Freedom in South Vietnam

Free elections—or, to be more precise, electoral processes that approach accepted democratic norms—require that the press be free to criticize government leaders and policies, and free to endorse alternatives to those leaders and policies. The voter needs a press that not only supports preferred candidates but also supplies sufficient "objective" news so that he can choose among candidates on rational grounds. And he should not be forced to buy an armload of newspapers to find out what he wants to know.

Most American and western European newspapers offer their readers enough straight reporting to meet these basic needs. The public in developing countries often is forced to depend on a very different brand of journalism. Newspapers are not always free to state their views on public matters, and there are very few papers with established reputations for objectivity. Sometimes, as in North Vietnam, all newspapers are published by the government or, what amounts to the same thing, by the controlling party. In other developing countries, where some newspapers are at least independent of the government, they tend merely to be the instruments of a politician or party, or of a religious sect, or of some other special interest. These papers offer their readers only limited information and even that slight amount is directed primarily to the support of preferred candidates and policies. The boundary between news and editorialization is ambiguous at best.

The government in such a country is likely to censor prior to publication, delete objectionable material, confiscate offending issues, or in some other manner to limit the freedom of the opposition press. (All governments make some effort to "manage" the news, so that form of control is not considered censorship here unless it is accompanied by one of the more blatant forms of control noted above.)[1]

The effort of the government to limit press freedom may vary with the presence of an external or internal threat. It may also vary with the nature of the attacks on government policies and personnel, or the government's sense of its own security, or other comparable reasons. The level of any of these variables may change from year to year; so too may the government increase or decrease its efforts to control the output of the press.

Thus, any description or evaluation of press freedom in country X that suggests more or less freedom in year Y may have little relevance for the year Y-plus-one when the situation may have significantly changed. For example, Banks and Textor, drawing primarily on the 1961 and 1962 Associated Press annual summary of curbs on press freedom around the world, described India as a nation with complete freedom of the press.[2] Yet, in 1962, a press control law was enacted that provided the basis for serious repression of foreign correspondents and, in short order, of domestic newspapers as well. Had Banks and Textor been writing in 1968 or 1970, they might have rated press freedom in India less generously—which is simply to say that any satisfactory judgment of press freedom must be based on analysis through time. Except in long-established regimes, totalitarian or democratic, unanticipated and dramatic shifts in the status of the press are common. Studies through time will not eliminate all errors of judgment or prediction, but they at least improve the chances of coming close.

The remainder of this chapter is devoted to an examination of the press in South Vietnam and its relations with the government as an essential part of the context within which parties and candidates conduct their campaigns and, if elected, develop policy. Surprisingly, in view of the prevailing interest in South Vietnam, very little has been written on this subject. The literature on the domestic affairs of South Vietnam

---

[1] In thus limiting the analysis to exclude problems of "managed" news, this book is following the practice of Arthur S. Banks and Robert B. Textor, *A Cross-Polity Survey* (Cambridge, Mass.: M.I.T. Press, 1963), p. 68.

[2] Ibid., see FC Numbers (Finished Characteristic Numbers) 50, 51, 52. The Associated Press summaries were made available for use in this book through the kindness of Ted Boyle of the New York office. The reports range from about 1,500 to 3,000 words in length and make no claim to completeness. Occasionally reports for one year repeat information from the previous year. Nevertheless, the summaries are useful in providing some picture of trends within the countries that are included in all or almost all the annual editions.

either says nothing at all about the press, and therefore nothing about government control or influence over the reporting of news, or it contains a page or so on the subject but only for the period prior to the coup d'etat of 1963.[3] Observations on press freedom under the present regime are dependent on personal observation, the Associated Press summaries, reports of U.S. officials and others who have observed the South Vietnamese press while in Saigon, and the occasional items that appear in the American press.

**The Constitution and the Press.** The constitution of 1967 provides that "the state respects freedom of thought, speech, press and publishing as long as it does not harm personal honor, national security or good morals." The same Article 12 states that "press regulations will be prescribed by law."

The National Assembly got around to establishing press regulations only toward the end of 1969. In the intervening years, the government continued to act under the provisions of two "decree laws" issued by the military regime in the spring of 1964.[4] These decree laws had replaced the strict regulations of the latter days of the Diem regime. The first decree law "recognized freedom of speech and freedom of the press." The second dealt with "free publication and organization of the press." Operating within the limits of these rules, the government allowed the press to regain much of the independence it had enjoyed during the most moderate period of Diem's leadership.

The government of Premier Ky promised the press freedom from all censorship during the presidential election campaign of 1967. The promise was kept, although some publishers claimed that the regime had threatened them with a reduction in newsprint. In the days immediately following the election, five Vietnamese-language papers were shut down. The 1967 Associated Press report noted, however, that "despite the pressures, newspapers have been noticeably more free in their criticism of the government." The summary also added that "the foreign press remained unfettered by censorship" though outgoing stories were read by the government.[5]

---

[3] The longest sections on the press even during the Diem period amount to no more than a few pages and are found in Joseph Buttinger, *Vietnam: A Dragon Embattled,* 2 vols. (New York: Frederick A. Praeger, Inc., 1967).

[4] Decree Law No. 2/64, February 19, 1964, and Decree Law No. 10/64, April 30, 1964.

[5] Associated Press annual summary of curbs on press freedom for 1967, undated.

In 1968 and 1969, the last two years under the decree laws, the Associated Press summaries noted the continued freedom of foreign correspondents but observed that occasionally the government "let its displeasure with a foreign correspondent be known. . . ." In the 1968 summary, it was reported that there was "no official censorship of news by the South Vietnamese government, but it has suspended various newspapers for printing material it found unpalatable."[6] In 1969, the summary reported that 14 newspapers had been temporarily suspended by government action. The same summary carried a note on North Vietnam (for the first time since 1966) which stated simply, "North Vietnam barred American reporters."[7]

**The Press Law of 1969.** The law establishing press regulations was promulgated December 30, 1969. The original draft was developed in the office of the president and sent to the National Assembly for its consideration. The assembly, according to U.S. officials who followed the legislation closely, made a number of changes in the original proposal. When President Thieu asked for a return to the original, the National Assembly refused to accept "perhaps half" of the proposed modifications. To block presidential proposals at that time meant that the opposition had to muster an absolute majority of both houses.

The 1969 press law provides, under the heading of "fundamental principles," that press freedom "shall not be harmful to personal honor, national security and traditional morality," that no publication can be suspended without judicial action, and that "press censorship is prohibited." The law authorizes the minister of interior for the region of Saigon and Gia Dinh and the executive officers in other provinces and autonomous cities to confiscate copies of newspapers and periodicals under the rules laid down in the law. Officers ordering confiscation, however, are required to bring the case to court within eight days (Article 19). If the publishers are acquitted of any charges, they may bring counter suits for losses incurred as the result of confiscation. Indemnities to publishers are paid from public funds (Article 20).

The law specifically authorizes the press to keep secret its sources of news. It also provides that there is "the right to criticize government

---

[6] Ibid., for 1968, undated.

[7] Ibid., for 1969, undated. From that time to June 1972, the North Vietnamese have let in a limited and select group of reporters. Reporters who have been notably sympathetic either to U.S. or South Vietnamese policy have not been invited to Hanoi.

policies and projects, provided that the criticism is not aimed at propagandizing for communism or pro-Communist neutrality" (Article 24).

Persons who have been mentioned in a newspaper by name, presumably critically, may demand an opportunity to reply without charge in the columns of the paper. Failure of a daily newspaper to print such replies within the next three issues may subject the owner to a fine and still leave him vulnerable to a civil suit instituted by the injured party.[8] The courts are ordinarily obligated to act in such cases within 10 days after the charges are brought and within 24 hours if the allegedly libelous material appears during a political campaign and is directed against a candidate.[9]

Several articles of the 1969 press law limit the kinds of stories that a newspaper may print. In general, these prohibitions fall within the category of U.S. constitutional law traditionally referred to as "clear and present danger." The press may not, according to the law, incite persons to commit certain crimes of violence, or "incite the people to violate domestic or external security," or urge "military men to disobey military discipline" (Article 27). The press may not jeopardize "national security or public order," the economy, military morale and discipline, or "sow division between religions, localities and races" (Article 28). Nor may the press "publicize" or "extoll" communism or pro-Communist neutralism (Article 29). Some limits are placed on what can be said about any private person—for example, about his private life, or actions taken by him more than 10 years earlier, and so on (Article 31). The press may not insult major public officials or visiting foreign officials (Articles 32 and 33). Finally, an anti-pornography clause states that the press "shall not be used to publicize articles, pictures and drawings infringing upon traditional morality" (Article 35).

---

[8] This provision duplicates the French rule which, since 1881, has allowed aggrieved citizens access to the columns of offending newspapers.

[9] This provision corresponds roughly with the French rules aimed at protecting candidates from scurrilous press attacks in the late stages of a campaign. The French rules are rigorously enforced. In 1965, in the last week of the campaign for city council in Marseille, Mayor Gaston Deferre was charged with falsely claiming a role in the Resistance. The mayor brought suit against a major newspaper in the city, *Meridional*. Within 48 hours, on the night before the election, the paper was forced to print a front-page retraction and a statement by M. Deferre, and pay him for the libel. At least in France, the law has served as some protection for candidates against sensational charges.

The courts may order the suspension of publications and impose jail sentences on officials of newspapers that have violated Articles 27, 28 or 29. The newspaper, in practice, may not be shut down nor the editor jailed while awaiting trial, or while the case is on appeal. Clearly, however, the law includes provisions that could be used by the regime to silence opposition papers—if, of course, the courts were to uphold such executive action.

**Enforcement of the Press Law.** The most obvious fact about reporting in South Vietnam is that there has been no censorship of outgoing reports by foreign correspondents. Even in the strictest days of the Diem regime, American reporters filed their stories without blue-pencilling by a bureau of censors. The Associated Press has noted in its annual summaries that a few correspondents have reported such pressure from the government as the loss of news sources, but only two cases where more has happened. In 1970, one American reporter was expelled and, in 1971, the visa of another was not renewed. The 1970 Associated Press summary reported that "Michael D. Morrow of the Dispatch News Service International was forced to leave the country, November 24, 1970." In both the 1970 and the 1971 summaries, the AP mentioned the refusal of the South Vietnamese government to renew the visa of Don Luce of the Ecumenical News Service, who was described in the 1971 report as "a parttime writer and social worker." The 1970 AP report stated, "Both men were accused of interfering in the internal affairs of South Vietnam."[10] In other words, it was "extracurricular" activity that got both reporters in trouble. The annual summaries mention no other disciplinary action against foreign correspondents during the preceding decade. Since the last AP summary, an Italian photographer has been expelled from South Vietnam allegedly for hoarding grenades, other weapons, and "documents harmful to the national security" in his Saigon apartment. The documents were North Vietnamese propaganda.[11]

The number of daily newspapers in South Vietnam varies considerably from year to year and even within a single year. In 1971, according to an American source, 30 newspapers were founded and 23 of them had failed within the year. American news stories have referred to as many as 50 South Vietnamese papers or as few as 30 during the six years

[10] See the annual AP summaries for 1970 and 1971.
[11] *Washington Post,* May 28, 1972.

of the present regime. As of April 1972, according to an American who has followed developments in the South Vietnamese press for several years, there were three English-language papers and 27 Vietnamese-language papers—five progovernment, eight antigovernment, nine independent, and five religious. This classification placed *Chinh Luan,* the most generally respected Vietnamese-language paper, in the progovernment category even though it has often been critical of particular actions and programs of the regime.

The "independent" newspapers are frequently of poor quality. Some are sensationalist in style and, when dealing with political matters, often antigovernment. Some of the papers have a style not unlike the so-called "underground" press in the United States,[12] combining a disdain for factual accuracy with a bent to pornography. In Vietnam, both pro- and antigovernment papers sometimes suffer from these same disabilities.

The government has enforced the 1969 press law with varying degrees of vigor. During the 30 months since its passage, however, no daily newspaper has been suspended and no editor or newsman jailed or fined. The Associated Press reported after the first year under the law that "domestic publishers who don't toe the line face confiscation of their newspapers and court trials, but they are better off than last year. . . . In 1970 there were no closures or suspensions, but more than 200 editions of various newspapers were confiscated by the government."[13] The 1971 summary was silent on this matter.

The grounds for the confiscation of individual editions of papers are most often found in the general prohibitions of Article 28. A few editions have been confiscated as pornographic, in violation of Article 35. U.S. embassy observers report that confiscations under Article 28 often relate either to disclosure of military operations or to alleged support of North Vietnam or the National Liberation Front. A frequent reason for confiscation is the publication of stories suggesting that the United States is about to desert South Vietnam, that President Nixon plans to shift support from President Thieu to some other political leader, or that Nixon now favors a coalition government.

---

[12] The term "underground press" is, of course, a misnomer in the United States. Such newspapers are sold on the street corners of every large city. The term is used, perhaps, to add a certain romantic quality to otherwise rather grubby products.

[13] Associated Press summary for 1970, undated.

In late 1971, editions of two papers were confiscated for carrying a story that Vice President Tran Van Huong had committed suicide in general revulsion against having to serve in a government headed by President Thieu. (As of publication date, Vice President Huong was very much alive.)[14]

During the 12 months preceding the 1971 presidential election, the number of confiscations ranged from a low of 14 in October 1970 to highs of 82 in June 1971, when the Laotian offensive was still in progress, and 83 in September 1971, just before the election.

Gross figures can be misleading in several ways. The number of confiscations does not fall evenly across the range of independent and antigovernment papers. In one month in the summer of 1971, for example, some 31 different issues were confiscated. But of that number, 17 were issues of one paper and seven were issues of another. No other paper was confiscated more than twice, while most papers were left wholly untouched. In another month when 48 issues were confiscated, editions of but four newspapers accounted for 33 of the instances. Again, most of the opposition and independent press was untouched, and many of these carried on vigorous anti-Thieu campaigns. Very occasionally a progovernment paper is confiscated—usually for printing pornographic cartoons.

There is another sense in which confiscation figures per se are misleading. Confiscations take place only after the newspapers are on the streets. Whether because of corruption, or inefficiency, or for whatever other reason—perhaps the government really is not that keen on censorship—officials making the confiscations take only those actually on display. As soon as the official leaves, other copies are put on sale. Confiscations may have greater impact on distribution to the provinces than in the Saigon-Gia Dinh area where, in 1971, all Vietnamese newspapers were published.

Confiscation rarely has much impact on the economics of publication. It is often the strong papers—whose sensationalism has been a factor in the size of their sales—that are picked up. Such papers may even flaunt their confiscations, as a "come-on" to draw more readers. One paper regularly published a box score of its confiscations during the

[14] It is ironic that Huong should have suffered from these stories in 1971, because it was a paper in which he had an interest that falsely announced the withdrawal of Phan Khac Suu from the presidential race of 1967 just 24 hours before the voting was to start and too late for Suu adequately to reply.

year. *Dien Tin*, one of the strongest opposition papers, edited by left-oppositionist deputy Ly Quy Chung, carried a headline after one confiscation, "We will continue to print in spite of Government suppression."

As noted earlier, no daily newspaper has been suspended under the current law. Only one publication of any kind, a Catholic magazine, has been suspended and an officer sentenced to jail. The priest-editor of *Doi Dien* wrote a series of articles in February 1971 discussing the merits of the economy of North Vietnam. The judge trying the case found the stories so objectionable that he ordered the suspension of the magazine for three months and the priest-editor jailed for six months. The latter has been active in the Catholic Worker Youth Movement, a leftist organization that has been associated with support for the National Liberation Front. The group is small, with perhaps 15 priests and 300 lay members, but it has received considerable publicity in Paris and elsewhere as an example of Catholic support for a coalition government to negotiate the end of the war. The decision against *Doi Dien* and its priest-editor was upheld by the court of appeals in Saigon, and has since been appealed to the Supreme Court. It may be still another year before a final decision is handed down, but *Doi Dien* has been published without interruption and the priest-editor continues to write.

The editorial columns of the Vietnamese-language press are often used by opposition members of the National Assembly. This custom may help account for the provision in the press law that at least one of the top three officers of the paper—publisher, editor, manager—"may not be a Deputy or Senator" (Article 6). If all three were members of the National Assembly, legislative immunity would clearly raise questions of the executive authority's right to confiscate. Certainly it would create problems for the courts. As long as one official is not protected by legislative immunity, the executive and the courts have more freedom of action.

During the first 12 weeks after the 1972 invasion of South Vietnam by the North Vietnamese regular army, there were no changes in the basic handling of the press. There is still no prior censorship. The papers still must appear on the newsstands before the government can act. The South Vietnamese military follows the same policies as those laid down by their U.S. counterparts: no newspaper should announce troop movements until the operation has actually begun, and there are restrictions on the reporting of certain other military information. To the annoyance of some American reporters, there are also restrictions on the travel of newsmen to the front. Most of the domestic press has rallied to the support of the government. As a result, there has been no striking increase in the number of issues confiscated and no new court cases.

The experience of the first 30 months of the law regulating the press suggests: (1) that foreign correspondents remain free to send any dispatches to their papers; (2) that there is relative freedom for domestic newspapers to criticize the government and propose alternative candidates and policies; (3) that the enforced restrictions generally deal with apparent support of policies and organizations that fall within the very broad prohibitions of Article 28 against stories that jeopardize "national security and public order" (in practice, often meaning support for the NLF or coalition government or articles concerning alleged withdrawal of President Nixon's support of the regime and the system); (4) that most of the confiscations are of a very few papers even though more than three-fourths of the Vietnamese-language newspapers can be classified as independent or antigovernment in content and style; (5) that the courts have not so far as we know been pressured by the executive branch to force suspension of papers or jailing of management; and (6) that no newspapers have been suspended under the current law and only one magazine is under sentence of suspension, and even this one continues to publish while its appeal is pending.

The government's record with respect to press regulation falls short of the standards of Western democratic countries. But there is a second side to the coin: neither do most of the Vietnamese-language papers maintain the level of responsible reporting that marks most major newspapers in Western democracies.

**Recent Developments.** In mid-1972, the situation changed—although how radically is not yet clear. Under decree powers, the Thieu government announced significantly more threatening rules for the enforcement of the press law. Most newspapers were required to post bond of roughly $46,000 to assure the payment of any fines assessed for violating the provisions of the law. (Religious papers and certain others were exempt from the bond requirement, and papers of political parties were required to post only about $9,200.) For the first time, distributors were also faced with fines for distributing offending issues of newspapers and their deposit was set at about $90,000 apiece. The real threat was to the poorly financed papers—perhaps two-thirds of the more than 40 papers being published at the time the decree was issued—which almost certainly could not scare up enough money to make the deposit.

The decree also provided that, after two editions of a paper had been confiscated, the newspaper could be suspended and the publisher jailed. Both the fines and the suspensions continue to require the same court action as in the past, but now the cases have to be decided at each level of the courts within 30 days. No longer can the appeals process delay enforcement by 18 months or more.

Publishers have denounced the law as a deliberate effort to drive all but the largest papers to the wall. At the end of the 30-day grace period for making deposits, only one newspaper had actually posted the bond. Several of the larger and more influential papers had flatly stated that, unless the rule was rescinded, they would simply stop publishing. President Thieu postponed the deadline by about two weeks and, according to some sources, he "had decided to ease certain provisions of the month-old law. . . ."[15]

The impact of the decree, as modified and enforced, is very much in doubt. The motivations behind it can only be guessed at. But in any case, the description of the 1969 law still stands, and *its* impact during the period of the assembly and presidential elections described in this volume is a matter of record.

[15] *Washington Post,* September 3, 1972.

# 9
# Political Organizations in South Vietnam

Preceding chapters have covered seven national elections in South Vietnam beginning with the selection of delegates to the Constituent Assembly in September 1966. Yet in these chapters there is only infrequent, mostly peripheral mention of political parties and their role in the electoral process. The reason is plain.

South Vietnam has had hundreds of political parties over the years but never anything approaching a party system.[1] System or no system, parties have played little part in campaigns for national office or in most local or provincial campaigns. The French made no effort to prepare the Vietnamese for independence and less than none for democracy. They suppressed indigenous political organizations that showed any interest in independence. The violence of the French efforts to abort or destroy political parties encouraged the Vietnamese penchant for clandestine organizations and, ironically, strengthened the hand of the most revolutionary of the parties—the Stalinists who controlled the Indochina Communist party and the Trotskyists who operated under various labels. The Trotskyists in turn were systematically eliminated by the Communists after World War II.[2] In any event, when indepen-

[1] Joseph Buttinger, *Vietnam: A Dragon Embattled,* 2 vols. (New York: Frederick A. Praeger, Inc., 1967), vol. 2, pp. 1234–1248. These pages provide a year-by-year listing of groups that called themselves political parties. It is almost certainly the most complete list available in English. U.S. Department of Defense, *United States-Vietnam Relations, 1945–1967* (Pentagon Papers), 12 vols. (Washington, D. C.: Government Printing Office, 1971), vol. 1, pp. B1–B32 and B57–B59, contains considerable information on parties in Vietnam between 1930 and 1954, with greatest emphasis on the Viet Minh.

[2] The Communists now play a role in the South only as the hard core of the People's Revolutionary party which provides the leadership for the National Liberation Front. In North Vietnam, the Communists or the Workers party (Lao

dence suddenly was thrust on Vietnam, there was no supply of leadership experienced in the politics of democracy.

### Parties and Organizations Within the System

**Parties under Diem.** In 1954 and immediately thereafter, numerous nationalist groups sprang up in South Vietnam to seek political power. Some could trace their lineage back to the period of World War II and two even farther than that. All were experienced in clandestine operations, not in open democratic campaigning.

The oldest of the parties, the Viet Nam Quoc Dan Dang (VNQDD) or Vietnam Nationalist party, suffered greatly under the French. It was founded in 1927 and suppressed in 1930 when many of its leaders were executed or jailed. Nonetheless, the VNQDD persisted—in Vietnam or in exile—throughout the difficult period of French domination, World War II, and the Viet Minh era.

In the years immediately after the war, other parties suffered at the hands of the Communists. The Trotskyist leader, Ta Thu Than, was a victim of Communist assassins as was the founder and leader of the Hoa Hao religious sect. The Communists also murdered the leader of the second oldest continuous nationalist party of South Vietnam, the Dai Viet party (Great Vietnam party).[3] The Dai Viets also suffered from internal divisions and factionalism as did the VNQDD and most of the other nationalist political groups of the period. Like weak and clandestine parties in any society, the demand for purity of party doctrine increased in inverse ratio to the likelihood of achieving political power.

Shortly after coming to power in 1954, Ngo Dinh Diem founded the National Revolutionary Movement (NRM). By the spring of 1955 at least 30 other parties had emerged. The NRM gained a majority in the 1956 National Assembly elections and, in the years that followed, the Diemists set up other parties to back the government. The most important of the new parties was the Can Lao Nhan Vi Cach Mang Dan,

---

Dong) control the government completely although, officially, the Socialist party and the Democratic party also have members in the National Assembly. Both these parties were created by the Communists and have no independent life of their own.

[3] A partial list of those eliminated by the Communists is to be found in Frank N. Trager, "The Impact of Marxism: Historical Overview and Judgment," in Frank N. Trager, ed., *Marxism in Southeast Asia* (Stanford: Stanford University Press, 1959), p. 267.

or the Personalist Labor Revolutionary party, which was founded by Diem's brother, Ngo Dinh Nhu. The organization is generally referred to as the Can Lao party. Initially it was intended to appeal to the nation's intellectuals but with little evident success. The party soon became a covert "holding" operation used by Nhu to manipulate the various front organizations that supported Diem.[4]

Diem and Nhu were accused of patterning the NRM after the Viet Minh and the Can Lao after the Communist party. Nhu certainly harassed or suppressed opposition groups but never with the thoroughness of the Communists in North Vietnam. By 1958, all parties except the Can Lao were operating underground. Still, new groups kept coming into existence both to denounce the regime and to work against it. Diem's may have been an authoritarian regime, but it stopped well short of totalitarianism.[5]

The coup d'etat of 1963 cast the Can Lao into temporary eclipse. Since 1970 there has been a revival of interest and respect for the late President Diem, and the Can Lao has shown some signs of renewed strength, among northern Catholics in particular.

Political parties were of almost no significance during the period of revolving military juntas that followed Diem's overthrow. When the government of Nguyen Cao Ky opened the way to political parties in 1965, more than 200 groups applied for recognition. Ky was probably not far wrong when he said at the time that there was "not a party in the country worthy of the name."[6]

**Political Parties under the New Constitution.** The 1966 constitution "recognizes that political parties have an essential role in a democratic system." Parties may, therefore, organize and "operate freely according to the procedures and conditions prescribed by law." Further, "the nation encourages progress toward a two-party system," and the consti-

---

[4] Buttinger, *Dragon Embattled,* pp. 1245–1248.

[5] Douglas Pike, *Viet Cong: The Organization and Techniques of the National Liberation Front of South Vietnam* (Cambridge: M.I.T. Press, 1966), p. 57, is more generous in his evaluation. Pike, who has perhaps studied South Vietnamese politics as carefully as any American, says: "The GVN was not a democracy, and the fact that Diem in interviews kept insisting that it was irritated Westerners, but neither could it in all fairness be called a tyranny. It was as good as most Asian governments at the time and better than some. If revolutions stemmed directly from absolutism, they would have developed in dozens of countries elsewhere in the world before Vietnam."

[6] Buttinger, *Dragon Embattled,* p. 1248.

tution points out the importance of "the formalization of political opposition." The National Assembly was mandated to write legislation to carry out these general propositions.

The assembly passed the "Political Party and Political Opposition Statute" and President Thieu promulgated the law in June of 1969.[7] It was intended, among other things, to "reduce the plethora of parties" that had grown up—parties in name only with no appreciable electoral strength.

Briefly, the law provided that all activities of "a political party or an alliance of political parties must be public, non-violent and lawful." Anyone 18 years and older could join a party except that military men were excluded unless they were already members at the time the act was passed. Each party had to file with the Ministry of Interior a declaration giving the name of the party, its national representative, headquarters, party rules (if any), full identification of all founders, and a report on the election of its central executive committee (if any). Founders had to be citizens of 10 years standing, 25 years of age, and must not have been convicted of a felony. If the Ministry of Interior rejected the application, appeal could be made to the courts. Once the application had been approved, the party had an 18-month probationary period during which it had to establish chapters in 10 provinces or autonomous cities, with at least 500 members in each. If the party had 10 or more members in the National Assembly, chapters were required in only five provinces or cities.

The law further provided that no party could receive money from any governmental unit except the funds provided for all parties for campaigns. The law established the position of "opposition leader" who was to receive the pay of a senator and the same immunities as members of the National Assembly. He had a role as adviser to the government but could not be appointed to any other public office. The opposition leader was to be selected in public meeting by members of parties or alliances represented in the National Assembly that had designated themselves as the opposition.

What criticism there was of the law focused, heatedly, on the requirement that the names of the 500 provincial or city charter members of the party had to be filed with the Ministry of Interior. First, party leaders believed that they and their members would be exposed to

---

[7] Law No. 009/69, June 19, 1969.

harassment by the government. The provision that any government official who disclosed the membership lists would be punished did not seem to be either realistic or dependable protection against possible bureaucratic oppression. Second, there was a real question whether most parties could sign up as many as 500 members in 10 jurisdictions. For the larger parties this was no problem. But for the "tea house" parties of Saigon, or for strictly localized parties, the 10 jurisdictions represented a very difficult hurdle. Some long-existing parties could not win 5,000 votes anywhere in South Vietnam let alone find that many members scattered evenly through 10 provinces.

For nearly a year, parties simply refused to file the necessary information. Finally, in August of 1970, the prime minister issued a "decree concerning political party activities."[8] The decree repeated the provisions of the law in every respect except that it stated, "The list of members may be replaced by a certificate of the regional administration testifying that the declaring provincial or municipal chapter has at least 500 members." Membership lists from the party chapters, attested to by the party executive committees, would be filed with regional offices.

This modification broke the jam. Parties were more willing to give information to provincial officials, who would presumably be more "flexible" in checking membership lists than the more impersonal Ministry of Interior in Saigon. (This new arrangement was something of a throwback to the days when the village council told the emperor the population of the village and the value of its resources, and the emperor accepted the council's statements without investigation.)

The first parties to fulfill the requirements of the law and receive permanent status were two large Catholic parties, which almost certainly called for no "flexibility" on anyone's part. By the summer of 1971, some 15 parties had met all the requirements. Six of them were grouped within the National Social Democratic Front which had been organized by President Thieu in the late spring of 1969, nearly a year before the passage of the law. Thieu had called simultaneously for the creation of an opposition alliance.[9]

No major coalition ever did develop among the opposition parties. But among the first group of parties to qualify under the 1969 law

---

[8] Decree No. 807/ND/NV, August 1, 1970.

[9] Joint U.S. Public Affairs Office, *Political Parties in Vietnam,* a special article on political parties for release to the media, September 1969, p. 5.

were five or six that were clearly oppositionist. These included the National Salvation Front headed by Senator Tran Van Don and the Progressive Nationalist Movement (PNM) led by Nguyen Van Bong. (Bong was assassinated in November 1971, almost certainly by the Communists.) Bong, who also headed the National Institute of Administration, was a moderate. Like Tran Quoc Buu of the Confederation of Vietnamese Workers (CVT), he supported President Thieu's decision to hold a presidential election in 1971 even after the withdrawal of Minh and Ky, although he was critical of the electoral law and the maneuverings that led to a one-man contest. Three splinter groups from the VNQDD qualified as well.

In addition to the 15 parties that were given permanent approval as of the summer of 1971, there were 14 other groups that had passed the initial screening by the Ministry of Interior but had not yet filed membership lists with provincial or city officials. Among these was the Worker-Farmer party under Buu, which later won 14 seats in the House elections of August 1971. One party representing several minority ethnic groups also gained preliminary approval. Three parties were rejected by the Ministry of Interior either because of Communist connections or other irregularities.

Failure to qualify as parties did not prevent all manner of ad hoc political groups from backing candidates in the 1970 Senate or the 1971 House elections. As noted earlier, the House elections attracted so many candidates that the obvious analogy was to unstructured U.S. nonpartisan local elections rather than U.S. general elections where parties play a major role.

Among active political organizations still without either temporary or permanent authorization is the Tan Dai Viet party (New Great Vietnam party), the smaller of the two factions that grew out of the breakup of the original Dai Viet party in 1964. The Tan Dai Viet party, like the parent organization and the very conservative Revolutionary Dai Viet party, is strongly nationalist—some would say zenophobic. The parent was vigorously anti-Communist but remained equally independent of the French and of the Chinese (whose military forces occupied much of northern Vietnam in late 1945-1946) during the postwar years. The Tan Dai Viets, by contrast with the Revolutionary Dai Viets, are primarily southerners. They also tend to be younger than members of most other nationalist parties.

The Tan Dai Viets were among the founders of the Progressive Nationalist Movement. They have opposed the Thieu regime in some domestic policy areas without indulging in violent denunciations, while supporting its efforts to assure Southern independence. Professor Nguyen Ngoc Huy, the secretary-general of the party, is a member of the South Vietnamese delegation to the Paris "peace" negotiations.

Stephen B. Young has described the Tan Dai Viet party as the "most potent of the nationalistic parties."[10] The party has been particularly active and successful in working with the peasants and villagers of the Delta. Young credits it with establishing the first Ministry of Pacification in 1964. Speaking of the Tan Dai Viets' efforts in pacification politics, Young asserts that they are committed to civilian government and to democracy as the route to modernization, and assume the village is the basic unit for organizing politically. They support the pacification program, which they see as assisting their own efforts in the rural areas. Crucial to the success of the Tan Dai Viets' program, according to Young, has been President Thieu's support—whatever his reasons might be.[11]

The Tan Dai Viets have been particularly effective in the post-Tet period—during which time the pacification program has recorded conspicuous successes. They have taken advantage, as most parties have not, of the new vitality in the villages of the Delta. Whether and to what extent they can increase their effectiveness at the province and then the national levels is not clear, but they have a foundation in the villages if they choose to make the effort.

**Non-Party Electoral Politics.** Religious and communal groups are stronger than most political parties at the local level, and some have had an impact on elections and policy making nationally. Sometimes they have worked through parties and sometimes directly.

The An Quang Buddhists, once referred to as the extremist wing of the United Buddhist Church, have received much of the attention of the foreign press because of their early and determined opposition to President Diem and their later conflict with the military regimes and the

[10] Stephen B. Young, "Power Towards the People: Local Development in Vietnam: 1968–1971," a paper prepared for the South East Asia Development Advisory Group seminar on the role of elections in Vietnamese political development, December 1971. The next paragraphs draw heavily on Young's study.

[11] Ibid., p. 5.

Thieu government. The internal debate in South Vietnam about relations with the DRV was sparked a good part of the time by the An Quang leader, Thich Tri Quang. The An Quang call for a boycott of the 1967 elections was only partially effective, but Buddhist-supported candidates led the balloting in the heavily Buddhist cities and provinces of I Corps. The Tet offensive helped change the public and private position of the An Quang leaders. The murder of thousands of civilians—most of them Buddhists—in Hue during the Viet Cong occupation made political neutrality and even a pro-NLF line of an earlier day difficult to maintain.

In the 1970 senatorial elections, the An Quang Buddhists put up their first slate of candidates for national office. The slate led all others. In 1971, the Buddhists again supported candidates, this time for House elections. Twenty-two of the 24 winning candidates in I Corps had Buddhist support. Opposition to the Thieu administration continued, but there was increasing evidence of Buddhist recognition of the relevance of operating within the existing system. Nonetheless, the Buddhists did call—some say only *pro forma*—for a boycott of the 1971 presidential election after it became a one-man contest. The vote was conspicuously low in Hue and Danang and the number of spoiled ballots high.

The North Vietnamese invasion of April 1972 once more nudged the Buddhists of I Corps closer to the system. News dispatches have noted cooperation between the Buddhists and other groups in the I Corps area in assisting refugees and have reported Buddhist denunciations of the invasion.

Richard Ehrlich has noted that the Hoa Hao, the Cao Dai, the Catholics, and the Buddhists have "demonstrated a higher degree of political development than any of the other competing political groups, with the sole exception of the Communists." All of them, including the Communists, have a village base and an organization that reaches out and maintains communications with a mass base; all offer an opportunity for upward mobility of talent; and all have a "professed devotion to an ethical value system backed up by a sophisticated apparatus for recruiting and indoctrinating converts. . . ." Each of these groups, says Ehrlich, fulfills the following political functions:

> political socialization and recruitment, interest articulation, interest aggregation, political communication, rule-making, rule application and adjudication [—a fact that] clarifies the aggressive manner in which each attempts to dominate the

polity, either regionally, as the Hoa Hao and the Cao Dai, or nationally, as the Catholics, Buddhists and Communists are attempting to do. It should also explain the tenacity and resilience each has shown in competing with the others.[12]

Studies of the politics of the Delta, where the Communists once were very strong, make the point that they were virtually frozen out of the Hoa Hao and the Cao Dai villages and provinces. In these same jurisdictions, the government of South Vietnam was also very weak under the Diem regime. The opposition of these groups helped point up Diem's inability to draw the villages and rural provinces into the national orbit. The Thieu programs for the villages since 1970 have been aimed at rectifying these mistakes.

It was the internal cohesion of the Hoa Hao that gave An Giang province the highest security rating in the country in 1967. It was the only province with a rating above 4.00 on a scale of 0 to 5.00.[13] Its rating of 4.24 was even more remarkable because An Giang is no more than 30 miles from the Cambodian border, and it is surrounded by provinces whose security ratings are among the lowest in the country. All other Delta provinces rated below 4.00. Chau Doc, another province with strong Hoa Hao influence, situated directly on the Cambodian border, had the next highest rating with 3.22. Nine provinces were rated between 2.00 and 3.00; the remaining five were below 2.00. All security ratings in the Delta went up sharply after Tet, but none yet matches An Giang. Some ratings have declined since the 1972 invasion—most obviously in provinces like Binh Dinh where security was never high and the pressure of invasion greatest.[14]

**Current Status of Parties.** There still is no party system in South Vietnam. There are only stray bits of evidence that a few parties are becoming more than tiny debating clubs and are beginning to perform some of the traditional functions of parties in mature democracies. The An Quang Buddhists, for example, are no longer just a religious pressure

[12] Richard Ehrlich, "Village and Hamlet Elections as a Means of Political Socialization," a paper delivered at the South East Asia Development Advisory Group meetings, December 1971, pp. 11–13. The Communists are today the weakest of the communal groups listed.

[13] Only the big U.S. base city of Cam Ranh rated above 4.00, and it managed but 4.07.

[14] Hamlet Evaluation System of the U.S. Military Assistance Command (Saigon), Civil Operations and Revolutionary Development Supports (CORDS).

group that has no broader interests. Candidates running with An Quang support are also pushing nonreligious issues. The same seems to be true of candidates of larger Catholic parties. The Buddhists and the Catholics have not discarded their religious interests, but neither are they limiting themselves to programs of parochial focus.

The Worker-Farmer Association, under Tran Quoc Buu, also operates more or less like a modern party. Its base, however, remains small, and it has not yet added greatly to its limited worker constituency. Some of the other older parties that are permanently qualified under the law may also be taking on modern party characteristics.

If the picture of the Tan Dai Viet party drawn by Stephen B. Young is accurate, then that party may well offer the best hope for a rapidly developing modern democratic party. The Tan Dai Viets, unlike members of most other parties except the communally based organizations, live in the villages and are beginning to build local bases, which will aid them not only in winning village elections but also in working successfully at the provincial and National Assembly level.

Neither the constitution nor the law requires that a candidate for the House of Representatives live in the province or city from which he is elected. A check of the stated residences of the 1971 winners elected from provinces outside the capital area shows that 50 representatives lived not in their constituencies but in the Saigon metropolitan area. Some of them may have moved into the Saigon area after the election. But many who lived in this area ran elsewhere for a variety of reasons. Some chose provinces of their birth or of their ancestors. Others chose their constituencies for symbolic reasons. Former Senator Tran Van Don, for example, decided to run in the strongly Buddhist province of Quang Ngai although he could very well have led the list in Saigon or almost any other province. His senatorial slate, after all, had led the field in 1967, and his name was generally and favorably known. At the other extreme, the "solid gold" deputy, Nguyen Quang Luyen, left his 1967 constituency to run in Binh Long for highly practical reasons. His problem was not lack of name recognition in his home district but precisely the reverse. He moved to the boondocks to escape the notoriety that followed him in the Saigon metropolitan area—and lost anyway!

The custom of living in Saigon and casually campaigning in a constituency only during the weeks before election may have helped take a toll of incumbents in the 1971 House elections. There were doubtless other reasons for the high mortality rate, but figures compiled by Allen E.

Goodman suggest that "working a constituency" or taking care of the "case work" may have paid electoral dividends in Vietnam just as it does in Wisconsin or in Bouches-du-Rhone or in a thousand other districts in a dozen long-time democratic countries. Checking the 1971 House elections, Professor Goodman found the following: [15]

| | *Percent reelected* | *Percent not reelected* |
|---|---|---|
| Service oriented | 41 | 59 |
| Not service oriented | 23 | 77 |

Professor Goodman's data obviously make no conclusive case for constituency service as a sure means of winning elections. Other variables may be of equal or greater importance. Name recognition, support by the province chief, and membership in the major ethnic or religious group in the constituency are a few of the possibilities. Nonetheless, his figures are suggestive and have a strong common-sense appeal. Some deputies are likely to note the apparent coincidence of reelection and constituency service, and they may be encouraged to try it out for themselves.

There is no assurance that a party system or even several serious parties will develop in the immediate future. The insecurity of the whole nation in the face of continued aggression is itself a deterrent. The fact that candidates for the House run at-large in the provinces hinders the development of local bases. There are other problems of tradition that may delay the development of viable modern parties. But for the first time, there is at least some slight evidence of progress in that direction.

## Parties and Organizations Outside the System

**National Liberation Front.** A rundown on political organizations in South Vietnam can scarcely ignore the Communists even though they have never openly participated in elections. Indeed, they are excluded from doing so both by the constitution and the laws, on the ground that their goal is to destroy the system and the independence of the country itself. In any case, the Communists have never looked on the electoral process as a preferred route to power in Vietnam: Communist organizations are not parties but revolutionary instruments. They provided most

[15] Letter to the author, dated March 9, 1972.

of the muscle for the civil war in the South until the North Vietnamese greatly expanded their own role after 1965. And it is the Communist organizations that will provide the personnel if a coalition government is forced on the South as part of a negotiated "political" settlement.

The Indochina Communist party (Lao Dong) and the Viet Minh were not as strong in Cochinchina as elsewhere in the country during the period between the end of World War II and the Geneva accords of 1954. Still, there were perhaps 10,000 Viet Minh who remained and went underground with the onset of the Diem regime.[16] During the next six years, the Lao Dong apparatus carried out some propaganda activities and, in 1959-1960, increasingly resorted to violence—including kidnapping and assassination of village leaders—directed at weakening the cohesion of the local communities.

In late 1960, the Communists announced from Hanoi the formation of the National Liberation Front.[17] They claimed that, while they had aided in its foundation, the NLF was "not dominated by them." They also said that the NLF was created to protect the people of the South from the repression and terror of the Diem regime. The new organization was not made up exclusively of Lao Dong members but, in its early period, was openly aligned with Lao Dong.

In Douglas Pike's estimate, the NLF is "a true Communist-front organization." It has performed the functions that were carried out by the Viet Minh during the first Indochina war (1945-54). It serves as the mass organization through which the Communists have carried on their work. Among its members have been both Southerners who went North after the Geneva accords and later returned secretly to South

---

[16] Estimate by Wesley R. Fishel, quoted in Douglas Pike, *Viet Cong,* p. 75.

[17] The two best books on the Viet Cong or the NLF are by Douglas Pike, including *Viet Cong,* cited above, and his more recent *War, Peace and the Viet Cong* (Cambridge, Mass.: M.I.T. Press, 1969). All of the relatively recent books on Vietnam treat the NLF. Among these are Bernard Fall, *The Two Vietnams* (New York: Praeger Publishers, Inc., 1967); Joseph Buttinger, *Dragon Embattled;* and Robert Shaplen, *The Road From War: Vietnam, 1965–1970* (New York: Harper and Row, 1970). Many articles and papers of importance have also appeared on the topic. Without attempting to list them all, the reader would do well to check the last six or seven years of the files of *Asian Survey,* the magazine that has most consistently carried authoritative and scholarly articles on South Vietnam. The papers delivered at periodic seminars of the South East Asia Development Advisory Group have also been of generally very high quality. (The papers are originally prepared for discussion at the seminar only, but sometimes have later been published in *Asian Survey* or in some other form.) An excellent article documenting the relationship of the NLF to the DRV was Joseph H. Weiss, "How Hanoi Controls the Vietcong," *The Reporter,* January 11, 1968, pp. 27–28.

Vietnam and other Communists who remained covertly in the South, post-Geneva. Some members were not Communists at all but simply persons who were deeply dissatisfied with the Diem regime. Jeffrey Race provides a fascinating description of the role of the Communist party in the NLF and the army in forwarding the party's cause:

> The Party now emphasizes the need to neutralize these intermediate classes by means of a broad national front, thus splitting the ranks of the enemy and easing the advance of the Party's core forces: the workers and the peasants. This role of the front has been formalized in Communist doctrine in . . . [the] three instruments of revolution of Mao Tse-tung: the Party, the army, and the front. The Party is the brain, the army is the muscle, and the front is the means of fracturing the society in such a way that the army can do its job with least resistance.[18]

Total NLF membership grew rapidly during the first two years to about a quarter of a million. The membership dropped sharply after the coup d'etat but climbed again in 1964–1965. At its peak, the Communists claimed that the NLF and all its affiliated groups numbered seven million. This figure is obviously a wild exaggeration.[19]

The NLF worked hardest and most successfully in the rural areas. It administered some villages that had once been dominated by the Viet Minh and secured control over more hamlets and villages in the Delta and elsewhere to which the government could not offer adequate protection. In its organizational efforts, the NLF sought to accomplish specific and often limited objectives: a demonstration against landlords in the area to unify the peasants, the consolidation of opposition to the village chief, meetings to "unmask" enemies in their midst. Ideally, whole segments of the village who had grievances would become involved. These gatherings generally called for some immediate actions that were not to be frivolous and would not unnecessarily expose the NLF leadership.

Violence was an essential if not a primary feature of NLF operations. It was used as an instrument to promote the political goals of the

---

[18] Race, *War Comes to Long An: Revolutionary Conflict in a Vietnamese Province* (Berkeley: University of California Press, 1972), p. 121. The whole of Chapter 3 of his book provides a good picture of NLF functions and the dominant role played by the Communist party in manipulating the NLF.

[19] Pike, *Viet Cong*, pp. 114–115.

movement, not simply as a random threat. Nevertheless, violence was very widely used in the period 1959–1963 when literally thousands of hamlet and village officials were kidnapped or murdered. The execution of unpopular mayors was sometimes accepted as a happy deliverance by the villagers, but many village and hamlet chiefs were murdered neither for their administrative failings nor because they had been unresponsive to known village wishes, but because their deaths would serve as a warning that the NLF had the power and the will to destroy in order to achieve its goals.[20] NLF violence served to terrorize possible dissenters into submission, to make possible or strengthen control of the village, to aid in the collection of taxes and rice, and to make easier the forced draft of young men into the VC.[21]

An important further effect of the murder of hamlet and village officials was the destruction of a generation of trained personnel, already in short supply. More than that, the threat of renewed terror was an effective deterrent to the recruitment of replacements, even after the NLF had lost power either because of the success of pacification programs or because of the decimation of NLF cadres during the Tet offensive. This shortage of available leadership from the preferred age group—Vietnamese view age as the handmaiden of wisdom in governance—was one reason for the relatively small number of candidates in the village and hamlet elections of 1967. More candidates turned up in the 1969 and 1970 village contests when the NLF was less able to pose a credible threat. Even then, in some areas there was a shortage of those who fit the Vietnamese villagers' image of the kind of person who should be in leadership positions.

A mass organization in its own right, the NLF was also the umbrella for other functional organizations that supported Communist programs in South Vietnam. Among these other organizations were the Women's

---

[20] Race, *War Comes to Long An,* p. 40, notes that persons who previously served on the village councils were no longer anxious to do so because it was too dangerous to hold such a "position in a society whose day had passed forever. The daily sight on the village roads of those who had killed landlords was a powerful reminder of that fact."

[21] Ibid., p. 135, where Race quotes a former province chief as saying, "The Vietcong use terror to instill fear. In a hamlet they will pick out a couple of people who they say cooperate with the Americans, and shoot them to set an example. From the Vietcong viewpoint this is legal and if they make a few mistakes, nevertheless the person who does is not punished. But after they kill a few people, the whole hamlet is afraid and the Vietcong can force them to cooperate. . . ."

Liberation Association, the Farmers' Liberation Association, and similarly labeled associations for workers, youth, and students. Farmers were obviously the most important interest group to organize in the rural areas of South Vietnam; thus, the Farmers' Liberation Association was the first organized and received priority attention by the party faithful.

Another association—the Cultural Liberation Association—was organized for scholars, artists, and so on. This reflected the recognition of Communists everywhere that intellectuals play an essential role in a revolutionary movement. Any modern or modernizing society depends heavily on their support. If their loyalty is transferred to the revolution, they become the core of destructive propaganda, planning, and organizational opposition to the existing government. They are leaders of the effective chaos-producing groups, excellent instruments for what has been called "creative disorder"—disruptions in the normal processes of society that in turn play into the hands of revolutionaries.

The NLF also gave special attention to the military. The purpose was to subvert members of the ARVN or, if that failed, to destroy them. Prior to the Tet offensive of 1968, NLF efforts were particularly effective among the Regional or Popular Forces in areas most vulnerable to the Viet Cong.

**People's Revolutionary Party.** The NLF, like the Viet Minh, provided a rallying point for opponents of the regime without demanding that they join a Communist organization. At the same time, precisely because it did draw into its membership some non-Communists, the NLF could be thoroughly reliable as a Communist instrument only with firm internal control and direction. To that end, the North Vietnamese in January 1962 created the People's Revolutionary party (PRP) which, as the press releases put it, was founded following "a conference of Marxist-Leninists . . . under the guidance of veteran revolutionaries." [22] Uncon-

[22] *The Communist Party in South Vietnam* (1966) prepared by the United States Mission in Vietnam, provides a brief, good account of the founding of the PRP. The next few paragraphs draw heavily on this document. One of the stated reasons for creating the PRP is of general interest because it describes the problem of the marginal member of any "true believer" organization (p. 14):

> Defectors . . . professed to having been Marxists. . . . Many indicated they felt cut off from the mainstream of communist thought, surrounded by nonbelievers, unable to suppress their doubts about the correctness of their actions, particularly those involving violence. . . . At first, one cadre said, everything had been simple and understandable; capitalism meant poverty and slavery; communism, abundance and freedom. Then he

firmed stories have suggested that not only were the North Vietnamese government and the Lao Dong party involved but that Le Duan (since Ho Chi Minh's death in 1969, the first among equals in the DRV) came South and himself contributed to the founding of the PRP. Within the year, the Committee for the Supervision of the South (COSVN), headed by Le Duc Tho, was created in Hanoi.

The PRP has been described by the North Vietnamese theoretical journal, *Hoc Tap,* as

> the soul of the NLF. . . . The PRP is a revolutionary party of the working class in South Vietnam, a Marxist-Leninist Party. . . . The PRP maintains that the revolutionary struggle of the southern people must necessarily use the revolutionary violence of the masses . . . to advance toward smashing the reactionary government and replace it by a genuinely revolutionary government. . . . Straying from this path can lead only to failure.[23]

A PRP training manual of 1965 states that it is "the vanguard of southern workers dedicated to achieving a patriotic, democratic and national revolution in order to introduce Socialism and then Communism in Vietnam." The same manual speaks of leading the "people toward the establishment of Communism. Communism will be practiced as it is in the Soviet Union. . . ." [24]

Locally in South Vietnam the PRP cadres downgrade the party's ties with the North Vietnamese Communist party. Yet the PRP flag and its Youth League flag feature the white hammer and sickle against a red background.

The PRP is built from a base of cells within the villages or cities and is controlled hierarchically like any other Communist party. There are a very few members of special importance who are to be found outside the cell structure. As always is the case with Communist organizations, the party is highly centralized. "The minority obeys the deci-

---

> came South and found prosperous villages, more so than in the North, and people who seldom felt the touch of a governmental hand, unlike the omniscient government of the North. Events swirled about him and with his inadequate grasp of Marxism, realistic explanations began to slip away. Uncertainty entered, followed by doubt, followed by a break in faith, followed by defection. . . .

The PRP was created to prevent the spread of these defections as well as give direction to the NLF.

[23] Ibid., p. 12.

[24] Ibid.

sion of the majority . . . the lower echelons obey the decisions of the upper echelons, all elements of the Revolution obey the Central Committee. There is one shout and a thousands echoes. . . ." [25]

**The NLF and the Future.** In spite of PRP efforts within the NLF, there has been a steady erosion of membership. A loss of faith in the movement and a shift toward nationalism, and even a middle-class outlook, have characterized the views of more and more once loyal NLF supporters. The PRP may have slowed the rate of defection, but it has not stopped defections. The most devastating blow to the NLF was the disaster that resulted from the Tet offensive of 1968. Not only were cadres lost, but the long promised "general uprising" that was finally to bring them to power in the summer of 1968 never materialized. Meanwhile, the reforms that the NLF said would never come from the government began to take hold, and the peasant was offered actual title to his land—not just an insubstantial NLF promise of title. As the NLF lost ground, the peasant paid less in taxes and his sons were not threatened by NLF conscription.

On the political front, the NLF was exposed as ineffective by the elections of 1970 and 1971. In the presidential election of 1967, for example, the NLF could turn out voters to support Dzu's candidacy—at any rate, Dzu carried or ran well in the areas where the NLF was a significant factor. By the time of the 1971 presidential election, by contrast, the NLF had neither the power to hold down the size of the vote nor the influence to cause the spoiling of ballots by those who did go to the polls.

This record helps to explain why the NLF and the Democratic Republic of Vietnam have generally rejected the U.S.-South Vietnamese proposal for open and internationally supervised elections to be held in the South. All parties to the discussion know that the NLF is now the smallest of the communal groups in the country and that a genuinely free election would show no significant support for NLF candidates. They and their supporters outside the country can make any claims they wish about the NLF's massive base of support—but, clearly, these are claims they are loath to put to the test, and advisedly so.

There is another reason for opposition to elections. The NLF has always claimed that in a real sense it *is* the government of the South.

[25] Ibid., p. 21.

Only the North Vietnamese government and the NLF as the vanguard of the workers have the "right" to rule. The coalition that the DRV and the NLF would find acceptable means first of all the exclusion of President Thieu—thus removing the one leader with any legitimacy—and the creation of cabinet or committee government with the NLF holding such key positions as it chose, and with the remaining posts in the hands of easily controllable political ineffectives. A coalition regime would in any case be only a way station on the route to total domination by the DRV at a time of its own choosing. There is, after all, no hurry. If the world prefers a fiction of independence in the South, that would be a perfectly acceptable facade until such time as the new Vietnamese government were to "demand" reunion with Hanoi.

# 10
# Summary and Conclusions

## Evaluation of the Electoral Process

In the opening chapter, a number of questions were posed about electoral processes in general and those of South Vietnam in particular. The answers, drawn from an examination of the seven elections of "modern South Vietnam," should in some significant degree measure that country's success, since 1966, in developing viable institutions that reasonably approach the norms of a democratic system.

> *Question 1:* Is the electorate constitutionally and legally defined in a manner that is generally inclusive of adults and therefore of potential voters, or are large numbers of them excluded arbitrarily from casting ballots for national and local candidates?

Constitutionally and legally the electorate includes most of the adult population of South Vietnam. Article 13 of the constitution provides that "every citizen has the right to vote, run for public office and participate in public affairs on an equal basis and in accordance with conditions and procedures prescribed by law." A separate law has been passed to govern each election since the adoption of the constitution. Provisions dealing with voting, however, have remained essentially the same. They give the vote to all persons of Vietnamese nationality who, "irrespective of sex, [were] 18 years of age as of December 31 [of the preceding year] and who [are] inscribed on the electors' list and holders of regular electors' cards except those deprived of the rights of citizenship." This latter category includes criminals, the insane, and Communists.

*Question 2:* Is the registration of voters conducted in a manner that assures the maximum listing of legally qualified voters, thus making heavy participation at the polls possible?

The registration process virtually duplicates that of France and most other European democracies. The government has the responsibility for registering all eligible voters. But, as in France, the system does not assure 100 percent inclusiveness. In the villages where officials know the residents, most everyone is registered on reaching age 18. In the cities, however, the government simply is unable to be sure. Hence the provision in the law that all citizens have an opportunity to check the lists for accuracy between a first and second public posting, a couple of weeks apart. Because any man eligible to vote for the first time is also old enough to be drafted, not all young men are interested in calling the government's attention to the omission of their names. Still, the system is reasonably accurate; it assures a more complete listing of eligible voters than is the case where the voter himself must take the initiative.

Alain Lancelot has estimated for France that about 7 percent of those who are otherwise eligible to vote have not been registered.[1] The figure for South Vietnam is almost certainly higher because there are limited facilities for making a thorough check, a relative lack of experience in preparing voting lists, and a large and shifting population of refugees who have been forced out of their homes and have not yet been registered in a new city or village. There probably is also a higher percentage of young men who are simply seeking to avoid the draft.

Census figures for South Vietnam at the close of 1970 showed a population of 17,333,000. Of that number, perhaps 9,150,000 were of voting age.[2] After subtracting from the latter figure the number of adults still living in regions under National Liberation Front control and those excluded from voting as felons or the institutionalized insane, it would require a registration failure rate of only about 11 percent—

[1] Alain Lancelot, *Abstentionisme Electoral en France* (Paris: Armand Colin, 1968), pp. 20–36, discusses the problem of the unregistered voter in France. Figures for non-registration from 1954–1964 are on page 26.

[2] All population figures are estimates or extrapolations from the 1964 census, but there seems to be general agreement that the population of South Vietnam increased by about three million between 1964 and 1970. Most of this increase was due to a population explosion, increase in life expectancy, et cetera. The annual growth rate had been only 1.3 percent for the years 1960–1965, but for the next five years it increased sharply to 2.9 percent. This increase has not yet been reflected in the number of new voters, needless to say.

reasonable in the circumstances—to arrive at the 1971 voter registration total of 7,192,660.

*Question 3:* Is secrecy of the vote protected for the citizen casting his ballot?

Voting booths in South Vietnam are very similar to the voting booths in France and make possible complete ballot secrecy. The envelope within which the ballot or ballots are placed is opaque. No one can see for whom the vote is being cast or whether, indeed, there is any ballot at all in the envelope. Some observers insisted that polling officials could discover how the voter voted in the 1971 presidential election by seeing whether he had discarded his ballot in a box or bag placed just inside the voting booth. But few observers reported that the receptacles were visible enough for officials to keep an accurate check of discarded ballots, and no observer claimed to know whether the receptacles had been positioned deliberately or whether the officials actually made a serious surveillance effort. Even granting every suspicion more than its due, there is no reason to conclude that secrecy of voting has been widely violated in the seven national elections since 1966. Absentee voting, which in many countries is a major source of fraud and provides an easy opportunity to violate the secrecy rules, is not allowed in South Vietnam.

*Question 4:* Is there adequate protection against multiple voting and other forms of voting fraud?

The major charge against the honesty of the 1967 presidential election related to the possibility of multiple voting, especially by members of the armed forces. The charge was repeated prior to the 1971 presidential "race." But it never amounted to much, perhaps because the latter was a one-man election. Critics have rarely alleged multiple voting in elections to the House or Senate.

There is, in any case, little or no evidence to back up the charge although there may have been isolated cases of persons voting more than once. Such violations of the law still occasionally occur in Western democracies, and it would be surprising if they did not also occur in South Vietnam.

The principal protection against multiple voting is the requirement that South Vietnamese voters must show both their regular identity card (with name, picture, and fingerprints) and their voter card (also with name, address, et cetera). These are checked against the voter registration list for each district and only then does the voter receive a ballot.

After he has cast his ballot, the appropriate part of the card (in the 1971 presidential election it was block "B") is clipped off, which renders the card useless elsewhere in the district.[3]

Multiple voting is possible but not probable even if a voter has more than one voter card. There is no doubt that both in 1967 and 1971 some persons, often soldiers, received more than one voting card. Soldiers could receive one for their home address where they had been registered before entering the service and another for the military unit where they were stationed. Because no absentee voting is allowed, because soldiers are confined to their units on election day, and because they can use only their military unit voting cards, there is no reason to believe that soldiers have been involved in multiple voting no matter how many cards they may have had.

In 1971, there was a verified case of two elderly women in Saigon who received two voter cards apiece. They brought their cards to public attention and General Minh used this as "evidence" that the 1971 elections were "rigged." As it happened, the two women lived at the same address. It seems probable, as the chief of the registration program suggested, that the computer spewed out two cards for each of them instead of one. Presumably there were other such cases, just as there must have been instances when the computer drew a blank. All of which says more about the wonders of technology than it does about the incidence of fraud.

*Question 5:* Is the system for counting the ballots open and public so that an honest count is probable?

The law provides that the counting of ballots must occur at the polling place immediately after the polls close. There were exceptions to this rule here and there in 1967 where ballot boxes were moved to secure locations because of a danger to the boxes themselves or to the official counting in areas contested by the Viet Cong. (In later elections there were very few such cases because there were so few areas where the VC had the necessary strength to interfere with the counting process.) Charges of fraudulent counting were made in some instances in 1967 when ballot boxes were removed—as it happened—to police stations. According to the critics, opponents of the regime were not allowed to follow the ballot boxes to the stations for the count and so tangible

[3] For reproductions of the voting cards issued in 1967 and 1971, see pages 53 and 114 respectively.

evidence was lacking; but, they said, the circumstances suggested fraud. In any case, the circumstances were so rare that such miscounting, if it occurred at all, would have had no effect on the outcome. As indicated in Chapter 4, if all charges of fraud had been upheld and the votes from those polling places thrown out, the Thieu-Ky margin of victory over Dzu would have increased, not decreased.

At least eight officials are present for the counting of the ballots. Poll watchers for each candidate, and any citizen who wants to, also may observe the count. Reports from every polling place are filed at three different governmental levels, which makes it relatively easy to trace any misrepresentation of results. The figures are ultimately reviewed by the bureaucracy and by the Supreme Court (in the case of presidential elections) or by the National Assembly (in the case of elections to that body).

There were some instances in the 1971 elections to the House of Representatives, as noted in Chapter 6, where the courts found polling officials guilty of deliberately miscounting the votes or otherwise fraudulently seeking to affect the outcome. Possibly the courts were more independent by 1971 and therefore more receptive to charges of fraud than in earlier elections. If so, this augurs well for future electoral honesty. But there is no generally accepted evidence that miscounting or other dishonest actions of election officials were widespread or that they prejudiced the outcome of these earlier elections. Because the counting must take place immediately after the close of the polls and the results reported the same evening, it is easy for candidates and watchers to stay around to determine whether the counting is legitimate.

*Question 6:* Do constitutional and legal rules make it possible for a reasonable number of candidates to compete for voter support?

In 1967, some 480 candidates (48 slates of 10 each) campaigned for 60 Senate seats. Three years later, 160 candidates (16 slates) sought 30 seats. In the 1967 elections to the House, there were 1,172 candidates for 137 seats or 8.7 per seat. So numerous were the competitors that only seven received 50 percent or more of the popular vote in their districts. In the Saigon metropolitan area, no winning candidate received more than 20 percent of the vote and half of them won with less than 10 percent. In spite of more stringent qualifying requirements in 1971, there were 1,242 candidates seeking the 159 House seats. The ratio of candidates to seats was 7.8 to 1, down slightly from 1967. All of which may still leave open the question whether absolutely everyone may seek public office; but, at the very least, the field for legislative seats has been crowded.

Much more controversial than the competition for National Assembly seats is the level of competition for the presidency. Eleven candidates presented themselves to the voters on election day in 1967. The Constituent Assembly had blocked seven other would-be candidates, either because they did not submit all the required information for filing or, in at least two instances, for failure to meet the basic constitutional and legal rules requiring candidates to be native-born citizens, to have no record of convictions for felonies, and to have no background of Communist affiliation or neutralist/pro-Communist activity.

The 1971 election law, as described above in Chapter 7, required that a candidate have the endorsement of 40 members of the National Assembly or 100 members of provincial or autonomous city councils. And, because President Thieu secured over half the National Assembly endorsements and 452 of the possible 550 provincial signatures (there were four vacant provincial seats), only General Minh was able to qualify. When he refused to run in a two-man race in which he seemed certain to be badly beaten and when Vice President Ky, made eligible in a last minute Supreme Court ruling, also refused to make the race, the result was a one-man presidential contest.

The law, as now interpreted by the South Vietnamese Supreme Court, makes it possible for as many as nine candidates to enter a future race by preventing any one candidate from collecting vastly more signatures than he needs.

The law as originally interpreted by the three-judge Supreme Court panel and the administration of the law by election officials were at best unfortunate. President Thieu apparently also made an error in judgment and tactics when he tried to force a two-man race. Nevertheless, both Vice President Ky and General Minh had an opportunity to run against President Thieu and both—evidently unwilling to meet him head-to-head—declined to take up that opportunity.

Professor Lucian W. Pye of the Center for International Studies, Massachusetts Institute of Technology, while not assessing blame for the lack of a contest for the presidency of 1971, said that

> the year . . . did not bring the open, competitive election that many had hoped it would; instead President Thieu ran without

opposition. As a consequence the democratic dream was not realized in Vietnam, but compared with most Asian societies South Vietnam still remains relatively open.[4]

*Question 7:* Does the system provide for roughly equal opportunity for candidates who have been nominated to compete for support?

The government assumes the costs of posters, some public meetings, radio and television time, and various other election activities on an equal basis for all candidates for the same office. In 1967, after some early confusion and controversy, the government also supplied transportation for presidential candidates to all meetings outside Saigon. How much money, if any, could be effectively spent beyond the amount supplied by the government is hard to say. The American observer has to remind himself that Vietnamese campaigns are short, there is no long series of costly primaries, and, with no commercial broadcasting, the expensive 30- or 60-second television spot is simply unknown. Potential opponents of President Thieu in 1971 spoke of the need for vast sums but never specified any precise amounts. When Truong Dinh Dzu claimed in 1967 that he had spent $350,000 before and during the election period to support his candidacy, long-time observers of the South Vietnamese political scene were dubious. They did not believe that he could profitably have spent so much money, short of outright vote buying. The expensive items—radio, television, posters, transportation—were already paid for by the state, and individual candidates could not buy more of them, money or no money.

In general, there seems to be an equal opportunity for all candidates. The obvious exception is that the incumbent, as in all systems, has a great advantage—assuming, of course, that things are going reasonably well in the country. This advantage is particularly obvious for the president. He has access to the press and to television and radio news simply because, as head of state, all that he does is news. Further, he has considerable patronage powers not available to others—and there are always orphanages to dedicate and chickens to distribute during the campaign period.

Candidates for the National Assembly also receive equal support from the government. The incumbent, however, has the advantage of a four- or six-year term during which he may have helped constituents

[4] Pye, "Asia: Profound Change," *Freedom At Issue,* January-February 1972, p. 5.

and gained some name recognition. The latter is especially important in a system that lacks strong political parties. That advantage was apparently not worth a great deal in 1971, to be sure: only 40 of the 119 House incumbents seeking reelection were successful.

If an appointed province chief (or the president who appointed him) is opposed to any House candidate in his district, incumbent or not, the candidate is at a disadvantage. The province chief has the provincial and much of the national patronage at his disposal. He may also use the civil service as his political machine. Three province chiefs were so heavy-handed in their efforts to control elections to the House in 1971 that the Supreme Court recommended they be fired.

The power of the president and the province chiefs, however, is not overwhelming. In 1971, the House elections produced 84 progovernment deputies, 60 oppositionists, and 15 independents. Of the 35 oppositionist incumbents, 57 percent were reelected, while only 23 percent of the 84 progovernment incumbents who sought reelection were successful. These figures are somewhat misleading: President Thieu and the province chiefs sometimes backed younger, abler candidates against progovernment incumbents of limited competence.

> *Question 8:* In the case of the legislature, where there are many positions to be filled, does the system encourage the selection of candidates representing the various religious, ethnic, and other minority groups in the society?

Election rules for the Senate do not make any special provision for minority groups. Because candidates run nationally in slates of 10, however, an effort is made to present balanced tickets. As a result, after the elections of 1970, there were four Cao Dai members (out of 60 senators), one Animist, two Hoa Hao, and one Muslim, in addition to the larger numbers of Buddhists and Catholics and those for whom no information was available. There were also at least two Montagnards.

For the House, the law explicitly provides that six Vietnamese of Cambodian descent must be elected, six of Montagnard descent, two of Cham descent, and two Vietnamese of North Vietnamese Montagnard descent. The law assigns the ethnic seats to specific provinces where particular ethnic groups are especially numerous, and only those of the designated ethnic background may seek these seats. Actually, the ratio of seats to the number of ethnics is somewhat higher than is the case for the Vietnamese generally. (Chinese are not given any special advantage because they are concentrated in Cholon and can elect their own Chinese deputies if they want to do so.) Persons of those backgrounds were elected in the numbers required in both 1967 and 1971. The rules do not prevent more of these ethnics from winning, but they require no less than the designated level of representation.

The religious affiliation of House members, to the extent known, showed the following distribution: Buddhists 49, Catholics 21, Hoa Hao 12, and Cao Dai 3. Almost certainly some of the Montagnards are Animists, but there was no such classification in the published lists. There is no way to be precise about it—but one rough mark of a free and open electoral system may well be the degree to which a numerous legislative assembly mirrors the distribution of major population groups. On such a scale, South Vietnam ranks well up.

> *Question 9:* Is the press free to criticize the government and its policies and to offer alternatives to the personnel and programs of the incumbent regime?

The chapter on the press indicated a good measure of freedom to criticize government programs and personnel—up to mid-'72 at any rate. The law of December 1969 authorizes the suspension of newspapers and periodicals but only after a court has so ordered. There has been only one such case: it began in February 1971, went through the lower courts, then was appealed to the Supreme Court, and had not yet been decided by August 1972. All this time, the magazine was still being published and the editor was still writing columns critical of the regime.

While only the courts can order suspensions of periodicals and newspapers, the executive may confiscate individual editions *after* they have reached the newsstands. The number of confiscations in the year just prior to the election of 1971 ranged from a low of 14 in October 1970 to a high of 83 in September 1971. Most confiscations have been justified by a catch-all prohibition against articles that undermine the morale of the military, jeopardize "national security or public order," or "show division between religions, localities and races." Articles praising the National Liberation Front or the Communist regime of North Vietnam [5] and stories suggesting that President Nixon plans to

[5] Curiously, quotations from NLF propaganda broadcasts and North Vietnamese publications may be printed and the editions not confiscated. In fact, the law explicitly protects the publication of direct quotations from other publications.

desert President Thieu in favor of a coalition government have been frequent grounds for confiscations in recent years.

There is no censorship of reporting by foreign correspondents. During the last six years, however, the government has expelled one American newsman and refused to renew the visa of another for "interference in the internal affairs" of South Vietnam. In the spring of 1972, an Italian photographer was expelled for overt security violations.

In short, the press in South Vietnam is, not surprisingly, less free than in Western democratic countries. As compared with the press in North Vietnam or even in nontotalitarian traditional or modernizing countries in Asia or most any other place, however, it is quite surprisingly free both to report and to criticize—even though its standards of professionalism are not noticeably rigorous. (The effects of the new press decree simply cannot yet be measured.)

> *Question 10:* To what extent does the political party system provide the organization and perform the functions generally thought to be required of parties in a democratic system?

The Tan Dai Viet party, at least in the villages of Long An and the Delta, performs some of the functions of a modern political party.[6] The same can be said to a greater or lesser degree of the An Quang Buddhists, the Worker-Farmer party, and some of the Catholic parties. These groups have sought to broaden their support beyond their original special-interest bases. Still, there is no party "system" in any accepted sense. Most candidates compete for House seats as individuals rather than party representatives. The artificial senatorial slates of 10 lead more to the selection of well-known personalities than to adherents of the same party. The further fact that, particularly at the presidential level, antigovernment candidates often perceive American newsmen and senators as their primary constituency is hardly conducive to the emergence of party organizations.

---

[6] See Chapter 9 and particularly Stephen Young's analysis of the Tan Dai Viet operation in Long An and elsewhere. It is worth noting that this analysis is in conflict with that of Jeffrey Race, *War Comes to Long An: Revolutionary Conflict in a Vietnamese Province* (Berkeley: University of California Press, 1972), Chapters 4 and 5. Mr. Race's analysis is based primarily on his research prior to the Tet offensive of 1968 and the major thrust of land reform in 1970. The reaction of the peasants to their opportunity to join in support of the North Vietnamese invasion of 1972 would seem to raise questions about the validity of the Race thesis.

There are in both houses of the National Assembly significant opposition forces to executive leadership, but that opposition has never coalesced. There is no unified party-based opposition to the incumbent president or to presidentially supported assembly candidates. Still, as Professors Ranney and Kendall suggested many years ago, coalitions in the legislature may develop into external coalitions or parties for electoral purposes, thus in turn expanding on their effective legislative strength.[7]

Once the United States has pulled completely out of South Vietnam, or its contribution to Vietnam's military and economic stability has been so regularized that neither U.S. press nor politicians involve themselves in that country's internal affairs (analogous to the situation, e.g., in South Korea), South Vietnamese political figures will probably begin cultivating their own indigenous constituencies. And they may see the advantages of organizing new parties or strengthening old ones—thus giving added impetus to the development of a viable party system.

Scattered through the foregoing answers are comments going to the obvious alternative to the electoral institutions of the existing South Vietnamese system. Suffice to say that the North Vietnamese government maintains total control over the people and institutions of the North. The Communist party is unchallenged, and there is no comparable institution in the South. The practical choice—as distinct from the full range of blue sky alternatives—comes down to a totalitarian regime, on the one hand, and an approach, however imperfect, to a democratic system on the other hand. In these terms, the fact that the people of South Vietnam have apparently opted to support the existing regime—which, if only by historical coincidence, is virtually interchangeable with the existing system—is not particularly surprising.

## Support for the South Vietnamese System

The future of this system, and of its electoral processes, is difficult to forecast: it is contingent on military, economic, and international developments, themselves difficult to forecast. How long, in what numbers, and with what contingent strings will U.S. forces and U.S. aid continue to be supplied to South Vietnam? Will the Democratic Republic of Vietnam continue to attack the South directly or indirectly every few years, or will the DRV shift its strategy and allow an indepen-

[7] See Austin Ranney and Willmoore Kendall, *Democracy and the American Party System* (New York: Harcourt, Brace and Co., 1956), p. 88 ff.

dent South Vietnam to develop? If the attacks continue, what will their impact be if U.S. aid has been withdrawn in the meantime—which is to ask, can and will South Vietnam "hack it" on its own?

A different, rather more fundamental kind of question is just as difficult to answer. Have the people of South Vietnam developed commitments to South Vietnam as a nation? Have they developed a loyalty to the emerging democracy of the last six years? What are their attitudes toward the current regime and toward available alternatives to that regime, and can they yet distinguish (or afford the luxury of distinguishing) the regime from the system per se?

Survey research data may be available in the files of both the U.S. and South Vietnamese governments that could provide hard evidence as to public attitudes. But even if they exist, such data are not available to outsiders. One is forced back on circumstantial evidence.

In the first place, areas of pacification have increased. More people are thus able to make a realistic choice, either way. Voters have turned out in relatively large numbers. They elected a majority of the House of Representatives in 1970 that supports the president, but the margin is relatively thin. In the presidential election, neither Vice President Ky nor General Minh, whose supporters apparently checked voter opinion in August of 1971, was willing to meet President Thieu head-to-head. One may surmise that a poll, if taken, apparently showed that the public preferred Thieu to either of the alternatives.

Turning to a second measure, the number of defections from the ranks of the National Liberation Front has gone up since 1963. The peak in the province of Long An was 2,453 in 1969, after the major Communist defeat in Tet. In 1970, the number of defectors dropped to 952. But this lower figure probably reflected the drop-off in NLF supporters rather than any change in the defection rate. The estimated military strength of the Viet Cong in 1968 in Long An was 3,100. In 1970, it was only 427.[8] Nationally, defections have followed a similar curve. They reached a peak of 47,023 in 1969, post-Tet. That number dropped to 32,565 in 1970 and to 20,357 in 1971.[9]

Surrender and defection rates are not, of course, clear tests of the attitudes of those who surrender or defect. They may quit to stay alive. They may or may not be reliable supporters of South Vietnamese inde-

---

[8] For Long An defection figures, see Race, *War Comes to Long An,* pp. 284–285.
[9] The figures for defection at the national level were made available by the Department of Defense.

pendence, and may even covertly continue to support the NLF. Still, the number defecting from the NLF has depleted its membership without any comparable rate of defection from the government side.

The government of the South, as Professor John Roche has often pointed out, had sufficient confidence in the South Vietnamese people that in the late '60s it gave out some 2,000,000 guns for self-protection against the Viet Cong. In the months since the 1972 North Vietnamese invasion, another 50,000 guns were put in civilian hands in Hue alone. Both Tet and the 1972 invasion afforded excellent opportunities for the South Vietnamese to switch sides, taking their guns with them, but they did not do so.

The gift of guns to the citizens of Hue was particularly impressive because it was in Hue that President Diem, Premier Ky, and later even Premier Tran Van Huong were so bitterly opposed by the An Quang Buddhists. It was there, as recently as 1966, that the Buddhists mounted major demonstrations against the government. But later events have sharply changed this relationship. The occupation of Hue during the Tet offensive ended with the murder of at least 3,000 civilians—the vast majority of them Buddhists. This may well have crystallized the views of some who had previously seen little to choose between the governments of the North and the South. In 1970, the Buddhists moved to join the system, as it were, by entering a slate of candidates in the senatorial elections. Their slate led all others in the voting.

In 1971, the An Quang Buddhists were well represented on the Central Election Council. Buddhists who had been barred from House candidacy by local election committees were generally restored by this national "appeals" body. Furthermore, the government made no special effort to defeat the Buddhist candidates, concentrated in I Corps. Some 22 of the 24 winners from that area were Buddhists. To be sure, the Buddhists officially opposed President Thieu's candidacy for reelection in 1971, and his support level in I Corps was lower than in any other area except Saigon. Nonetheless, much of the bitterness was gone. Knowledgeable observers see no irreconcilable conflict between President Thieu and Thich Tri Quang and his followers; and, judging by their actions, the Buddhists now feel more at home within the political system in the South.

Nearly all members of the National Assembly sprang to the defense of South Vietnam's independence when North Vietnam invaded in 1972. They gave blood for the wounded and led the people in contributing money to the cost of defending the country. The Senate, however, did refuse to grant certain extraordinary powers to the president for the duration of the crisis. This refusal ultimately led 26 progovernment senators to hold a rump minority session to approve President Thieu's emergency request. The conflict between President Thieu and the majority of the Senate was not a matter of preference for the North: it involved major differences on issues of public policy and the fear of some senators that powers given the president might not be returned when the crisis was over. The most important of these issues were the latter's request for more power to control the economy, to increase taxes levied on the wealthy to help defray the costs of the war, and to equalize the draft rules.[10]

President Nixon, among others, noted in the case of the 1972 invasion that "not only has there been no domestic uprising in South Vietnam, but the stream of refugees has all been away from the 'liberators' and toward safety behind the South Vietnamese lines." Elsewhere in the same article, the President pointed out that

> the government and people of South Vietnam have been working hard at establishing new and more representative constitutional processes, even while fighting a war for national survival. Few countries in history have experimented with the development of representative institutions in the midst of war, and even fewer have done so with the degree of success that South Vietnam has achieved.[11]

Another kind of evidence suggests the absence of fundamental opposition to the political system of South Vietnam. Anticipated popular support has simply not been available to the invading armies of the North. During the 1968 Tet offensive, the long promised "general uprising" never arose. In 1972, very few members of the National Liberation Front and the People's Revolutionary party gave help to the armies of the North. The failure was so obvious by early June that Liberation Radio, the outlet of the People's Revolutionary government, editorially questioned whether its supporters had the "firm determination" called

---

[10] It is risky to grant extraordinary power to the executive but, as Professor Robert A. Dahl has pointed out, the executive must have considerable power and freedom of action in times of crisis so that the processes do not overwhelm the needs of the system. See his *Polyarchy: Participation and Opposition* (New Haven: Yale University Press, 1971), pp. 320–321.

[11] Richard M. Nixon, "The Real Road to Peace," *U.S. News and World Report,* June 29, 1972, p. 37.

for. It admonished "cadres, combatants, and compatriots [to] understand the general situation and the concrete situations in their localities and to adopt a firm determination to fight to the end to change their lives. . . ." [12]

The Thieu regime has been able to bring a semblance of order and stability to the greater part of South Vietnam. Not since independence from France in 1954, has so much of the country been under the relatively firm control of the government in Saigon. Professor Samuel P. Huntington has emphasized the importance of such a development in new countries. "The primary problem," he has written of the modernizing state,

> is not liberty but the creation of a legitimate public order. Men may, of course, have order without liberty, but they cannot have liberty without order. Authority has to exist before it can be limited, and it is authority that is in scarce supply in those modernizing countries where government is at the mercy of alienated intellectuals, rambunctious colonels, and rioting students.[13]

By election time in 1971, the government had reached such a level of security that it could contain student riots within a limited area of Saigon, shrug off the few hundred demonstrating veterans directed by Vice President Ky's lieutenants, and absorb the criticism of the intellectuals—all without risking the overthrow of the regime *or* the system. No previous government in South Vietnam had dared allow such freedom. Again, it should be emphasized that the restraint of the Buddhists (and/or their commitment to the system) was a major factor in this new stability.

The growing pains of modernization may be slowly subsiding. Developing democratic institutions may be getting stronger. Professor Huntington has argued that

> the older an organization is, the more likely it is to continue to exist through any specified future time period. The prob-

[12] Quoted in the Washington *Evening Star,* June 7, 1972.

[13] Huntington, *Political Order in Changing Societies* (New Haven: Yale University Press, 1968), pp. 7–8. Just prior to the statement quoted, Huntington cites James Madison who, in *Federalist 51,* had made much the same point 180 years ago: "In framing a government which is to be administered by men over men, the great difficulty lies in this: you must first enable the government to control the governed; and in the next place oblige it to control itself." Professor Dennis Duncanson has repeatedly stressed this point in his work on Vietnam.

> ability that an organization which is one hundred years old will survive one additional year, it might be hypothesized, is perhaps one hundred times greater than the probability that an organization one year old will survive one additional year. . . .[14]

Some years ago, to repeat a point noted at the outset, Professor I. Milton Sacks first argued that the "continuation of the . . . effort to create an elected government in South Vietnam and to 'make the Constitution work' might create the conditions of stability." [15] Unlike some who worried about the difficulties of carrying on elections in wartime, Professor Sacks argued that the very fact of elections in the crises of a transitional society might itself have a stabilizing influence. He continues to argue this position.

The current *system* in South Vietnam has survived and grown stronger over the last six years, and the Thieu *regime* has managed to rule for five of them—years of increasing internal stability. Challenges to survival have been dangerous enough to test any government. Yet it did survive the Tet offensive and, so far, it has survived the 1972 invasion. It has exercised increasing authority over the nation's affairs. New territories have been brought under its jurisdiction as pacification has proceeded. Land reform has transferred real wealth and power in the rural areas from a limited number of landlords to an increasing number of peasants. The fact that the regime has done as well as it has, in the face of major opposition both internal and external, may itself have strengthened the chances of the system surviving. But the problems of peace, when it comes, may be as obstinate as the problems of military crises; the record of six years of "evolving" democracy is no adequate basis for any firm prediction of a durable democratic society a decade hence.

Some years ago, the late James Thurber is supposed to have responded to the question, "How is your wife?" with the counterquestion, "As compared to what?"

The people of South Vietnam are not faced with a choice between the existing system and some ideal model of a liberal democracy. Academic analysis can sometimes be served by comparing existing institutions against a normative model. Reformers may also find it useful to

---

[14] Ibid., pp. 13–14.

[15] Sacks, "Restructuring Government in South Vietnam," *Asian Survey,* August 1967, p. 520.

establish a model as a goal for ultimate reform efforts. Neither of these purposes is particularly relevant to the very practical and immediate problem of the South Vietnamese: they must choose to live under the current system of South Vietnam (more or less as it is) or under the only system that can predictably replace it, i.e., that of North Vietnam. And, like it or not, the Thieu regime is so far the only one the system has ever produced.

A few South Vietnamese intellectuals, possibly encouraged by the policy debates in the United States, have followed the path of the Italian intellectuals described by Professor Dahl. They have demanded perfection for the South Vietnamese system as the price of their support. Perhaps because North Vietnam's aggression against the South has become so blatant, the number of intellectuals who insist on "perfection now" appears to have decreased sharply. If the prospects for greater democratization in South Vietnam are still uncertain, the likelihood of continued totalitarian control in North Vietnam is very high indeed for the foreseeable future.

In the years since the 1968 Tet offensive and particularly since the invasion of 1972, the vast majority of South Vietnamese appear to prefer the uncertainty: it is leavened at least with hope.

# Appendix A

## ELECTIONS IN NORTH VIETNAM

An election in a Communist country is less a process for selecting government leaders than it is an occasion for rallying the faithful. Elections in North Vietnam are cases in point. They exhibit—at least within limits—the forms of democracy. But the substance is totalitarian.[1]

Early in November 1945, a few months after proclaiming the Democratic Republic of Vietnam (DRV) to be the independent government of all Vietnam, Ho Chi Minh issued a call for elections to a national assembly. These elections were the first of four that the DRV, now the government of North Vietnam, lists as official elections and the only ones that involved participation by voters outside the boundaries of North Vietnam.

---

This article appeared in substantially the same form in *World Affairs* (Washington, D. C.: American Peace Society), vol. 135, no. 1, Summer 1972, and is included here with the permission of the American Peace Society.

[1] North Vietnamese official publications and broadcasts are the sources for most of the data used in this appendix—particularly for the National Assembly campaigns and elections of 1964 and 1971 and for the description of the National Assembly at work. *Nhan Dan,* the official newspaper of Lao Dong (Workers' party), reprints many reports of the National Assembly, including the results of elections to that body, the record of its actions, and reports of the number and length of assembly sessions since its inception in 1946. *Nhan Dan* and other official journals, or Radio Hanoi broadcasts, are sources for descriptions of the selection of assembly candidates by the Fatherland Front and of the official campaign rallies. These articles or broadcasts are translated into English by U.S. government agencies and are to be found in (1) *Vietnam: Documents and Research Notes,* a "service of the United States Mission in Vietnam," which may be requested from the Minister-Counselor for Public Affairs, American Embassy, Saigon, Vietnam (hereafter cited as *Documents and Research Notes*); and (2) the publications of the Joint Publications Research Service, Office of Technical Services, U.S. Department of Commerce, available through the U.S. Government Printing Office (hereafter cited as *JPRS*).

Descriptions of party rallies and actions of the Fatherland Front were intended for North Vietnamese consumption and may well be idealized versions rather than literal reports of the events.

Excerpts from the 1960 constitution of the Democratic Republic of Vietnam and the National Assembly election law of the same year are official North Vietnamese translations that have been reprinted in American publications.

At the same time, Ho Chi Minh announced the dissolution of the Indochina Communist party (ICP), "in an effort," as George Carver has noted, "to make the Viet Minh government more palatable to non-Communist Vietnamese and to the Chinese Nationalist forces then occupying Viet Nam down to the 16th parallel." [2] The Viet Minh was the Communist-controlled umbrella organization or front that dominated the government of the newly announced DRV. The ICP was immediately replaced by the Association for Marxist Studies, and control of the Viet Minh remained in exactly the same hands as before.[3]

Initially, the elections were scheduled for December 13, 1945, but they were later postponed to January 6, 1946, as part of an agreement with the Nationalist Chinese that extended also to slating some unopposed candidates. (Ho Chi Minh, claiming that communications were too difficult, never did postpone the elections in some parts of the country.)[4] The Viet Minh-Nationalist Chinese agreement committed 70 assembly seats in advance to candidates of two non-Communist parties. Twenty were given to the Dong Minh Hoi, a Kuomintang-like group of which Ho Chi Minh had once been a member, and 50 more went to the Viet Nam Quoc Dan Dang (VNQDD) or the National Democratic party, the oldest continuous party in Vietnam, also patterned (and named) after the Kuomintang. Bernard Fall has argued that, because the two parties had to agree not to compete under their own

---

[2] George Carver, "The Faceless Viet Cong," reprinted from *Foreign Affairs* (April 1966) in Wesley R. Fishel, ed., *Vietnam: Anatomy of Conflict* (Itasca, Illinois: F. E. Peacock, 1968), p. 313. See also Carver's footnote on the same page which reads: "Despite the Vietnamese Communists' claim that their party did not 'exist' under any name from 1945 to 1951, on August 31, 1953, the Cominform journal noted that the Vietnamese Communist Party membership increased from 20,000 in 1946 to 500,000 in 1950."

[3] Of the major writers who discuss the rise of the Viet Minh, only Joseph Buttinger, in *Vietnam: A Dragon Embattled* (New York: Frederick A. Praeger, 1967), pp. 361 and 593-594, accepts at face value the "dissolution" of the ICP. Curiously, in an earlier book on Vietnam, *The Smaller Dragon* (New York: Frederick A. Praeger, 1958), p. 449, Buttinger took a rather different view of the ICP. Then he said that their "stormtroopers were ordered to murder anyone who tried to use [democratic] liberties and institutions against the Viet Minh." He put quotation marks around "dissolution" in indexing the event. I. Milton Sacks, "Marxism in Vietnam," in Frank N. Trager, ed., *Marxism in Southeast Asia* (Stanford: Stanford University Press, 1959), p. 158, quotes the dissolution statement of the ICP in full, including a clear indication to ICP members that they were to join the Association for Marxist Studies.

[4] Bernard Fall, *The Viet Minh Regime* (Ithaca: Cornell University Press, 1956), p. 11.

names as the price for uncontested seats, they "sealed their doom." Voters could not identify their candidates, and they lost their identity.[5]

"The Dong Minh Hoi and the VNQDD," according to John T. McAlister, "continued to lead a campaign against elections, hoping ultimately to sabotage them by not putting up any candidates. This had little effect, and the resulting vote for the Viet Minh was massive. In Hanoi, Ho Chi Minh received 169,222 votes or 98 percent of the 172,765 cast from the 187,880 registrees." McAlister questioned the entire affair, noting that the total population of Hanoi was listed at the time as only 119,000. In the country as a whole the Viet Minh claimed more than 90 percent of the votes. These claims "aroused such passions from the opposition that they were not published for three months." [6]

In some provinces where no elections were held and where the VNQDD controlled the villages, Viet Minh members were declared "winners" anyway and were seated in the assembly. Voting was not secret, and voters were under great pressure to support Viet Minh candidates. This pressure was the more effective because ration cards were used for voter identification and had to be stamped at the polls to validate them for later food purchases. "Under the conditions of food scarcity and near-famine then existing in the north, this was undoubtedly an extremely effective means of bringing the urban population more firmly under the Viet Minh's control." [7]

The National Assembly, in Professor Fall's words, "with its 'elected' members convened six weeks before the election results were officially known and confirmed. Indeed, the assembly met for the first time on March 2, 1946, while the official election results were published in the Official Journal on April 13." Even then, the announced results were incomplete. Only 272 winners were listed although another 100 presumably were also elected.[8]

When the assembly met for the second time in the fall of 1946, its original membership had shrunk to 291. In response to a question, the minister of agriculture stated that 33 opposition members had been arrested. By the end of the session, less than two weeks later, the

---

[5] Bernard Fall, *The Two Vietnams* (New York: Frederick A. Praeger, 1967), p. 65.

[6] John T. McAlister, *Viet Nam: The Origin of Revolution* (Garden City, N.Y.: Doubleday Anchor Books, 1969), p. 22.

[7] Ibid., pp. 222-223. See also Robert G. Scigliano, *South Vietnam Under Stress* (Boston: Houghton-Mifflin Company, 1963), p. 13. Later elections in North Vietnam have offered voters no greater privacy.

[8] Fall, *The Viet Minh Regime*, p. 13.

number of opposition members had dropped to two and the progovernment members to 240. During its brief session, the assembly wrote and adopted a new constitution.[9] Its official job done, the assembly remained in office for 14 years.

According to the "Pentagon Papers," the new government established under the constitution in the fall of 1946 "preserved the facade of coalition; although the key cabinet positions were filled by communists, the government included independents, democrats, socialists, and even one nominal VNQDD. . . . Ho Chi Minh throughout the period [1946-1949] preserved a coalition, at least *pro forma;* the DRV (Democratic Republic of Vietnam) included one VNQDD and one Dong Minh Hoi."[10] Both the Socialist party and the Democratic party which were represented in the cabinet were founded by the Communists and have been under their continuous control.[11]

**Local Elections.** Our concern here is with national elections, but a few words about the local variety will help complete the picture of "representation" in North Vietnam. A 1945 Viet Minh law provided for "two categories of organs of authority" at the local level—people's councils and administrative committees. The councils of 20 to 30 members were elected by village residents age 18 or older who had not been judged insane or classified as "traitors or reactionaries." George

---

[9] Ibid.

[10] U.S. Department of Defense, *United States-Vietnam Relations, 1945-1967* (Washington, D. C.: U.S. Government Printing Office, 1971), vol. 1, pp. 49-50.

[11] See Dennis J. Duncanson, "Two Vietnams or One?" *The World Today,* September 1969, p. 411, where he asserts that the fact that some members of the NLF politbureau are from the Democratic and Socialist parties "is a distinction without a difference: the statutes of the former describe its purpose as 'representing the bourgeoisie and helping it to participate in the struggle for creation of a peaceful, unified, powerful, and prosperous Vietnam, in accordance with the policies of the working class and the Workers' Party,' while the Socialist Party represents 'intellectuals in close association and tight unity with the Workers' Party.' " The first quotation appeared in *Doc Lap,* Hanoi, December 3, 1960, and the second in *Nhan Dan,* July 28, 1961, on the occasion of the Socialist party's 15th anniversary.

In a letter to the author, June 11, 1972, Professor Duncanson listed nine more citations providing further evidence of Lao Dong control over the Socialist and Democratic "parties." One citation from *To Quoc* (June 1, 1960) stated, in giving biographical data on the preferred candidates for the National Assembly of the DRV, that "Comrade Hoang Minh Giam was a founder of the Democratic Party and as such was Minister of Interior in 1945-46; since 1954 he has been Deputy Secretary-General of the Socialist Party and, as such, Minister of National Education." Satellite parties and their officers apparently are interchangeable parts.

Ginsburgs, who has written the most thorough description of local government in North Vietnam, has noted that both these broad categories of disqualification offered great flexibility of interpretation under a Communist regime.[12] The administrative committees were neither elected by the people nor controlled by them.

Council elections were to be held every two years, but this arrangement was soon changed to elections every six months. Professor Ginsburgs speculates that the change may have been made because the Viet Minh did not initially control all the councils and, by reducing the length of the terms, found it easier to extend control without clearly violating the law. He also suggests that holding frequent elections opened the way for constant propaganda campaigns. Finally, he says that it allowed the Viet Minh to take credit for "having originated democratic government in the area." [13]

The basic law of 1945 provided that the council should elect from "among the literate cadres on its own staff an administrative committee of five persons (chairman, vice chairman, secretary, treasurer, and a member) and two alternates." In rural areas, where virtually all peasants were illiterate, the requirement of literacy forced the selection of Viet Minh cadres to these committees. Ginsburgs concludes that "effective power . . . was vested not in the theoretically supreme elective organs of local authority—the People's Councils—but rather, in small, indirectly chosen executive bureaux." [14]

Control of the administrative units was highly centralized. The village committee, both as to membership and action, was subject to the approval of the province committee, whose membership and actions, in turn, were subject to the approval of the council of ministers in Hanoi. In other words, power in the villages was in the hands of executive committees that were controlled by other nonelective officials at a higher level. Both the elected councils and the executive committees could be dismissed by higher units for reasons vague enough to allow the latter great freedom of action.[15]

---

[12] George Ginsburgs, "Local Government and Administration Under the Viet Minh, 1945-1954," in P. J. Honey, ed., *North Vietnam Today: Profile of a Communist Satellite* (New York: Frederick A. Praeger, 1962), pp. 138-139 and 146-147.

[13] Ibid., p. 139. Scigliano, *South Vietnam Under Stress,* p. 13, makes somewhat the same point.

[14] Ginsburgs, "Under the Viet Minh," pp. 147-148 and 142-143.

[15] Ibid., pp. 140-141.

The popularly elected councils held open meetings "barring extraordinary circumstances." The more powerful administrative committees "were in permanent session and their meetings were invariably conducted behind closed doors." [16]

After a few years, the councils lost all review powers over the executive committees. By 1948 the appointment of local council members by higher governmental units was widespread, "thereby in fact ensuring ultimate control by the Viet Minh faction of all the lower agencies of public authority." The Viet Minh insisted, however, that these changes "did not affect the democratic nature of the reforms." [17]

Writing in the early 1960s, Ginsburgs noted that after independence (1954 and after) the DRV continued its local government system almost unchanged. The general forms and the methods of control of the local units were, he said, similar to those in the Soviet Union.[18]

**The Constitution of 1960.** Between 1946 and 1960 there were no national elections in North Vietnam, by which time the DRV had adopted a new constitution that has governed all subsequent elections.

After a lengthy preamble that praises the Viet Minh and its leaders for their heroic revolution against the imperialist powers of France and the United States, the DRV constitution of 1960 provides in a general way for the institutions of government and their powers.[19] It asserts

---

[16] Ibid., p. 145.

[17] Ibid., pp. 156-157. For a different picture of the councils under the Viet Minh, see Buttinger, *Dragon Embattled,* p. 347. He says that "the undemocratic councils of notables were abolished September 5. They were replaced by committees also selected by universal suffrage. The Vietminh *even insisted* that the 'middle class' be adequately represented on these committees." (Emphasis added.) Gerald C. Hickey, *Village in Vietnam* (New Haven: Yale University Press, 1964), p. 183, says that two members of the committee in Khanh Hau were "brothers from a relatively well-to-do landowning family" and like the other members were active Viet Minh cadres. Hickey makes no mention of selection by universal suffrage. As noted in the text, George Ginsburgs says that power in any case had shifted from the councils to the executive committees. He quotes Soviet descriptions of the local governments to the effect that the organizations "include representatives of the workers, peasants, intelligentsia, lower and middle bourgeoisie, as well as progressive elements from among the former big landowners" but makes no mention of any *requirement* that the "middle class" *must* be included in either the councils or the committees.

[18] Ginsburgs ("Under the Viet Minh," p. 165) quotes a Soviet analyst on the subject of "people's democracies" who says that North Vietnamese local organs "are socialist in type and in this respect are related to the local organs of State rule in the U.S.S.R." even though differing in "political form and level of development."

[19] The text of the constitution is reprinted in Fall, *Two Vietnams,* pp. 417-434.

that all power belongs to the people who exercise that power "through the National Assembly and the People's Councils . . . elected by the people and responsible to the people."

The National Assembly is granted normal legislative powers. It also selects the president of the DRV and a number of other national executive officials, the president of the Supreme Court, and the Standing Committee of the National Assembly. This committee is given very extensive powers by the constitution and, in addition, may exercise powers given to it by the National Assembly; it exercises all the powers of the assembly when that body is not in session—and, because the National Assembly very rarely is in session, the Standing Committee *is* in effect the legislature.

National Assembly members are elected for terms of four years, but the life of the assembly may be extended in periods of crisis. Citizens 18 and over have the right and duty to elect "deputies and the People's Councils at all levels . . . on the principle of universal, equal, direct and secret suffrage." Those who are 21 years of age have the right to stand for election. These rights may be suspended by the courts.

The constitution provides a bill of rights that guarantees freedom of speech, press, assembly, association, religion, et cetera, and also places limitations on these guarantees. "The state forbids any person to use democratic freedoms to the detriment of the interests of the state and the people." (Article 38) "Citizens of the Democratic Republic of Vietnam must abide by the Constitution and law, uphold discipline at work, keep public order, and respect social ethics. . . ." (Article 39)

After stating that public property must be respected and protected and that citizens must pay taxes, the constitution asserts that "to defend the Fatherland is the most sacred and noble duty of citizens of the Democratic Republic of Vietnam." Further, "It is the duty of citizens to perform military service in order to defend the Fatherland." (Article 42)

**Electoral Provisions.** The election law that has governed national elections since 1960 outlines registration rules that, as in the case of South Vietnam, follow French forms. The law, like the constitution, asserts that voters have the right to elect delegates to the National Assembly by "universal, equal, direct and secret ballot." *Nhan Dan* stated in 1971 that "the secret suffrage principle enables voters to decide by themselves and freely choose their representatives. Disabled and illiterate people may allow other people to vote for them."[20] But, in practice, the voter does not have the privilege of casting his ballot in the privacy of a closed booth.

The constitution provides that there shall be one delegate to the National Assembly for every 50,000 persons—with "proportionate" representation for some ethnic groups—except that "in areas of the collective industries and *in the cities under the control of the Central Government* there shall be one delegate for every 10,000 to 30,000 people." (Emphasis added.)

*Nhan Dan* explained this deviation from the one man-one vote concept by pointing out that

> the working class always assumes a heavy share of our revolutionary responsibilities. However, since our industry is just newly developing, there are as yet few workers. We must assure that the number of working-class representatives is in proper proportion to the responsibilities of the working class. Because of this, the National Assembly election law has stipulated that in the large cities and industrial zones, 30,000 people will elect one representative. . . .

The law therefore allows a number of concentrated industrial areas to "organize themselves into special electoral units."[21] Elsewhere *Nhan Dan* provided a slightly different explanation:

> Every fifty thousand citizens elect one representative. In order to enable the working class to serve as the vanguard and to lead the national liberation revolution and socialist construction, the rules specify that: In the collective industrial areas and urban centers where workers are most numerous from ten to thirty thousand citizens can elect one representative. This regulation means that our state is a people's democratic state founded on the worker-peasant alliance and led by the working class.[22]

During the early years of the DRV, another reason for reducing the relative power of rural voters was the fact that they provided much of the opposition to the new regime. It was the peasants who suffered

---

[20] Quoted in *Documents and Research Notes,* no. 95, part 1, p. 55.

[21] *Nhan Dan,* March 27, 1964, translated and printed in *JPRS,* #24571, p. 6.

[22] *Nhan Dan,* February 13, 1971, quoted in *Documents and Research Notes,* no. 95, part 1, pp. 55-56.

most grievously from the centralization of the economy. Some commentators estimate that the number of peasants who were executed ran at least as high as 100,000. Other peasants committed suicide or were driven from their land. The tumult associated with the DRV land-reform program and the subsequent alienation of the peasants may also have been major reasons for the failure to hold any national elections between 1946 and 1960.

It is worth noting that the problems of the DRV were heightened in the late 1950s by the opposition of the intellectuals. The government banned all except official publications after a brief experiment with open criticism. It also purged some intellectuals who had participated in the criticism. By 1958, the government instituted a program for sending all "cultural workers" to the "countryside, factories, mines, and army units, to perform manual work and to study the practical life of the people." [23]

Electoral councils, committees, and cells are to administer the elections at various government levels. The powers granted to these units include the power "to survey the casting of ballots at the voting booths" and the power "to secure order inside the voting booths." But, according to another provision of the law, "nobody, including Electoral Cell officials, shall have the right to watch a voter closely when he shall be writing on his ballot." (Descriptions of the conduct of elections suggest that this last rule was followed half-heartedly at best.)

Cell officials also are to be responsible for counting and reporting the vote. According to the law, their reports must indicate the number of registered voters, the number who cast ballots, the number of acceptable and unacceptable ballots, the number of blank ballots, the number of votes cast for each candidate, and finally the complaints filed with election officials. At each level similar reports are required. (Again, law and practice seem to have gone their separate ways. At any rate, only the percentages of the vote received by the winning candidates are published—not the number of votes cast nor the percentages for the losers nor the actual figures for the winners.)

---

[23] See P. J. Honey, "Ho Chi Minh and the Intellectuals," reprinted from *Soviet Survey* in Fishel, ed., *Anatomy of Conflict,* p. 165. For another discussion of intellectuals in the DRV see the essay by Nhu Phong, "Intellectuals, Writers and Artists," in Honey, ed., *North Vietnam Today,* pp. 70-92. For a full discussion of the tyranny of land reform and of the repression of the intellectuals see Hoang Van Chi, *From Colonialism to Communism: A Case History of North Vietnam* (New York: Frederick A. Praeger, 1964), passim.

The law states that candidates are elected if they receive a majority of the votes cast in any multi-member district and finish within the number of delegates allotted to the district. If there is a tie for the last position, it goes to the older of the candidates. If fewer than the allotted number receive a majority, then there must be a second election within two weeks to choose from among those candidates who failed to win 50 percent plus one in the first round. Because no winning candidate has ever received less than 60 percent of the votes cast in his district, there never has been any reason to invoke the run-off rule.

### Assembly Elections: 1960-1971

Three elections have been held under the constitution and election law of 1960, all of them conducted in essentially the same manner. Campaigning, balloting, and the announcement of results have followed the same pattern in each. Some aspects of the elections of 1960 and 1964 will be noted briefly, and then the 1971 elections will be described in some detail.

**1960.** Bernard Fall has described the 1960 elections.[24] He noted that under the apportionment formula favoring the cities, Hanoi received 36 seats, or roughly three times the number to which it would have been entitled under a system that allotted seats strictly according to population. Fall described the circumstances of the election as follows:

> There were no electoral booths or other means of ensuring secrecy of voting. Ballots were written out in full view of all persons in the voting station, at open tables with aides standing ready to help the comrades who had difficulty in making out the ballot. . . . A total of 458 candidates had presented themselves for the 362 seats; in other words, less than one-third of the seats were contested.[25]

There were, in addition to the 362 seats mentioned above, 89 southern deputies whose terms were simply extended for the length of the new or Second Legislature. (Originally there had been 91 southern deputies but two had died by 1960.) They had been part of the

---

[24] Bernard Fall, "North Vietnam's Constitution and Government," reprinted from *Pacific Affairs,* vol. 23, September 1960, in Fishel, ed., *Anatomy of Conflict,* pp. 148-157.

[25] Ibid., p. 149.

legislature since 1946. Their presence in the National Assembly continued the myth that all of Vietnam was one nation and that the National Assembly was representative of and governed the whole area.

Radio Hanoi announced that 99.85 percent of the voters turned out in 1960. Ho Chi Minh led all candidates with 99.91 percent of the vote in his district. Other leading Communists won with 98.75 and 99.6 percent.

Fall noted the curious fact that Truong Chinh, whose position in the Lao Dong or Workers' party—the post-independence name for the Communist party—had dropped sharply after the "initial land reform fiasco," still received a slightly higher percentage of the vote than did Le Duan, the man then most frequently mentioned as Ho Chi Minh's probable successor as leader of the Lao Dong apparatus.[26] Fall further pointed out that the government-approved satellite parties, the Socialist party, the Democratic party, and the endorsed associations of Patriotic Buddhists and of the Resistant and Peace-Loving Catholics, all won some seats. Their candidates, however, "won their electoral seats by majorities that were somewhat less lopsided than those of their Communist colleagues, since they ranged from only 87.8 to 93 percent."

**1964.** The 1964 elections (for the Third Legislature) were little different from those of 1960. This time there were 366 deputies to be elected from among 448 candidates—an average of 1.22 candidates per seat. Of 8,755,002 registered voters, 8,580,002 or 97.77 percent turned out. Hoang Van Hoan, vice chairman of the National Assembly Standing Committee, proudly reported that "the percentage of many areas was 100%, such as: of Hanoi's 634 precincts, 433 achieved 100%; 379 of Quang Binh's 520 precincts had a 100% voting record. One hundred percent of the voters in Ninh Binh city voted." Only three of the 31 provinces, zones, and cities in the DRV had turnouts of less than 95 percent, six had 96 percent turnouts, eight 97 percent, six 98 percent, and eight 99 percent-plus. Hoang Van Hoan reported that even in some Catholic districts 100 percent of the voters cast ballots.[27]

---

[26] Ibid., p. 148. Le Duan did, in fact, become the secretary of the Lao Dong. The conflict between Le Duan and Truong Chinh has continued in the decade since, as the discussion of the 1971 election will show.

[27] *Nhan Dan,* June 28, 1964, quoted in *JPRS,* #2779, pp. 41-44. Hoan's announcement was made to the National Assembly and the entire speech was printed in *Nhan Dan.*

The elections were held on April 26, but the results were not known until May 11. The results were free of surprises. Sitting members won reelection by overwhelming majorities. Chairman Ho Chi Minh again led all candidates. He received 99.92 percent of the vote in his district.[28]

Before the conclusion of the last session of the Second Legislature, the National Assembly again provided for the continuance in office of all deputies who "represented" the South. Not all of them had really been elected, even in 1946, but they had held their assembly seats for 18 years, presumably speaking for the people of South Vietnam.

**1971.** The constitution provides for elections every four years but "in the event of war or other exceptional circumstances, the National Assembly may decide to prolong its term of office and take necessary measures to ensure its activities and those of the deputies."

In 1968, when elections for the Fourth Legislature should have been held, the National Assembly decided to "prolong its terms and entrusted the National Assembly Standing Committee with the task of organizing the election of delegates . . . when conditions would permit." Elections could not be held as scheduled, it was said, "because of the war of destruction." [29]

At the time many analysts felt that the decision to postpone the elections meant that no more would be held until the end of the war. Surprisingly, however, the Standing Committee issued a call for elections in early February 1971. On February 10, *Nhan Dan* offered this explanation:

> The election of deputies to the National Assembly, Fourth Legislature, has very important significance. The National Asembly, Fourth Legislature, will certainly further consolidate our people's democratic dictatorship, perform the heroic task of the proletarian dictatorship, mobilize our people and army to completely defeat the U.S. aggressors, simultaneously conduct the three revolutions, of which the technical revolution is the key, and further advance the socialism-building task in the North.[30]

[28] Ibid.

[29] Quoted in *Documents and Research Notes,* no. 95, part 1, p. 5.

[30] Ibid., p. 6, *Nhan Dan,* February 10, 1971.

A few days later, *Nhan Dan* noted that "the U.S. imperialists" were fighting against the North. "Yet, our party's Political Bureau has realized that in the current situation, we need and are able to organize elections. . . ." [31]

Still later, according to *Nhan Dan,* Ton Quang Phiet, secretary general of the Standing Committee of the National Assembly, spoke of the progress in the South with the creation of the Provincial Revolutionary Government (PRG) and suggested that this was the reason for holding a new round of elections in the North. In line with this argument, the Standing Committee called for an end to the terms of the deputies from the South who had held their assembly seats since 1946. This news was broadcast on March 5, 1971. It was also announced that the National Assembly had voted unanimously during its final session, March 2-4, to support the proposal of the Standing Committee. (All votes of the National Assembly's seventh session were unanimous.) The PRG had existed since 1969, of course, and had not previously been invoked as a rationale for new elections. Cancelling the tenure of the 89 southern deputies at least served to remove one contradiction in the position of the DRV. For two years the DRV had contended, on the one hand, that the PRG was an entirely separate and independent government in the South which was recognized by 20 countries and, on the other hand, that Vietnam was one nation and that the South was represented by the delegates in the DRV National Assembly.[32]

Other explanations have been offered for holding the elections in 1971 and for dropping the southern deputies.[33] Some saw it as a part of a continuing struggle between Truong Chinh, chairman of the Standing Committee, and Le Duan, secretary of the Lao Dong. Truong Chinh has emphasized internal economic development in North Vietnam rather than the conquest of the South. As head of the Standing Committee of the National Assembly, he has also stressed the legitimizing functions of the assembly. Le Duan, on the other hand, has allied himself with Vo Nguyen Giap in the quest for an early military victory

---

[31] Ibid., pp. 4-7, *Nhan Dan,* February 13, 1971.

[32] Ibid., part 2, pp. 88-90. Some southern deputies were later cleared by the Fatherland Front for candidacy from North Vietnamese districts. After the North Vietnamese invasion across the Demilitarized Zone in 1972, the DRV once more asserted that all of Vietnam was one country and that the DMZ was not a valid international dividing line.

[33] Daniel Southerland offered some possible explanations for the elections in the *Christian Science Monitor,* April 14, 1971.

even at the expense of North Vietnamese economic development. The very fact that elections were held at all may have been a victory of sorts for Truong Chinh. The massive invasion of South Vietnam in 1972, however, demonstrated the strength of the Le Duan-Giap faction. In any case, both Truong Chinh and Le Duan were reelected and the showdown between these two leaders, if there is to be one, must come another day.

The number of constituencies was increased in 1971 from 50 to 80 and the number of deputies to be elected from 366 to 420. Some 529 candidates were in the final competition, for an average of 1.26 candidates per seat. Only seven were "independents." The rest were from organizations that were part of the Fatherland Front, whose central committee had to approve all candidates. In turn, the Fatherland Front was guided by the Lao Dong. Fatherland Front committees at the municipal and provincial level proposed candidates to the front's central committee for final approval. As described on Radio Hanoi's domestic service, the Hanoi committee unanimously recommended persons to be candidates; all were accepted by the central committee, which itself added 10 more names to the list. Ultimately there were 55 candidates seeking 42 seats from Hanoi. The process was virtually the same for each of the other constituencies in the country. Article 24 of the 1960 election law reads: "in each electoral unit, the major parties and the people's groups shall be able to introduce [nominate] the candidates in a collective or individual manner." [34] Radio Hanoi's English-language service asserted that "by virtue of this provision, the Vietnam Fatherland Front, the broadest mass organization embracing the various social classes and strata of the people, has nominated 522 candidates." [35] *Nhan Dan* was quoted to the effect "that if the front did not choose candidates, 'inconvenience would occur.' " [36]

Once nominated, the candidates met with the Fatherland Front local committee. The chairman of the Hanoi committee, according to Radio Hanoi's domestic service, "warmly welcomed and greeted the candidates who are inflamed with patriotism and ready to shoulder the glorious and heavy responsibility of the forthcoming Legislature of the National Assembly." He also enumerated their duties and thanked

---

[34] Quoted in *Documents and Research Notes,* no. 95, part 1, p. 25.

[35] Ibid., part 2, p. 148.

[36] Henry S. Bradsher in the Washington *Evening Star,* April 4, 1971.

them on behalf of the people of Hanoi for accepting the nominations. In reply,

> Comrade Hoang Quoc Viet, on behalf of the comrades who have offered their candidacy for election . . . thanked the Hanoi Fatherland Front Committee, the Hanoi Administrative Committee, and the other election committees for organizing the present meeting. He warmly hailed the election committees for their positive activities and for having created favorable conditions allowing the candidates to meet the voters. Then the candidates held talks with the election committees of the respective units to discuss plans for getting in touch with the voters in their units.[37]

Radio Hanoi devoted most of one "campaign" broadcast to Truong Chinh's long address to a Hanoi rally. During the course of his speech, Chinh contrasted the legislatures of capitalist countries, with that of the DRV. In the capitalist legislatures, he said, the bourgeois and landlord representatives fight fiercely with each other for their special interests. "On the other hand," he went on,

> there is always unity and unanimity of opinion among our National Assembly representatives because all these representatives are willing to defend the interests of the various strata of working people whom they represent. If there is any disagreement on a certain problem at the beginning they will surely come to an agreement through democratic debate. This is the basic difference between the National Assembly in our country and those in capitalist countries and between our National Assembly and capitalist National Assemblies.[38]

The report of Truong Chinh's speech at the Hanoi rally closed by noting that "the meeting took place in an atmosphere of solidarity and enthusiasm. Everyone returned home conscious of being the master of the state and knowing that they must elect worthy delegates to the National Assembly." [39]

Day after day, Radio Hanoi told its domestic audience some variation of the same story. The superiority of socialist society, the evils of American warlords, and the successes of the Vietnamese army and peoples were stressed. Always there was unanimity among the candi-

---

[37] *Documents and Research Notes,* no. 95, part 2, pp. 116-118.
[38] Ibid., pp. 122-125.
[39] Ibid., p. 131.

dates, who were "deeply moved [as they] expressed their profound gratitude to the people for having reserved for them a boundlessly great honor. . . ." In reply, "voters' representatives" manifested "their confidence in and enthusiasm over the forthcoming National Assembly election" and vowed to work harder and achieve more for the nation.[40]

After two weeks of these rallies, the election brought out 98.88 percent of the voters. In Hanoi, the turnout reached 99.53 percent. The nationwide figure for valid votes of those cast was 99.36—which may well be accurate in view of the fact that "voting is still done openly, without the secrecy of choice." [41] On the other hand, since voting required "writing on his ballot," it is remarkable that fewer than one percent of the voters erred in marking ballots. Normally, more errors than that occur even in countries where voting has long been part of the democratic tradition.

Only four of the winning candidates received fewer than 70 percent of the votes in their constituencies; 147, or over a third, received in excess of 98 percent. More than two-thirds of the winners received over 95 percent, as the following figures show:

| *Categories of Winning Percentages* | *Percentage of Candidates in Category* |
|---|---|
| 95-100 | 67.3 |
| 90-94.99 | 18.3 |
| 85-89.99 | 8.3 |
| Below 85 | 5.9 |

Needless to say, most of the losers lost big. The available reports provide only percentages for the winners which makes it impossible to be sure how most individual losers came out, but the average for all losers was well below 20 percent.[42] National leaders, of course, were all in the top bracket. Le Duan received 99.46 percent; Pham Van Dong, the prime minister, 99.30 percent; Truong Chinh, 99.29 percent; and

[40] Ibid., pp. 143-144.

[41] Washington *Evening Star,* April 4, 1971.

[42] The official figures were printed in *Nhan Dan* over a rather long period—from April 13 to April 23, quoted in *JPRS,* #53403, pp. 1-31. "Thus," according to a South Vietnamese source, "the returns can be said to have come in quite 'normally' for an underdeveloped country like North Viet-Nam." The same source noted that reports for Lai Chau and Ha Giang came in especially late and commented that in these two places "it is rumored that the North Vietnamese authorities are having some difficulty 'pacifying' the restless population."

Ton Duc Thang, president of the DRV, 98.89 percent. General Vo Nguyen Giap, minister of national defense and the great national military hero, received the highest vote in the election, 99.54 percent, from his constituency in Quang Binh province. The other leaders were all from districts in Hanoi. All 366 incumbents from the Third Legislature were reelected; and this suggests than the Lao Dong may have used the 54 new seats to provide representation for some younger citizens and some minorities which had previously been unrepresented.

The problem of North Vietnamese legislative elections, in contrast with that of South Vietnam, is obviously not a lack of organization. As noted, the winners won big and the losers lost big in spite of the fact that there were only 129 more candidates than seats to be filled. The party leaders clearly must have given the word on candidates to support, or the counting must have left something to be desired, or the losing candidates were chosen because they could not claim popular support—but this seems unlikely. To have been chosen by the Fatherland Front was itself an honor that would not lightly have been given to total incompetents or undesirables.

## The National Assembly in Action

What did the voters get for their efforts on election day? If they expected to select their governors, not a whole lot.

The National Assembly is described in the constitution as the source of all power in the government. In fact, it offers little to the policy-making process other than the rubber-stamping of decisions made elsewhere, and it does not always have an opportunity to do even that much.

The constitution provides that the National Assembly shall meet twice each year. In fact, it has averaged only one meeting a year since coming into existence in 1946, and the frequency of meetings has not improved in recent years. During the Second Legislature, from 1960 to 1964, the National Assembly maintained the constitutional two-a-year routine. But the Third Legislature, from 1964 to 1971, dropped back to one a year and in 1967 it failed to meet at all.

The sessions themselves are much too brief to allow the National Assembly to play a serious role as a policy-making body or even as a critic of policies made elsewhere. During the entire period from 1946 to 1971, there were 26 sessions of the assembly. The shortest meeting was the first one which lasted only one day. The longest was the sixth meeting in December 1956 and January 1957 which lasted 29 days. The average length of the sessions was 7.95 days. Figures on the length of National Assembly sessions are set forth below: [43]

| *Days of Each Session* | *Number of Sessions* |
|---|---|
| 1-5 | 9 |
| 6-10 | 12 |
| 11-15 | 4 |
| More than 15 | 1 |
| Total Sessions: | 26 |

The Third Legislature (1964 to 1971) not only cut the number of sessions it held, it also held shorter ones. Four of its seven sessions were of four days duration or less. The remaining three ran for six, eight, and nine days. The average length of each session was only 5.28 days.

The Fourth Legislature apparently is following in its predecessor's footsteps. The constitution requires that the National Assembly hold its first meeting within two months after the election. In compliance with this rule, the National Assembly was convened on June 7; by June 10, it had adjourned.

In 1965, the National Assembly turned over to the Standing Committee most of its largely unused powers. The assembly now has so little importance as a policy-making body that a *Nhan Dan* article entitled "Some Important Events and Some Memorable Documents from the National Assembly" mentioned only one "memorable event" for the years 1964 to 1971: "On 23 September 1969, during the fifth meeting of the third term, the National Assembly named Ton Duc Thang as President to replace Ho who had just died. Nguyen Luong

[43] These figures almost certainly exaggerate the length of the sessions of the National Assembly. In the first place, both the opening and closing days have been counted as full days of work, which is, in fact, highly unlikely. In the second place, the dates given in a *Nhan Dan* article of April 11, 1971, quoted in *JPRS,* #53598, pp. 16-17, have been followed. This article listed the last session of the outgoing legislature as March 1-4, 1971. All other references in *Nhan Dan,* quoted in *Documents and Research Notes,* no. 95, part 2, p. 91, including the final communiqué of the seventh session itself, speak of the session as having taken place March 2-4, 1971. A similar difference for the other sessions would, of course, reduce the total days by 25 and the average by roughly one day.

Bang was named as vice president."[44] Under the heading, "Some Memorable Documents," seven items were mentioned for the 1964-1971 period, but *all of them described actions of the Standing Committee, not of the National Assembly.*[45]

The communiqué summarizing the latest three-day session of the National Assembly made abundantly clear the character of its work load.[46] The communiqué noted that all members were present. Chairman Truong Chinh opened the session. He was followed by Premier Pham Van Dong who read "a political report of the Government." Further national level reports were made by Minister of Defense Vo Nguyen Giap, the People's Supreme Court President Pham Van Bach, the People's Supreme Procurate Chief Procurator Hoang Quoc Viet, and the Secretary of the National Standing Committee Ton Quang Phiet, who provided the National Assembly with reports of the work of the Standing Committee.

At a plenary session, 20 delegates made reports to the assembly. The action of the National Assembly was then described:

> During the debates, the National Assembly unanimously approved:
>
> (1) A resolution on the political report of the Government;
>
> (2) A resolution approving the decisions taken by the National Assembly Standing Committee from the Sixth Session to this session, in accordance with the authority entrusted by the National Assembly;
>
> (3) A resolution ending the term of the National Assembly Deputies elected by the South Vietnamese people on 6 January 1946, and the term of the National Assembly of the Third Legislature;
>
> (4) A statement of the National Assembly.
>
> The National Assembly then elected the President of the People's Supreme Court and the Chief Procurator of the People's Supreme Procurate, whose terms have ended. Comrade Pham Van Bach has been reelected President of the People's Supreme Court, and Comrade Hoang Quoc Viet reelected Chief Procurator of the People's Supreme Procurate.

---

[44] *Nhan Dan,* April 11, 1971, quoted in *JPRS,* #53598, p. 12.

[45] Ibid., pp. 14-15.

[46] The communiqué was broadcast in Vietnamese to South Vietnam on March 6, 1971. It is printed in full in *Documents and Research Notes,* no. 95, part 2, pp. 91-93.

> After these elections, DRV President Ton Duc Thang made a speech, to which the National Assembly resounded with applause. At the end, Chairman of the National Assembly Standing Committee Truong Chinh made a speech closing the Seventh Session of the National Assembly of the Third Legislature.[47]

It is clear from the National Assembly's own description of its activities that it is neither a policy-making body nor even an instrument for serious discussion. It hears reports of government actions (some of which have been taken in its name); when requested to do so, it ratifies these actions; and it appoints or reappoints the officials it is expected to. When officials with real or only ceremonial authority speak to the assembly, the members make "the hall resound with applause" and then they go home, their work done.

Whatever ritual functions North Vietnamese elections may perform for the community, it is not particularly surprising that most Western scholars take them less than seriously as the process for choosing national leadership.

[47] Ibid.

# Appendix B

## NOTES ON THE PRESIDENTIAL CANDIDATES' CAMPAIGN APPEARANCE IN MY THO, AUGUST 26, 1967*

For the first time during the campaign, a member of the Thieu/Ky slate has appeared on the campaign tour. General Thieu joined members of nine other slates in a lively meeting on August 26 before some 5,000 people gathered on the main boulevard in the center of My Tho. The crowd was liberally interspersed with ARVN soldiers—perhaps 30-40 percent of the total—who took an active part in the question-and-answer portions of the program. Thieu was treated just like the other candidates (although his late arrival and early departure created some disturbance, partly because of the attention given him by the press). Thieu was his usual dignified self, handling questions calmly and ably. In the main, civilian candidates repeated their general campaign lines and we did not detect any change in the content or delivery of their presentations because of the presence of the chief of state. There was some jostling around the questioners' microphone and occasional hooting and jeering, but the atmosphere throughout the meeting was generally relaxed. The crowd was attentive and good humored despite a stiff breeze and occasional rain showers. An unusual note was added to this exercise in democracy by sporadic heavy artillery fire from the nearby U.S. base at Dong Tam, plus occasional bursts of mortar and small-arms fire clearly audible from across the My Tho river in Kien Hoa.

The chief of Dinh Tuong province, Lt. Col. Tran Van Phuc, told this embassy officer that he had not learned of Thieu's arrival until 45 minutes before the scheduled meeting time of 0900. All the candidates traveled 65 miles to My Tho by car except for Thieu who arrived by VNAF helicopter. Province officials had scheduled the dedication of a new public eating facility for the same morning, at which Minister of

---

* These notes were prepared by an officer of the U.S. embassy and made available to election observers. They are reprinted here as written with minor editorial changes to cast them into more formal style.

Public Welfare Phong was to have presided; a bandstand was set up near the market and a crowd assembled, mostly school children. On Thieu's arrival he went to that ceremony first where he presided briefly in place of Phong. This accounted at least in part for Thieu's late arrival at the candidates' meeting (he arrived at 1020 during Truong Dinh Dzu's presentation). Col. Phuc said he had provided additional security for a portion of Route 4 (from Saigon to My Tho) in Dinh Tuong, as well as security for the meeting itself, of course, but no other special preparations had been made because of Thieu's presence.

The meeting began promptly at 0900. The crowd had reached about 2,500 and was rapidly growing. Some ARVN soldiers were on hand and others arrived in a group later. At this point, Ha Thuc Ky placards were most numerous in the crowd. Several Thieu/Ky posters were displayed on the speakers' platform itself, but so were posters for the Senate slate of the Movement of the Renaissance of the South (the "Sowing Wheat" list). Perhaps this was a result of a trade-off between the Thieu/Ky and the Huong/Truyen members of the local campaign committee. Many foreign press were present and very much in evidence, particularly while Thieu was on the scene.

1. Ha Thuc Ky was the first speaker. He kept to his familiar format, first briefly rehearsing his revolutionary past and service to the nation, then inviting questions. He was asked about the prime minister's alleged statement in Da Nang that democracy is nonsense. Ky replied that a government which professes to wish to build democracy should show goodwill toward democracy, but that the prime minister obviously has contempt for democracy. So, he asked, how can we believe his posters which say that the Thieu/Ky government, if elected, will be democratic?

Ky was asked to reconcile his statement that, if elected, he would include members of all parties and factions in his government with his behavior as minister of interior when he appointed only Dai Viets as province chiefs. Ky replied that it had not been his responsibility to appoint province chiefs. That had been the business of the corps commanders. No one person and no one party can carry the burden of government alone, Ky said; his would be a government of national union with room for all.

Ky was then asked if he had planned a coup against Nguyen Khanh. He replied, How could I?—and maintained that Khanh had the army with him. To a petulant question that everyone talks well but no one does anything for the people, Ky said, Look at my revolutionary record.

Next Ky was asked why, as the newspapers have reported, he had called on President Johnson to intervene in our election: Ky said he had only stated that the elections must be fair, not that any foreign government should intervene to make them so.

Referring again to Ky's stint as minister of interior, a questioner asked if Ky could point to any positive accomplishments he had achieved, or had he just worked for himself? Ky replied that he had been minister of interior for two months only, which was not enough time to do much, not even to release political prisoners, a step he had recommended to Nguyen Khanh.

Ky was next queried (this question may have been planted) about an incident in Hue in which, Ky had alleged, RDV [Revolutionary Dai Viet] campaign workers were mistreated by the police. Ky recounted his version of the incident and said that the refutation of his charges by the chief of Thua Thien province, which had appeared in the press, was not sufficient. Before Ky had exhausted the subject his time ran out and he was cut off by the timekeeper, the chairman of the local campaign committee. Ky was well received: several of his replies were applauded and he was warmly applauded when he stepped aside.

2. Lieu Quang Khinh spoke for the Binh/Khinh slate. He apologized for Binh's absence, saying he was campaigning in central Vietnam. Khinh then began to explain the slate's campaign platform but was shouted down by the crowd which allowed it had heard the platform already. Khinh nevertheless managed to restate several points, including proposed constitutional amendments to provide for election of the prime minister, to revise the manner in which the Senate is chosen, and so forth.

The crowd, which apparently did not take the Binh/Khinh candidacy very seriously, cheered when the first questioner asked what, in addition to talk, did Khinh propose to do if elected? Khinh said the most important thing was to have a good constitution—everything would depend on a good constitution—so his first step would be to amend it. He was interrupted by the next questioner who asked why Thieu and [Nguyen Cao] Ky had felt it necessary to assure President Johnson that the elections would be free. Khinh replied that he did not know, that the question should best be put to them. He received little applause.

At this point, Thieu/Ky placards began to appear. They were carried onto the scene largely by pedicab drivers, one of whom told this embassy officer later that they were acting at the direction of their union.

3. Next to speak was Vu Hong Khanh, who vigorously attacked the GVN [government of South Vietnam] for alleged campaign misconduct. Khanh, speaking with dignity and considerable presence, said that people have the right and responsibility to use the ballot. However, the GVN ticket [Thieu/Ky ticket] has all the advantages in this race, he asserted, and the civilian representatives are being "trampled." Dai Viet and VNQDD party workers are being arrested, beaten, and even kidnapped. How can we call this democracy? And what has the Thieu/Ky regime done to help the people? The people must recognize this and act. If things continue as they are, this will not be a good election *(khong tot dep lam)*.

Khanh then turned the platform over to the local representative of his slate who began to recite Khanh's background. He was interrupted by a questioner who asked for evidence of GVN misconduct during the campaign—places, names. The local representative said he had not been allowed to finish the prepared portion of his speech. The questioner shot back that, if speeches were dragged out forever, there would not be time for questions. At this point Khanh intervened to say that he, of course, had the evidence and that it had been presented to the public in a press conference.

The next question was why had Khanh served the French by working for them as minister of youth. Khanh began his reply—stating that at that period in history the Vietnamese people had two enemies, the French and the Communists—when his time ran out. The crowd applauded politely.

By this time, the crowd had grown to nearly 5,000, a considerable number of whom were military personnel from the 7th Division. A group of them moved forward as Khanh concluded his delivery and more or less surrounded the microphone used by questioners. At no time were civilians totally barred from the area, but there was a considerable press from this point on and most questioners had to do a little pushing and shoving to gain access to the microphone.

4. The Suu/Dan slate had the floor next. Suu spoke briefly in generalities, saying people must choose their leaders carefully. He also denied that he had ever been pro-French. Dr. Dan then took over with a forceful presentation. There are two problems, he said: war versus

peace, and the elections themselves. Dr. Dan commented that on his way to My Tho that morning he had noted how rich the Dinh Tuong countryside is. Vietnam is rich enough to need no foreign aid, if only there were peace. How to bring peace? The use of force has failed, Dr. Dan said. The other way to bring peace is with an independent Vietnam, as the British had done with an independent India and Pakistan. The Communists are only a minority. (Note: this remark was not clear in the given context.) Dr. Dan continued: This past year the war has been escalated unnecessarily. One million men, planes, tanks, all have been added, and our strength is greater than North Vietnam's. We have not won. (At this point artillery fire from the nearby U.S. base at Dong Tam, which had been heard throughout the morning, increased slightly, but Dr. Dan made no allusion to the unscheduled sound effects.)

Dr. Dan was interrupted then by a question: The candidates are trying to defame each other; is that virtuous? The questioner was hooted down. There was some commotion around the speakers' stand, with jostling between civilians and the military. The next question was not heard, but Suu's reply was: The junta tore up the constitution, so why should I have stayed in power? I withdrew to keep my self-respect.

Suu was then asked what he thought of Dan's statement that Suu was indecisive in small things but decisive where the issues are important. Suu answered, A person is indecisive when he does not have a position of his own. But I have a policy, and I will not be indecisive. When I was arrested I was tortured and beaten for not mentioning other members of the conspiracy. Time ran out at that point. The crowd, which had alternately hooted and applauded both questions and answers when they could hear them, gave Suu and Dan polite but not enthusiastic applause.

5. Crowd interest was increasing as Truong Dinh Dzu rose to speak. There was quite a press around the speakers' platform and the questioners' microphone; additional Thieu/Ky placards were to be seen. Dzu, speaking with his usual flair, thanked the audience for coming to hear him and reminded them of the need for decorum. Dzu said: I am known as a peace candidate. The war must be decided by the Vietnamese. Peace, however, must be with honor, and not like the peace obtained at Geneva in 1954. Peace is for the people of both North and South Vietnam. There must be a logical peace, concluded on the basis of mutual concessions by North and South Vietnam. Some people say that

to talk about peace is to talk about surrender to the Viet Cong. Why, after so many years of war, can we not appeal for peace?

The first questioner asked what Dzu would do if the VC would not agree to negotiate. Dzu replied: Peace or not, we must have a just cause. Up to now, our cause has not been just. We have asked the Americans to help us, but we have no mutual assistance agreement *(hiep uoc ho thuong)*. If elected, I will obtain such an agreement. If Hanoi refuses to negotiate, then I could call on the people to fight because we would have a just cause. But now, the soldiers do not know what they are fighting for.

Dzu was next asked about the law abrogating the Buddhist charter and promulgating a new charter. As Dzu began his reply, General Thieu made his appearance, walking to the platform through the crowd. He was accompanied by Nguyen Van Loc and one or two guards. Crowd and press attention immediately focused on the chief of state, although he did nothing special to attract it. As Thieu was making his way to the platform, Dzu replied to the question about the Buddhist charter. He said that, as a lawyer, he considers the new charter unconstitutional. General Thieu, as chairman of the National Leadership Committee, does not have the right to promulgate the new charter. There has been no Buddhist convention. According to Article 35 of the old charter, there must be a two-thirds vote in such a convention to validate a new charter.

The next series of questions and answers was accompanied by mixed cheers and jeers by claques. A questioner shouted that he rejected Dzu's concept of peace because there were no preconditions stated. Dzu replied he did have preconditions, one of which would be to stop bombing the North. Someone shouted "Down with that!" The timekeeper, who had intervened mildly on several previous occasions, did so again but with little noticeable effect as the crowd seemed to enjoy the heckling. The next question that could be heard was, Well, what would you do? Dzu said he would ask the commanders of the U.S. and Vietnamese military forces to stop the bombing. Then, he said, I would ask Hanoi to talk. And I would have to talk with the National Liberation Front. This is my program. You can accept it or reject it. One man in the crowd shouted "The soldiers have shed too much blood to accept defeat so easily." As Dzu stepped down there were cheers and applause.

6. General Thieu spoke next, first striking a personal note. I am, he said, familiar to the people of Dinh Tuong. I have been stationed in IV Corps. I hope the people consider me as a fellow citizen and the

soldiers a comrade. I have tried to keep my identity as a soldier and not to become a demagogue.

During these past two years we have seen our country invaded. There is need for a social revolution. We must both defeat the Communists and help the people in the countryside to develop a better life in freedom and democracy. Now, what has our government done these past two years? We have not, in this time, been able to complete the task of defeating the Communists and building democracy. Results have been small. But we have worked with devotion and goodwill. As a soldier, I do not like to talk nonsense. If you know that we have tried, that we have devotion and goodwill but that we have not yet had the time to finish the job, then you will continue to trust in us. That is what I believe. If we are elected, the four following years may not be enough. We cannot do everything. However, we will make every effort to achieve democracy, victory, and social progress.

I would like to repeat three things which you may have heard me say before. One is settlement of the war *(giai quyet chien tranh).* I do not think that it is easy to obtain peace, but I trust in your efforts. If I am elected, I will tell Hanoi: I am the legally elected representative of the people—which the NLF is not. I will send Hanoi a message demonstrating my goodwill and suggesting a settlement. If Hanoi accepts, and wants me to display some gesture of goodwill as a condition for negotiations, I will recommend a bombing pause of one week. But if Hanoi continues its infiltration, then we will have no choice but to continue to fight. Now, militarily we are strong, but politically we are weak.

At this point, Thieu was interrupted by a questioner who said, Your program sounds good, but can you guarantee that it will be carried out? Also, the civilian candidates accuse you of trying to rig the elections and unfair pressure tactics. Will you seek revenge on your enemies if you are elected? General Thieu answered that all the programs sound good. I depend on the support of the army and the people who know that I am both honest and sincere. As for unfair tactics, that does not depend on the authorities but on the people themselves. As for the specific charges themselves, I will ask for evidence. Suppose we are elected and there is evidence the elections were unfair. Then the National Assembly can invalidate the elections.

The next questioner, an ARVN enlisted man, said, I am a soldier and I know there is much injustice and favoritism in the army. And I know that our pay is too low to keep up with the cost of living. General

Thieu replied that each commander is responsible for the maintenance of justice in his unit. As for improvement in the soldiers' life, that takes time. I have planned not only to improve the pay of soldiers but also to help them after leaving the army. I have lived the life of a soldier and I know your problems. Thieu then reminisced a little on his experiences in Ca Mau, the leeches, et cetera.

The third questioner was a soldier in the Regional Forces. He said that, according to decree 16/66, personnel who have completed military service may be discharged. But it is not observed. Furthermore, the men are oppressed; therefore they desert and then are arrested and sent off as laborers to combat units. What do you think? General Thieu said that soldiers must remember that the maintenance of discipline is necessary. He said he had signed a decree to the effect that those who have violated military regulations but have been rehabilitated may have their rights returned to them.

The next questioner asked why General Ky had sent a letter to the U.S. Congress reporting on the Vietnamese elections, when this reflected on Vietnamese sovereignty? Thieu replied that the letter was in response to charges that the election was being unfairly conducted. It was in response to attempts to discredit the elections, but it was not a report.

The final questioner asked about Ky's alleged remark that he would stage a coup if a civilian were elected. Does that mean that Thieu and Ky do not respect the people? To this, Thieu replied that Ky had said something like that but he, Thieu, had just recently said that we [the ticket] would respect the election results and that the army would serve any elected regime.

Thieu was still talking when he was cut off by the timekeeper. He stopped, thanked the people for hearing him and sat down to a burst of cheers and applause. Most but not all of the soldiers in the crowd joined in the cheers, as did numbers of civilians.

7. Tran Van Huong followed Thieu, presenting his usual platform. He made the familiar point that the Vietnamese do not have enough facilities to fight the war so they have sought help from friends. However, military means alone cannot bring peace. We must have political means. A soldier must know for whom he sacrifices and he will not sacrifice for those making fortunes out of the war. To have peace we must negotiate and to negotiate we must have some advantage. Since we don't yet have an advantage, at present we could only negotiate on the enemy's terms.

In the first question, Huong was asked about the fact that the foreign press had found no evidence to support Huong's charges of local pressure on his campaigners. Huong replied he would produce evidence. A teacher asked why Huong didn't take the side of the Buddhists. [Huong is a Confucian.] Mai Tho Truyen replied that people making trouble in the name of the Buddhist church are only a small minority. Another person asked about promises to end corruption: Nothing has been done so far. When inspection teams go to the provinces the facts are distorted. If elected, what action will you take? Huong replied that he would make no promises and that the question should be referred to the GVN slate.

Huong was hard to hear, partly because he spoke softly and partly because there was some confusion on the platform caused by aggressive foreign press, mostly U.S. The crowd was sympathetic and the Huong/Truyen slate received warm applause.

8. Tran Van Ly came to the stand and went over points he had made on previous occasions. The nation has had troubles for many years but now we have a constitution. Choose carefully or the consequences will be serious. Ly's running mate Duong then read their platform. A member of the crowd asked if Ly's plan to sign a law clearing out the prisons might turn criminals loose on society. Ly replied with a Chinese proverb: rule by virtue is strong, rule by force is weak. Another person asked why the cost of living was rising, what would Ly do about it and how long would he take? Ly replied that the cost of living was high because the piasters had been devalued from 65 to 118 per dollar and because of insufficient internal production. He cited the need to import rice. The time it takes to improve things will depend on the type of program chosen, i.e., emergency, short range or long range. Ly said that, as an example, he would encourage people to raise pigs. The next question was how Ly would bring about peace. The situation at the battle front is not secure so how can you stabilize the rear and bring down the cost of living? Ly gave an ambiguous answer, saying that we give credit to the army for its achievements. As for the fact that Vietnamese are killing Vietnamese, that is not our fault.

The crowd began to dwindle after the Huong/Truyen presentation. The press conducted an informal interview with Thieu on the platform as Ly spoke. Thieu left during Ly's presentation, further distracting people who were not much interested in Ly anyway.

9. Nguyen Hoa Hiep was the next to the last to speak. About half of the crowd was left to hear him make his usual argument that war

cannot be settled by military means. He said that his objective is democracy and social improvement and then read his platform. Then he called on the people to make proper use of their right to vote and said he would not withdraw from the race no matter what the obstacles. His running mate Truyen followed with his customary speech about his familiarity with Communist leaders. He mentioned that Hiep had formed the Third Division which fought against the French. He stated that, if elected, he would have his friends suggest to Ho Chi Minh that he go to the conference table. The first question was asked by a man who said that he admired the VNQDD but disliked the Third Division because it had not fought the French, and besides it had executed his brother. Hiep claimed, in reply, that the Third Division had killed some French and that it had accorded prisoners a fair trial, killing only those who cooperated with the French. The next question was, Would Hiep think of young people if elected? He replied that, along with the release of political prisoners, he would correct the military service system and send aged men back to their families. Another questioner complained about Americans giving candy to children and was promptly shouted down with laughter by the last remnants of the crowd. Hiep said it was normal for children to take candy offered by Americans.

10. The last speaker was Nguyen Dinh Quat who ran through his usual platform. As Quat spoke, the crowd completed its departure.

# Appendix C

## PRESIDENTIAL ELECTION RETURNS, 1967 AND 1971

**Table 1**

1967 PRESIDENTIAL ELECTION:
VOTER PARTICIPATION, BY PROVINCE AND CITY

| Province or City | Registered Voters | Turnout | | Valid Ballots | |
|---|---|---|---|---|---|
| | | Number | % of Registration | Number | % of Turnout |
| I CORPS | | | | | |
| Hue | 54,827 | 45,203 | 82.4 | 43,335 | 95.5 |
| Da Nang | 116,053 | 94,364 | 81.3 | 89,894 | 95.7 |
| Quang Nam | 153,393 | 135,182 | 88.1 | 130,662 | 97.0 |
| Quang Ngai | 202,664 | 176,229 | 86.9 | 167,625 | 95.4 |
| Quang Tin | 94,483 | 88,013 | 93.1 | 87,102 | 98.8 |
| Quang Tri | 107,281 | 91,511 | 85.3 | 88,457 | 95.6 |
| Thua Thien | 183,160 | 156,086 | 85.2 | 151,876 | 97.4 |
| Total | 911,861 | 786,588 | 86.2 | 758,951 | 96.5 |
| II CORPS | | | | | |
| Dalat | 34,765 | 28,274 | 81.3 | 26,511 | 93.9 |
| Cam Ranh | 24,353 | 21,962 | 90.1 | 21,143 | 95.9 |
| Binh Dinh | 302,260 | 272,022 | 89.9 | 270,357 | 99.4 |
| Binh Thuan | 106,375 | 96,490 | 90.7 | 93,835 | 97.3 |
| Darlac | 78,099 | 67,842 | 86.8 | 65,793 | 97.0 |
| Khanh Hoa | 166,240 | 146,444 | 88.1 | 141,059 | 96.6 |
| Kontum | 47,998 | 42,611 | 88.7 | 39,770 | 93.4 |
| Lam Dong | 26,939 | 23,044 | 86.0 | 22,340 | 96.9 |
| Ninh Thuan | 67,400 | 63,497 | 94.2 | 62,026 | 97.8 |
| Phu Bon | 27,052 | 24,531 | 90.6 | 22,956 | 93.7 |
| Phu Yen | 116,107 | 101,079 | 87.0 | 98,314 | 97.3 |
| Pleiku | 77,572 | 63,235 | 81.5 | 60,757 | 96.3 |
| Quang Duc | 15,506 | 14,402 | 92.8 | 14,289 | 99.3 |
| Tuyen Duc | 41,696 | 36,806 | 88.2 | 35,585 | 96.8 |
| Total | 1,123,362 | 1,002,239 | 88.5 | 974,735 | 97.3 |

**Source:** *Public Administration Bulletin*, no. 41 (November 30, 1967), pp. 68-69 for registration and turnout, and pp. 64-67 for valid ballots.

Table 1 (continued)

| Province or City | Registered Voters | Turnout Number | Turnout % of Registration | Valid Ballots Number | Valid Ballots % of Turnout |
|---|---|---|---|---|---|
| III CORPS | | | | | |
| Saigon | 765,340 | 583,127 | 76.1 | 545,611 | 93.6 |
| Vung Tau | 35,787 | 30,861 | 86.2 | 29,739 | 96.2 |
| Con Son | 1,014 | 958 | 94.4 | 940 | 98.1 |
| Gia Dinh | 562,190 | 446,195 | 79.5 | 424,898 | 95.3 |
| Bien Hoa | 179,450 | 143,541 | 79.9 | 138,048 | 96.5 |
| Binh Duong | 113,065 | 88,256 | 78.0 | 84,854 | 96.1 |
| Binh Long | 28,218 | 24,385 | 86.4 | 23,200 | 95.1 |
| Binh Tuy | 27,068 | 23,817 | 88.2 | 23,202 | 97.5 |
| Hau Nghia | 63,439 | 50,955 | 80.3 | 49,656 | 97.6 |
| Long An | 75,303 | 63,918 | 84.8 | 62,427 | 97.7 |
| Long Khanh | 61,155 | 51,791 | 84.6 | 49,416 | 95.4 |
| Phuoc Long | 20,981 | 18,983 | 90.4 | 18,442 | 96.8 |
| Phuoc Tuy | 50,768 | 44,912 | 88.4 | 43,534 | 96.9 |
| Tay Ninh | 130,395 | 112,527 | 86.2 | 107,379 | 95.9 |
| Total | 2,114,173 | 1,684,226 | 79.6 | 1,601,346* | 95.1 |
| IV CORPS | | | | | |
| An Giang | 224,274 | 185,235 | 82.5 | 182,552 | 98.7 |
| An Xuyen | 42,245 | 35,703 | 84.5 | 34,017 | 95.2 |
| Ba Xuyen | 103,574 | 86,798 | 83.8 | 84,196 | 97.0 |
| Bac Lieu | 68,780 | 56,120 | 81.5 | 54,623 | 97.4 |
| Chau Doc | 184,301 | 165,942 | 90.0 | 161,537 | 97.4 |
| Chuong Thien | 52,984 | 44,199 | 83.4 | 43,830 | 99.2 |
| Dinh Tuong | 112,934 | 94,389 | 83.5 | 91,909 | 97.5 |
| Go Cong | 38,588 | 35,338 | 91.5 | 34,785 | 98.6 |
| Kien Giang | 132,967 | 110,756 | 83.2 | 108,117 | 97.3 |
| Kien Hoa | 118,857 | 102,715 | 86.4 | 101,345 | 98.3 |
| Kien Phong | 111,110 | 95,346 | 85.8 | 93,352 | 97.9 |
| Kien Tuong | 17,200 | 15,268 | 88.7 | 14,788 | 96.8 |
| Phong Dinh | 145,332 | 109,974 | 75.7 | 107,663 | 97.9 |
| Sa Dec | 97,662 | 88,019 | 90.1 | 87,667 | 99.6 |
| Vinh Binh | 95,791 | 80,806 | 84.3 | 79,184 | 98.0 |
| Vinh Long | 148,389 | 123,087 | 82.9 | 120,852 | 98.2 |
| Total | 1,694,988 | 1,429,695 | 84.3 | 1,400,417 | 97.9 |
| *Summary* | | | | | |
| I CORPS | 911,861 | 786,588 | 86.2 | 758,951 | 96.4 |
| II CORPS | 1,123,362 | 1,002,239 | 88.5 | 974,735 | 97.3 |
| III CORPS | 2,114,173 | 1,684,226 | 79.6 | 1,601,346 | 95.3 |
| IV CORPS | 1,694,988 | 1,429,695 | 84.3 | 1,400,417 | 97.9 |
| TOTAL | 5,844,384 | 4,902,748 | 83.9 | 4,735,449 | 96.6 |

* This total was erroneously cited in the source as 1,600,846.

## Table 2

1967 PRESIDENTIAL ELECTION:
CANDIDATE VOTES, BY PROVINCE AND CITY

| Province or City | Candidates | | | | | | | | | | |
|---|---|---|---|---|---|---|---|---|---|---|---|
| | Suu | Ky | Binh | Dzu | Huong | Co | Ly | Hiep | Thieu | Khanh | Quat |
| I CORPS | | | | | | | | | | | |
| Hue | 20,394 | 5,054 | 368 | 1,503 | 1,937 | 301 | 389 | 499 | 8,162 | 501 | 4,227 |
| Da Nang | 34,061 | 5,045 | 1,258 | 5,160 | 4,770 | 1,284 | 1,039 | 2,072 | 22,496 | 3,215 | 9,494 |
| Quang Nam | 20,716 | 15,764 | 3,776 | 12,779 | 5,289 | 3,018 | 2,381 | 4,790 | 28,378 | 17,187 | 16,584 |
| Quang Ngai | 31,468 | 8,806 | 4,582 | 44,323 | 7,073 | 2,830 | 2,491 | 4,288 | 41,609 | 2,911 | 17,244 |
| Quang Tin | 10,538 | 6,532 | 3,098 | 7,147 | 7,827 | 2,257 | 1,950 | 4,503 | 34,045 | 3,234 | 5,971 |
| Quang Tri | 14,287 | 16,008 | 2,197 | 8,991 | 2,580 | 2,020 | 1,482 | 2,630 | 20,911 | 8,016 | 9,335 |
| Thua Thien | 41,203 | 35,382 | 2,408 | 5,168 | 4,347 | 1,610 | 1,311 | 2,961 | 33,804 | 3,710 | 19,972 |
| Total | 172,667 | 92,571 | 17,687 | 85,071 | 33,823 | 13,320 | 11,043 | 21,743 | 189,406 | 38,774 | 82,827 |
| II CORPS | | | | | | | | | | | |
| Dalat | 2,314 | 1,672 | 508 | 2,846 | 5,561 | 497 | 539 | 773 | 9,723 | 768 | 1,310 |
| Cam Ranh | 4,717 | 1,287 | 450 | 921 | 978 | 538 | 559 | 1,203 | 7,324 | 524 | 2,642 |
| Binh Dinh | 27,151 | 17,601 | 5,522 | 46,076 | 10,293 | 5,809 | 4,940 | 13,021 | 118,232 | 5,922 | 15,790 |
| Binh Thuan | 6,169 | 4,867 | 2,006 | 19,588 | 7,766 | 1,992 | 1,955 | 3,531 | 37,924 | 2,811 | 5,226 |
| Darlac | 3,209 | 2,691 | 1,550 | 3,552 | 6,014 | 1,344 | 1,410 | 2,788 | 38,554 | 1,770 | 2,911 |
| Khanh Hoa | 30,043 | 7,199 | 2,732 | 9,270 | 7,619 | 2,929 | 2,919 | 4,897 | 56,192 | 2,946 | 14,313 |
| Kontum | 1,431 | 1,443 | 583 | 5,700 | 1,427 | 368 | 359 | 1,169 | 25,707 | 607 | 976 |
| Lam Dong | 2,312 | 1,505 | 540 | 1,039 | 979 | 475 | 410 | 880 | 12,048 | 825 | 1,332 |
| Ninh Thuan | 5,749 | 3,348 | 1,307 | 4,696 | 5,020 | 1,569 | 1,525 | 2,420 | 30,503 | 1,730 | 4,159 |
| Phu Bon | 1,197 | 992 | 716 | 1,116 | 1,248 | 416 | 309 | 2,327 | 11,717 | 548 | 2,370 |

*Table 2 (continued)*

| Province or City | Candidates | | | | | | | | | | |
|---|---|---|---|---|---|---|---|---|---|---|---|
| | Suu | Ky | Binh | Dzu | Huong | Co | Ly | Hiep | Thieu | Khanh | Quat |
| Phu Yen | 23,261 | 5,931 | 2,827 | 9,176 | 3,279 | 2,320 | 1,855 | 3,960 | 30,067 | 2,327 | 13,311 |
| Pleiku | 3,885 | 3,528 | 1,934 | 7,164 | 3,507 | 1,505 | 1,577 | 3,592 | 29,466 | 1,569 | 3,030 |
| Quang Duc | 948 | 706 | 333 | 697 | 505 | 424 | 444 | 540 | 8,519 | 440 | 733 |
| Tuyen Duc | 2,124 | 1,502 | 718 | 2,728 | 2,107 | 684 | 590 | 1,192 | 21,463 | 1,049 | 1,428 |
| Total | 114,510 | 54,272 | 21,726 | 114,569 | 56,303 | 20,870 | 19,391 | 42,293 | 437,433 | 23,836 | 69,531 |
| III CORPS | | | | | | | | | | | |
| Saigon | 59,371 | 34,007 | 13,995 | 87,670 | 137,962 | 13,159 | 10,010 | 14,910 | 135,527 | 15,300 | 23,700 |
| Vung Tau | 2,227 | 1,767 | 646 | 3,657 | 4,015 | 553 | 469 | 977 | 13,456 | 889 | 1,083 |
| Con Son | 49 | 21 | 16 | 30 | 85 | 4 | 16 | 25 | 658 | 17 | 19 |
| Gia Dinh | 36,472 | 21,580 | 9,078 | 63,934 | 69,949 | 7,968 | 6,774 | 11,694 | 171,123 | 10,422 | 15,904 |
| Bien Hoa | 7,878 | 7,102 | 3,140 | 31,494 | 13,546 | 2,965 | 2,531 | 4,343 | 55,488 | 3,570 | 5,991 |
| Binh Duong | 7,106 | 6,196 | 3,062 | 23,499 | 8,576 | 2,529 | 2,290 | 3,698 | 19,275 | 2,904 | 5,719 |
| Binh Long | 1,945 | 1,396 | 880 | 3,936 | 1,616 | 1,007 | 982 | 1,272 | 7,732 | 980 | 1,454 |
| Binh Tuy | 761 | 1,496 | 499 | 5,143 | 639 | 427 | 488 | 1,101 | 11,237 | 566 | 845 |
| Hau Nghia | 3,044 | 3,082 | 1,555 | 19,430 | 3,837 | 1,256 | 1,175 | 1,608 | 10,425 | 1,483 | 2,761 |
| Long An | 4,544 | 4,235 | 2,071 | 15,335 | 9,220 | 1,812 | 1,831 | 1,879 | 15,608 | 2,407 | 3,485 |
| Long Khanh | 2,580 | 3,975 | 1,159 | 5,746 | 3,270 | 898 | 823 | 1,961 | 25,624 | 1,403 | 1,977 |
| Phuoc Long | 832 | 802 | 599 | 1,008 | 961 | 617 | 556 | 895 | 11,004 | 514 | 654 |
| Phuoc Tuy | 2,176 | 2,170 | 1,120 | 12,002 | 4,268 | 933 | 820 | 1,291 | 15,705 | 1,229 | 1,820 |
| Tay Ninh | 6,696 | 5,013 | 3,607 | 39,947 | 6,543 | 2,284 | 2,157 | 3,133 | 30,830 | 2,825 | 4,344 |
| Total | 135,681 | 92,842 | 41,427 | 312,831 | 264,487 | 36,412 | 30,922 | 48,787 | 523,692 | 44,509 | 69,756 |
| IV CORPS | | | | | | | | | | | |
| An Giang | 11,502 | 22,456 | 6,567 | 43,483 | 12,215 | 3,546 | 3,291 | 4,737 | 62,035 | 4,968 | 7,752 |

| | | | | | | | | | | | |
|---|---|---|---|---|---|---|---|---|---|---|---|
| An Xuyen | 1,523 | 1,476 | 832 | 6,444 | 2,491 | 760 | 652 | 3,593 | 14,326 | 789 | 1,131 |
| Ba Xuyen | 4,601 | 6,378 | 2,896 | 20,574 | 8,823 | 3,553 | 2,662 | 3,665 | 21,738 | 3,878 | 5,428 |
| Bac Lieu | 4,241 | 5,290 | 1,923 | 9,729 | 6,191 | 1,902 | 1,555 | 2,582 | 15,717 | 1,954 | 3,539 |
| Chau Doc | 9,372 | 11,023 | 5,341 | 40,019 | 8,043 | 3,692 | 3,084 | 4,336 | 65,374 | 4,117 | 7,136 |
| Chuong Thien | 2,472 | 2,423 | 1,405 | 7,909 | 2,018 | 724 | 724 | 824 | 22,488 | 997 | 1,846 |
| Dinh Tuong | 6,352 | 6,844 | 2,977 | 14,240 | 15,492 | 2,479 | 2,288 | 3,955 | 29,732 | 3,265 | 4,285 |
| Go Cong | 1,657 | 1,726 | 892 | 2,879 | 4,581 | 798 | 583 | 1,543 | 17,594 | 1,238 | 1,294 |
| Kien Giang | 6,602 | 6,729 | 2,975 | 28,364 | 8,258 | 2,567 | 2,002 | 3,072 | 39,130 | 2,647 | 5,771 |
| Kien Hoa | 6,920 | 6,942 | 3,509 | 14,069 | 9,056 | 2,815 | 2,775 | 4,035 | 40,845 | 3,621 | 6,758 |
| Kien Phong | 4,850 | 6,351 | 3,332 | 34,160 | 3,812 | 1,891 | 1,750 | 2,524 | 28,448 | 2,301 | 3,933 |
| Kien Tuong | 648 | 557 | 396 | 4,283 | 732 | 321 | 283 | 434 | 6,125 | 414 | 595 |
| Phong Dinh | 10,772 | 9,007 | 5,393 | 24,103 | 11,846 | 2,825 | 2,697 | 3,403 | 28,072 | 3,336 | 6,209 |
| Sa Dec | 5,200 | 6,703 | 3,254 | 13,246 | 5,068 | 1,702 | 1,715 | 1,861 | 43,760 | 1,934 | 3,224 |
| Vinh Binh | 3,572 | 7,340 | 2,839 | 13,745 | 5,550 | 2,488 | 2,066 | 3,224 | 32,246 | 2,726 | 3,388 |
| Vinh Long | 10,232 | 8,523 | 5,698 | 27,402 | 15,311 | 3,652 | 3,121 | 4,189 | 31,401 | 3,972 | 7,351 |
| Total | 90,516 | 109,768 | 50,229 | 304,649 | 119,487 | 35,715 | 31,248 | 47,977 | 499,031 | 42,157 | 69,640 |
| *Summary* | | | | | | | | | | | |
| I CORPS | 172,667 | 92,571 | 17,687 | 85,071 | 33,823 | 13,320 | 11,043 | 21,743 | 189,406 | 38,774 | 82,827 |
| II CORPS | 114,510 | 54,272 | 21,726 | 114,569 | 56,303 | 20,870 | 19,391 | 42,293 | 437,433 | 23,836 | 69,531 |
| III CORPS | 135,681 | 92,862 | 41,427 | 312,831 | 264,487 | 36,412 | 30,922 | 48,787 | 523,692 | 44,509 | 69,756 |
| IV CORPS | 90,516 | 109,768 | 50,229 | 304,649 | 119,487 | 35,715 | 31,248 | 47,977 | 499,081 | 42,157 | 69,640 |
| TOTAL | 513,374 | 349,473 | 131,069 | 817,120 | 474,100 | 106,317 | 92,604 | 160,800 | 1,649,562 | 149,276 | 291,754 |
| TOTAL AS % OF VALID VOTES | 10.8 | 7.3 | 2.7 | 17.2 | 10.01 | 2.2 | 1.9 | 3.4 | 34.8 | 3.1 | 6.1 |

TOTAL VALID VOTES: 4,735,449

**Source:** Ibid., pp. 63-67.

## Table 3

1971 PRESIDENTIAL ELECTION:
VOTER PARTICIPATION, BY PROVINCE AND CITY

| Province or City | Registered Voters | Turnout | | Valid Ballots | |
|---|---|---|---|---|---|
| | | Number | % of Registration | Number | % of Turnout |
| I CORPS | | | | | |
| Hue | 62,558 | 42,045 | 67.2 | 27,059 | 64.3 |
| Da Nang | 160,842 | 122,081 | 76.0 | 90,829 | 74.4 |
| Quang Nam | 190,758 | 179,593 | 94.1 | 177,380 | 98.7 |
| Quang Ngai | 241,214 | 203,820 | 84.4 | 194,805 | 95.5 |
| Quang Tin | 154,588 | 146,062 | 94.4 | 143,249 | 98.1 |
| Quang Tri | 127,762 | 119,043 | 93.1 | 116,235 | 97.7 |
| Thua Thien | 192,936 | 159,435 | 82.6 | 137,028 | 85.9 |
| Total | 1,130,658 | 972,079 | 85.9 | 886,585 | 91.2 |
| II CORPS | | | | | |
| Cam Ranh | 43,462 | 36,607 | 84.2 | 33,754 | 92.3 |
| Dalat | 39,618 | 30,643 | 77.3 | 26,948 | 87.9 |
| Nha Trang | 79,448 | 66,213 | 83.3 | 53,841 | 81.3 |
| Qui Nhon | 67,693 | 59,017 | 87.1 | 58,395 | 98.0 |
| Binh Dinh | 269,487 | 255,137 | 94.6 | 251,642 | 98.6 |
| Binh Thuan | 117,074 | 96,478 | 82.4 | 90,872 | 94.2 |
| Darlac | 93,569 | 90,357 | 96.0 | 88,421 | 97.8 |
| Khanh Hoa | 91,298 | 84,481 | 91.5 | 81,906 | 97.2 |
| Kontum | 53,720 | 51,874 | 96.5 | 51,556 | 99.4 |
| Lam Dong | 36,452 | 35,368 | 97.0 | 34,637 | 97.9 |
| Ninh Thuan | 76,276 | 71,567 | 93.8 | 70,645 | 98.8 |
| Phu Bon | 30,580 | 26,542 | 86.8 | 26,162 | 98.6 |
| Phu Yen | 118,919 | 108,428 | 91.8 | 106,768 | 98.5 |
| Pleiku | 104,891 | 96,097 | 91.6 | 93,271 | 97.1 |
| Quang Duc | 15,778 | 14,002 | 88.7 | 13,904 | 99.4 |
| Tuyen Duc | 44,307 | 42,283 | 95.4 | 41,101 | 97.2 |
| Total | 1,282,572 | 1,165,094 | 90.1 | 1,123,823 | 96.5 |
| III CORPS | | | | | |
| Saigon | 674,824 | 516,315 | 76.5 | 432,099 | 83.6 |
| Vung Tau | 42,440 | 34,918 | 82.2 | 25,647 | 73.4 |
| Bien Hoa | 219,904 | 167,571 | 76.2 | 143,768 | 86.0 |
| Binh Duong | 110,702 | 100,183 | 90.5 | 92,135 | 92.2 |
| Binh Long | 35,801 | 32,350 | 90.3 | 30,879 | 95.4 |
| Binh Tuy | 32,456 | 31,428 | 96.8 | 30,956 | 98.4 |
| Gia Dinh and Con Son | 576,522 | 459,127 | 79.6 | 430,053 | 93.6 |
| Hau Nghia | 105,063 | 95,984 | 91.3 | 89,960 | 93.6 |
| Long An | 146,128 | 136,393 | 93.3 | 133,583 | 97.9 |
| Long Khanh | 73,146 | 57,147 | 78.1 | 55,646 | 97.4 |
| Phuoc Long | 24,380 | 22,263 | 91.3 | 21,554 | 96.9 |

*Table 3 (continued)*

| | | | | | |
|---|---|---|---|---|---|
| Phuoc Tuy | 55,338 | 53,206 | 96.1 | 50,607 | 95.1 |
| Tay Ninh | 151,418 | 140,935 | 93.0 | 135,286 | 95.9 |
| Total | 2,248,122 | 1,847,820 | 82.1 | 1,672,173 | 90.5 |
| IV CORPS | | | | | |
| Can Tho | 65,692 | 64,720 | 98.4 | 57,810 | 89.3 |
| My Tho | 41,756 | 36,879 | 88.3 | 33,980 | 92.1 |
| Rach Gia | 43,909 | 40,952 | 93.2 | 38,889 | 94.9 |
| Giang | 247,106 | 203,999 | 82.5 | 190,743 | 93.5 |
| An Xuyen | 81,540 | 80,406 | 98.6 | 79,124 | 98.4 |
| Ba Xuyen | 178,141 | 159,775 | 89.7 | 158,695 | 99.3 |
| Bac Lieu | 122,561 | 117,035 | 95.4 | 116,645 | 99.6 |
| Chau Doc | 235,667 | 223,817 | 94.9 | 219,758 | 98.1 |
| Chuong Thien | 100,774 | 91,438 | 90.7 | 90,242 | 98.6 |
| Dinh Tuong | 174,224 | 163,407 | 93.7 | 160,418 | 98.1 |
| Go Cong | 75,953 | 73,536 | 96.7 | 73,303 | 99.7 |
| Kien Giang | 122,100 | 121,063 | 99.1 | 120,666 | 99.6 |
| Kien Hoa | 238,411 | 212,696 | 89.2 | 208,571 | 98.1 |
| Kien Phong | 156,500 | 140,471 | 89.7 | 135,585 | 96.5 |
| Kien Tuong | 20,990 | 20,653 | 98.3 | 20,186 | 97.7 |
| Phong Dinh | 142,576 | 137,668 | 96.5 | 136,472 | 99.1 |
| Sa Dec | 121,019 | 113,273 | 93.5 | 113,079 | 99.8 |
| Vinh Binh | 140,120 | 135,673 | 96.8 | 134,814 | 99.3 |
| Vinh Long | 222,269 | 200,097 | 90.0 | 194,711 | 97.3 |
| Total | 2,531,308 | 2,337,558 | 92.3 | 2,283,691 | 97.7 |
| POLLING STATIONS IN CAMBODIA | | | | | |
| Krek (4 stations) | | 1,937 | | 1,893 | 97.7 |
| Chipou (2 stations) | | 1,290 | | 1,251 | 96.9 |
| Neak Luong (3 stations) | | 1,229 | | 1,157 | 94.1 |
| Kempong Trach (1 station) | | 624 | | 541 | 87.4 |
| Total | | 5,080 | | 4,842 | 95.3 |
| *Summary* | | | | | |
| I CORPS | 1,130,658 | 972,079 | 85.9 | 886,585 | 91.2 |
| II CORPS | 1,282,572 | 1,165,094 | 90.1 | 1,123,823 | 96.5 |
| III CORPS | 2,248,122 | 1,847,820 | 82.1 | 1,672,173 | 90.4 |
| IV CORPS | 2,531,308 | 2,337,558 | 92.3 | 2,283,691 | 97.6 |
| Polling Stations in Cambodia | | 5,080 | | 4,842 | 95.2 |
| TOTAL | 7,192,660 | 6,327,631 | 87.9 | 5,971,114 | 94.4 |

**Source:** "Returns of the Presidential Election as Reported to the Ministry of the Interior," News Release no. 66, Election Information Center, Ministry of the Interior, October 5, 1971.

# Index

Cover and book design: Pat Taylor